Beyond Transmission: Innovations in University Teaching

Beyond Transmission: Innovations in University Teaching

First published in 2011 by Libri Publishing

ISBN 978 1 907471 58 2

A CIP catalogue record for this book is available from The British Library

Cover design by Helen Taylor

Design by Carnegie Publishing

Printed in the UK by Short Run Press Ltd

Libri Publishing
Brunel House
Volunteer Way
Faringdon
Oxfordshire
SN7 7YR

Tel: +44 (0)845 873 3837

www.libripublishing.co.uk

Contents

	About the Editors	vii
	Foreword	ix
Chapter One	Effectiveness in Higher Education Demands Innovations in Teaching that Progress Beyond Transmission *Claus Nygaard, Nigel Courtney and Clive Holtham*	1
Chapter Two	Resisting Student Consumers and Assisting Student Producers *Eva Dobozy*	11
Chapter Three	A Research-based Approach to University Curriculum Development that Prepares Students for Subsequent Practice *Jesper Piihl and Kristian Philipsen*	27
Chapter Four	Innovation and Student Learning: ePortfolios for Music Education *Jennifer Rowley*	45
Chapter Five	The Sequence of Educational Innovation from University to Working Life *Pekka Räihä, Marja Mäensivu, Matti Rautiainen and Tiina Nikkola*	63

Chapter Six	Introducing a Pedagogy of Optimal Engagement and Transformation (POET) *Sam Elkington*	77
Chapter Seven	Learning through Innovation *Paul Bartholomew and Nicola Bartholomew*	99
Chapter Eight	Contextualised Iterations of Innovative Teaching Practices *Anne Herbert and Elyssebeth Leigh*	117
Chapter Nine	Implementing a Constructivist Learning Environment: Students' Perceptions and Approaches to Learning *Patrícia Albergaria Almeida and José Teixeira-Dias*	135
Chapter Ten	A Centralised Tutor System to Support the Affective Needs of Online Learners *Aileen McGuigan*	151
Chapter Eleven	Fostering High-quality Learning through a Scaffolded Curriculum *Kayoko Enomoto*	167
Chapter Twelve	The Use of RISK® for Introducing Marketing Strategy *John Branch, Lewis Hershey and David Vannette*	185
Chapter Thirteen	Poster Presentation: an Effective Assessment for Large Communication Classes? *Swapna Koshy*	203
Chapter Fourteen	"Be Original, but not too Original": Academic Voice, Text-matching and Concordancing Software *Michelle Picard and Cally Guerin*	221
Chapter Fifteen	Communal Roleplay: Using Drama to Improve Supervision *Katarina Winka and Tomas Grysell*	235
	Collected Bibliography	253

About the Editors

Claus Nygaard is Professor in Management Education at Copenhagen Business School, Denmark. Originally trained in business economics and administration, where he holds a PhD, he first became Associate Professor in Economic Sociology at Department of Organization and Copenhagen Business School. In 2000 he changed position to CBS Learning Lab, and began to work with Quality Enhancement of Higher Education. He was a driving force behind the formulation and implementation of the "Learning Strategy" for Copenhagen Business School in 2005. He has received distinguished research awards from Allied Academies, outstanding paper awards from Students in Free Enterprise, and he was voted "best teacher" at Copenhagen Business School in 2001. His research has resulted in several anthologies, and he has published in leading journals such as *Higher Education, International Studies of Management & Organization, International Journal of Public Sector Management,* and *Assessment & Evaluation in Higher Education.*

Clive Holtham is Professor of Information Management and Director of the Learning Laboratory at Cass Business School, London, UK. After taking a Masters degree in management, he trained as an accountant and was Young Accountant of the Year in 1976. Following six years as a Director of Finance and IT, he moved to the Business School in 1988. His research is into the strategic exploitation of information systems, knowledge management and management learning. He has been an adviser to the European Parliament on educational technology, and led a major EU project on measurement and reporting of intangibles as well as the highly rated QuBE project into quality enhancement in business schools. In 2003 he was awarded a UK National Teaching Fellowship, and is a board member of the Non-Profit E-learning Network (2008–2011), a major initiative to promote management education through informal online learning. He is author of a large number of publications, and lectures, broadcasts and consults in the UK and internationally. He was a founding member of the Worshipful Company of Information Technologists, the City of London's 100th livery company.

Nigel Courtney is Honorary Senior Visiting Fellow at Cass Business School, City University London, where he gained the MBA and was awarded his PhD. He is a Visiting Fellow at the University of Technology, Sydney. Nigel is a chartered engineer, a certified management consultant and a certified IT professional with extensive experience in project and general management. Clients of his firm Courtney Consulting include the European Commission, Deloitte & Touche, Metropolitan Police, Transport for London, The Post Office and the UK National Endowment for Science Technology and the Arts. Nigel co-authored PD7502 on Knowledge Management for the British Standards Institute and is co-originator of the Skills Framework for the Information Age (SFIA.org.uk). Nigel's teaching practice includes MBA programmes and MSc courses in Economics and on Information Leadership. His research interests include innovation in education, business innovation, the extraction of business value from ICT, and the use of communications technologies for social change.

Claus and Clive are the founders of LIHE, an international academic association for the enhancement of Learning in Higher Education. http://www.lihe.wordpress.com

Foreword

The current context is a nuanced and complex one. Internationally, Higher education systems are experiencing rapid and often turbulent change as nations seek to balance a desire to move beyond university education just for an elite subset of citizens while ensuring that systems remain of high quality and financially sustainable. Increasingly students are having a greater part to play in quality assurance and enhancement, and the nature of the student experience is changing as the relationship between them and academic staff shifts. At the same time, paradigms of learning are evolving, with concepts of "knowledge transfer" becoming less important and co-production of knowledge becoming more widely accepted. When students don't need to rely on lecturers as the principal sources of subject knowledge, with the ready availability of electronic means of sourcing information becoming ubiquitous, it is inevitable that teaching and learning in universities must change radically.

Higher Education institutions in the twenty-first century must find creative, powerful and positive ways of supporting student learning. Nowadays there needs to be significantly less emphasis on content delivery and a stronger focus on recognising and accrediting student achievement wherever this takes place (in the workplace, through independent study, in blended learning contexts). Programmes need to be constructively aligned (Biggs, 2003), to ensure that all elements work effectively together.

We also need to find new ways to support student engagement with the learning process, in particular helping to strengthen student skills, particularly in the area of information literacy. Finding information is no longer a problem, but learning to recognise what comprises good quality data from a mass of undifferentiated material, and being able to use and acknowledge it appropriately, is a more difficult issue for many students, particularly those from disadvantaged backgrounds. Students may need advice on approaches to reading for different purposes, writing in diverse registers, information retrieval and maximising social learning opportunities, as well as how best to manage the learning experience and form connections with fellow students that can make for lifelong learning and networking.

Assessment in universities is changing too, as HEIs recognise the importance of assessment as an integral part of the learning process rather than a bolt-on at the end of the curriculum design process (Gibbs 1999). Fit-for-purpose assessment (Brown, Rust and Gibbs, 1994) can be a powerful driver for learning when well designed and effectively implemented but poor assessment can seriously hamper learning when it is ill designed and badly implemented (Boud, 1995). Assessment needs to be *for* not just *of* learning and feedback needs to be used as a means to help students recognise good quality work as they are producing it (Sadler, 1998), so that they learn in the process of being assessed.

This volume is the result of an original collaborative process that aligns well with current imperatives. The authors have applied the principles that underpin good practice in higher education today, co-producing the text as a mutually developmental process and using the best of international evidence-based research to support their proposals to move beyond pedagogic transmission modes towards a truly creative way of working. I commend it to you enthusiastically.

Sally Brown, June 2011

About the author

Sally Brown is Emeritus Professor of Higher Education Diversity in Teaching and Learning at Leeds Metropolitan University where she was Pro-Vice Chancellor (Academic) until July 2010. Sally is also an Adjunct Professor at the University of the Sunshine Coast and a Visiting Professor at the University of Plymouth.

Chapter One

Effectiveness in Higher Education Demands Innovations in Teaching that Progress Beyond Transmission

Claus Nygaard, Nigel Courtney and Clive Holtham

The Case for Action

It has to be acknowledged that a key part of the success of universities, in their long-term survival over many centuries, has been an inbuilt distrust of radical innovation relating to their own structures and processes. However, periodically it has been necessary for more radical changes to take place. Notably the 19th-century developments in Germany relating to Humboldt's scientific method (Knobloch, 2006), and parallel growth in the USA following creation of the Land-Grant Colleges, of a much wider curriculum than the classical preoccupations which had hardly changed since medieval times.

In many countries today higher education enjoys a much wider range of participation in more diverse curricular areas than could have been imagined a century ago. However, higher education still faces challenges and these are of a different order to those which preoccupied academics in the 19th century. Higher education (HE) cannot assume the undivided attention of its students. This may be for economic reasons, for example where students need to take part-time work. It may be for social reasons, where the opportunities for friendship and connectivity extend well beyond the perimeter of the campus. It may also be for intellectual access reasons; a student today can and does instantly access written, audio or video materials from professors and public intellectuals all over the world.

It is too simplistic to suggest that technology alone presents the single greatest challenge to the pedagogic *status quo* in higher education. Student expectations are evolving, not least for reasons relating to the consumption of media generally. There are also changes in the nature of secondary education, which has become less diverse and more bite-sized in a number of countries over the last two decades.

So we argue that for many overlapping reasons, there is a strong case for challenging the continued dominance of transmissive education, perhaps best symbolised in the continued dominance of lectures in much of higher education.

Support for the Necessary Paradigm Shift

Blackburn *et al.* (1980) found that between 73% and 83% of faculty chose lectures as their primary method of instruction. Two decades later Lammers and Murphy (2002) reported that although other teaching techniques were becoming more popular, the lecture continued to be the most prevalent teaching technique in the university classroom.

Although those percentages have probably seen a further slight drop since then, our own interactions with faculty internationally suggest that lecturing is still by far the dominant mode of teaching in many faculties of many universities.

However, the last few decades have seen significant challenges to the lecture-heavy transmissive model. Of necessity, large-scale distance learning approaches have had to move away from this model; it is interesting to see how the UK Open University eventually dropped the "televised lecture" in favour of more constructivist approaches. Problem-based Learning (PBL) such as at McMaster and Maastricht Universities has demonstrated that face-to-face universities can make institutional commitments other than to a transmissive approach. But these remain outliers compared to the majority of universities.

The case for a shift from the traditional model is summarised well by Goodyear (1999) in Figure 1.

Information transmission	→	Design of learning tasks and environments
'Teacher' directed	→	Learner-managed learning
Subject centered	→	Learner-centered design & development
Individualistic learning	→	Learning communities
Inert knowledge	→	Usable knowledge
Atomistic, technology-focused approaches	→	Holistic/systemic approaches

Figure 1: Transitions Associated with the Growth of Constructivist, Learner-centred Approaches to Education

The chapters in this anthology unashamedly champion this shift from a transmissive to a constructivist approach (Bostock, 1998; Wilson, 1996).

Of course it is hardly surprising, given the historical reluctance of higher education to engage in radical change, that there is no shortage of critics of proposals to move away from the transmissive approach. Constructivism has itself attracted critics both from pedagogic and other perspectives (Irzik, 2001). Stunkel (1998) even argues that the lecture is a tool for "intellectual liberation". There is no reason why a well-crafted lecture or speech cannot challenge, stimulate or inspire students or listeners more generally. We do not advocate the demise of such lectures. What we are challenging is a higher educational diet substantially made up from a single approach. Many students approve of conventional lectures, in part because they allow for the whole gamut of attention, from complete engagement to totally passivity (if not actual or metaphorical slumber). However, even in a climate of educational consumerism it remains the responsibility of faculty to design challenging learning experiences, and the days of the lecture as the dominant vehicle of transmission of information are surely numbered.

A Forum for Sharing Best Practice

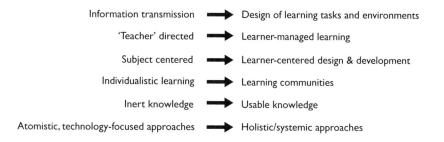

Having worked professionally with quality enhancement in higher education for more than a decade we, the editors, founded the International Academic Association for Enhancement of Learning in Higher Education (LIHE; www.lihe.info) as a forum for facilitating collaborative work between international researchers and practitioners working professionally with student learning. After publishing on student-centred learning, improving students' learning outcomes, creativity in teaching, and postgraduate education, it seemed natural to focus explicitly on the link between learning and teaching as a practice.

Consultations with members of the LIHE community revealed a growing feeling that innovatory teaching approaches are essential if teachers are to appeal to the new types of mindset displayed by people entering higher education today and to instil in them a love of learning. From this debate emerged the theme for this anthology "Beyond Transmission: Innovations in university teaching".

Identifying Characteristics of Teaching that Are "Beyond Transmission"

This anthology is the result of an international symposium on this theme. The call had elicited a wide range of proposed chapters and these were narrowed down by double blind review. The symposium began by bringing together the 17 selected authors to propose and explain their academic passions. These authors – who represent a broad cross-section of educational disciplines – hail from five continents and bring to bear ten national mindsets.

By discussion, exchange and combination they identified a number of jointly-held views. Their responses to the statement "Our joint academic passion is ..." included concepts such as:

- Induction into a wide learning community of academics and students;
- Construction of identity in academic environment / workplace;
- Improving student engagement by recognising varied learning styles through e-learning and practical applications;
- Changing roles of teachers and students to encourage the holistic development of students using various multimedia and extracurricular activities;
- Understanding student learning styles to develop inspirational and exciting, emotional and personally relevant deep learning that develops the essence of human education as a journey;

- Articulating the academic lifestyle combining research and teaching excellence with an explicit development and reward process from PhD onwards.

Having scoped areas of common ground each author set out to explain to the others the key message they intended their chapter to impart. This shared understanding enabled the group to identify linkages. The process culminated in the realisation that any innovatory teaching approach that goes beyond transmission shall be bounded by three essential facets, namely; vision, process and practice.

Of course, the extent to which each facet influences any particular solution will vary. This was proven when each author was readily able to map the centre of gravity of their chapter on a model distributing vision, process and practice at the apexes of a triangle. In this way the mapping enabled each author to highlight the facet with which their chapter is chiefly concerned and the extent to which it embraces the other two facets.

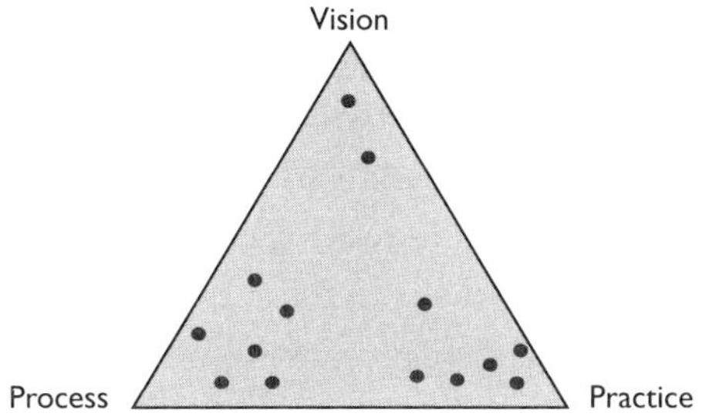

Figure 2: Clustering the Chapters in this Anthology

Navigating the Collection

We have used this clustering to arrange the chapters in a sequence that helps you, the reader, to go straight to chapters addressing the area that is of keenest importance to you at the moment. However, vision, process and practice are not mutually exclusive. So a feature of this anthology is that where our authors have seen that another chapter in this volume throws further light on their viewpoint they offer the reader a link. We hope that these links will bring you fresh insights.

On Vision for Going Beyond Transmission

Eva Dobozy's chapter opens the collection with a powerful appeal to teachers in higher education to develop their students as producers rather than as customers. Eva believes that in a globalised world the task of educating the next generation of knowledge workers means gaining awareness of the cost of the growing tendency of HE institutions towards this "businessification" of HE.

In chapter 3, the Danish authors Jesper Piihl and Kristian Philipsen recognise that the widespread emphasis on research-based teaching creates tensions because the great majority of graduates will embark on careers as practitioners rather than academics. In response they propose a theoretical model of new practice-research relations that bridges theory-of-application and modes of knowledge production.

On Process for Going Beyond Transmission

As shown in Figure 2, six chapters describe a process-based approach to innovations in university teaching.

Jennifer Rowley opens this section of the anthology by reporting her experience of teaching musicians to become music teachers. She finds that the deployment of online tools can enable the storing of evidence to document learning but the way these tools foster development of the student's learning story constitutes an even more valuable process.

In chapter 5, Pekka Räihä, Marja Mäensivu, Matti Rautiainen and Tiina Nikkola describe an innovative approach to educating prospective teachers in Finland. After eight years of deployment they investigate the extent to which their graduates have been able to transfer behaviours derived from the innovation into the way their employer institutions operate.

The next two chapters consider theoretical aspects underpinning innovative processes.

Sam Elkington's response to the need to increase and enhance engagement has been to devise an experiential perspective of teaching and learning that emphasises the cognitive, motivational, and emotional processes of learning. He describes how his pedagogy of optimal engagement and transformation ("POET") brings student learning journeys to life.

In chapter 7 Paul and Nicola Bartholomew describe and evaluate a staff development course they have pioneered in the UK to enhance institutional capacity for innovative teaching. Their examples and survey data demonstrate how effective their course has been in creating change agents.

Chapters 8 and 9 consider practical aspects of implementing process innovations in higher education teaching.

Anne Herbert and Elyssebeth Leigh reflect that negotiations with the possibilities and constraints in a particular classroom teaching context allow for new pedagogic practices to be implemented. In describing their experience with dialogic learning, formative assessment and transparent assessment they demonstrate that the implementation process is iterative.

Our focus on process concludes with chapter 9 by Patrícia Albergaria Almeida and José Teixeira-Dias. They highlight the importance of the learning environment. Their analysis of interviews with their chemistry students in Portugal reveals that those gaining the lowest grades tend to be surface learners; those gaining the highest marks are likely to be deep learners. The authors warn that assessment methods which focus on understanding do not necessarily promote deep approaches to learning.

On Practice for Going Beyond Transmission

In this set of six chapters the authors describe tools and behaviours and practical procedures that animate their teaching innovations. The emphasis is on innovative practices that lead to improved outcomes.

Aileen McGuigan notes that the growing popularity of online courses can mean that personal tutors become swamped by communications. In response, she has developed a centralised tutor system using Web 2.0 technologies to support the affective needs of online learners on a teacher education programme in Scotland. It has proved both popular and effective.

Kayoko Enomoto teaches Japanese in Australia to postgraduate students from diverse academic backgrounds. In chapter 11 she examines the effectiveness of a scaffolded curriculum to foster high-quality learning and develop transferable thinking skills which can be used by the learner to gain new knowledge.

The next two chapters look to theory to explain the effectiveness of some very practical tools.

In chapter 12 John Branch, David Vannette and Lewis Hershey offer a fascinating résumé of business games and simulations. They discuss the use of the board game RISK for introducing American business school students to marketing strategy and provide compelling evidence of its effectiveness.

Swapna Koshy teaches business communication courses to very large classes in Dubai. She describes the innovative way student poster presentations can be used as an aid to assessment. Her survey findings indicate clearly that as well as leading to efficient assessment it promotes active learning by students.

The closing two chapters on practice for going beyond transmission highlight the role of process for achieving results with practical tools and techniques.

In chapter 14, Cally Guerin and Michelle Picard reflect that research students today tend to struggle to distinguish between plagiarism and the acceptable recycling of language. They describe how the use of text matching software in conjunction with concordancing programs can help students use sources appropriately and develop their academic voice.

Katarina Winka and Thomas Grysell conclude the collection with a powerful description of their use of Communal Roleplay – an innovative pedagogical theatre method they have evolved in Sweden for developing the academic skills of postgraduate supervisors, teachers and students alike.

In Conclusion

We were delighted with the range and depth of chapter proposals for this anthology – from which the published collection was distilled by double blind and peer review. It affirms that across the world there is an increasing number of faculty members who are actively concerned with innovating in their own educational practice.

It also highlights that, although technology has an important role to play in innovation, technology is not a *sine qua non*. Indeed, Csikszentmihalyi (2002: np), who has criticised both traditional and over-technological approaches to education, reflects that:

> *"It has turned out that mass education is more difficult to achieve than we had anticipated. To close the gap between the rather dismal reality and earlier expectations, researchers and practitioners have placed their faith in teaching methods modelled on computers and other rational means for conveying information – which in turn were modelled on industrial production techniques and on military human systems design. The implicit hope has been that if we discover more and more rational ways of selecting, organizing, and distributing knowledge, children will learn more effectively.... The claim is that if educators invested a fraction of the energy on stimulating the students' enjoyment of learning that they now spend in trying to transmit information we could achieve much better results. Literacy, numeracy, or indeed any other subject matter will be mastered more readily and more thoroughly when the student becomes able to derive intrinsic rewards from learning. At present, however, lamentably few students would recognize the idea that learning can be enjoyable."*

We trust that the chapters in this collection will inspire you in your quest for one or more teaching innovations that address your particular needs and circumstances.

About the Authors

Claus Nygaard is Professor in Management Education at Copenhagen Business School, Denmark and Director of LIHE. He can be contacted at this email: lihesupport@gmail.com

Nigel Courtney is Honorary Senior Visiting Fellow at Cass Business School, City University London, UK and Visiting Fellow at the University of Technology Sydney, Australia. He can be contacted at this email: nigel@city.ac.uk

Clive Holtham is Professor of Information Management and Director of the Learning Laboratory at Cass Business School, City University London, UK. He can be contacted at this email: c.w.holtham@city.ac.uk

Chapter Two

Resisting Student Consumers and Assisting Student Producers

Eva Dobozy

Introduction

This chapter offers a conceptual consideration of two interrelated issues plaguing higher education (HE) in Australia and elsewhere: The first being the persistent and growing notion of student-as-customer. The second being the increasing push for quality assurance and with it a directed move to inquiry learning and generic skills building in support of new graduate competencies and identities.

My aim is to draw attention to the growing tension between two competing notions in global, market-driven systems of higher education in a number of Western nations. The first is the age-old pedagogical question of the level of students' engagement with and commitment to learning. The second is the need for universities to satisfy customer demands, not only for flexible access to curriculum material and lecturing staff but also in relation to course-related demands and degrees of difficulty of study material and processes. There is an imperative in Australia and elsewhere to provide what in a market-driven trade system is often referred to as "quality customer service" to develop brand loyalty among students enrolled in a particular program (Bowden, 2009). The alternative is that dissatisfied students will simply switch to another HE provider and complete their degree requirements there. There is growing concern within Australia that under the current system, which invites increased competition among universities for fee-paying students' satisfaction, the maintenance of quality education provisions may suffer as some HE providers may be tempted to offer a more convenient and less demanding course (Arkoudis, *et al.*, 2009; Dow, *et al.*, 2009). This problem is echoing Bailey's (2000:353) views that *"classes become popularity contests [and] pedagogy becomes entertainment [as] student desire drives programs."*

What are the potential snowballing effects and implications of this tension for quality teaching in HE? What follows is, firstly, a contextual snapshot of neoliberal deregulation policy developments impacting on Australian higher education provisions and the problematic nature of the corporatisation of HE as perceived from a critical pedagogy perspective. The aim is to illustrate the shifting nature of higher education and the possible impacts of the corporatised discourse, especially as it relates to the "higher learning" needs of the 21st-century globalised world (Giroux, 2010). Secondly, I provide a brief discussion of the usefulness of three interrelated metaphors: students-as-customers, students-as-clients and students-as-producers. Thirdly, an in-depth exploration is presented of the meanings of these metaphors and what it means to construct pedagogies for learning that are grounded in contemporary critical pedagogy and social constructivist learning theory. The conclusion is drawn that even if there is a growing acceptance that paying students should be able to take advantage of flexible HE offerings, and pick and choose their courses and mode of study, there is an inherent danger in viewing and describing them as HE "customers" or "clients".

Australia's Cost-sharing Higher Education Policy

Australia has a history of deregulation of HE. In the late 1980s, the Labor Government, through its then Minister of Education John Dawkins, introduced a cost-sharing system, moving from a "student aid" to a "student trade" system (Dobson & Hölttä, 2001; Smart & Ang, 1993). The policy introduced a higher education fee, initially the Higher Education Loan Program (HELP) and later the Higher Education Contribution Scheme (HECS), which was strongly influenced by neoliberal conceptions of what the then Prime Minister Bob Hawke (1983) claimed to be "*the capacity of markets to allocate resources efficiently, or the great productive power that is associated with this capacity*".

The expansion of the HE system was seen as a primary goal of Hawke's Labor government, but an unintended consequence of the "Dawkins Revolution" has been that full-fee-paying international students were recruited in increasing numbers by Australian universities in order to supplement their drastically reduced income since the policy shift (Arkoudis *et al.*, 2009; Milne, 2001). In addition to the previous measures introduced three decades ago, a further deregulation of the HE market place is commencing next year. The policy imperative for growth is intended to encourage domestic students from diverse backgrounds to apply for a university place and this is seen as vital to achieving the current Australian federal government's goal of increasing the target of a university-educated Australian workforce from 34.2% of 25 to 35 year olds in 2010 to 40% in 2025 (O'Keeffe, 2011). Fuelled by a globalised market perspective for the cost-sharing and an income generating higher education sector in Australia, student financial contributions to their higher education have steadily increased over the past decades. In addition, the latest developments of further deregulation and an anticipated increase in competition among universities for first-generation students from diverse backgrounds has strengthened concerns of the maintenance of quality in HE provisions (Dow, *et al.*, 2009).

Taking into account the increasing complexity of HE in Australia and elsewhere (Chevalier, 2007; Dobson, 2007), the critical scrutiny of the impact of globalised market forces on what counts as higher education, in the sense of transformational learning experience, becomes increasingly vital. This is accentuated by mounting evidence that the view of students as customers or clients is not confined to Anglo-Saxon nations but instead is also spreading rapidly on the European mainland (Kwiek, 2009) and in Asia (Dobson, 2007).

Critical Pedagogy for 21st-century Learning

Critical pedagogy is a historically grounded learning theory, which has its roots in social theory and the Frankfurt School of educational philosophy (Blake *et al.*, 2003). It provides a critique of neoliberal developments in HE and promotes a transformation of the individual and society through formative and developmental education grounded in the critique of ideology (based on the German notion of *Bildung* – combining personal and cultural maturation – as opposed to vocational training). Hence, the aim of education is to increase epistemological understanding that provides grounding for ethical social and cognitive behaviour through the deconstruction of taken-for-granted neoliberal values and attitudes, de-centring oppressive systems (Nash, 1990). Hence, critical pedagogy is seen as an ideal theoretical framework for the present analysis. The approach to critical pedagogy taken here is to problematise current educational practices in some HE systems that are a threat to "higher" learning. Henry Giroux (2007, 2010), a staunch critic of the market-based neoliberal rationality which is, so he claims, holding HE "hostage", treating students as customers, makes *"no distinction between schools and restaurants"* (Giroux, 2010:186). Focusing on narrow technical knowledge acquisition in conjunction with the domination of HE by market forces, is putting a misplaced emphasis on training at the expense of transformational learning. Tertiary education's mission in the current era of globalised knowledge economies is multi-faceted and needs to include opportunities for students to develop moral and political agency in parallel with the growth and practice of professional skills and knowledge which are vital for a vibrant democracy (Aghion *et al.*, 2008; Giroux, 2010; Trilling & Fadel, 2009). This extension of corporate logic and HE entrepreneurship leads to the "businessification" (Mayo, 2009) of HE which is undermining democracy (Giroux, 2007) and leading to hegemonic globalisation, with the aim of increasing the responsiveness of HE to *"the market order and to market interests of their customers"* (Olssen & Peters, 2005:326).

I offer three metaphors to assist in the deconstruction of neoliberal market forces on HE students' knowledge production processes. I argue that metaphors or analogies can be helpful tools in aiding understanding of unfamiliar or changing concepts. Metaphors work by relating novel ideas to already-known notions of a given concept, such as referring to a student as a customer. Thus, expressing the changing idea of a student to the specific term of a customer, supports the emergence of a new mental model. Metaphors can also be used to trigger an image schema (e.g. fee-paying student), or an "attention grabber" (e.g. value for money), which is intended to provoke a particular response (Aragno, 2009). However, metaphors are most commonly used to identify and explore widely recognised but ill-defined and fuzzy sets of relational concepts. Hence, they are effectively aiding personal and communal meaning-making processes, using organisational structures to influence perceptions. An example of powerful metaphoric images (conveying various connotations) is Bailey's (2000:353) conception of student-as-customer which he contrasts with conceptions of students-as-clients and, later on, with students-as-producers.

Student-as-Customer/-Client/-Producer Metaphors

The metaphor student-as-customer has become well used in the HE literature (Boden & Epstein, 2006; Franz, 1998; Little & Williams, 2010; Mandelson, 2009; McCulloch, 2009). However, it has been used variously and is greatly contested. Table 1 contrasts Bailey's (2000) definitions of the student-as-customer metaphor and the student-as-client metaphor

Student-as-customer	**Student-as-client**
A customer is a person who buys goods or services and expects his or her expressed preferences to be met with regard to the product or service being purchased • Passive recipients of a service that will need to meet quality approval as judged by the customer • Low degree of professional competence and ethics • Insignificant personal consequences for the customer • Transactional relationship: anonymous, value-for-money, and efficient	A client is one for whom professional services are rendered • Passive recipient of a service that is accepted as being performed "in the best interest of the client" and operating within professional standards • High degree of professional competence and ethics • Significant personal consequences for the client • Transactional relationship: personalised and effective

Table 1: Student-as-Customer and Student-as-Client Differentiation, Adapted from Bailey (2000:354).

Bailey (2000:355) asserts that there are distinct differences in conception of roles and expectations of customers and clients of education. He argues that these conceptions shape the thinking of lecturers and students as they engage in the learning and teaching process. However, the focus on conceptual difference *"does not preclude that there may also be some similarities"* between the roles and expectations of students as customers/clients. In essence Bailey (2000) notes that there is a qualitatively different relationship between students-as-customers and students-as-clients. For example, whereas a customer may expect that s/he has the right to judge the goods and services rendered based on her or his understanding of service and quality, the delivery may not necessarily require high professional standards or ethical behaviour. As long as the goods and services provided meet the expectations of customers, they are perceived as "quality" goods or services. However, a client would expect goods and services rendered to be in their best interest. However, in addition to their customer satisfaction expectations, clients also expect a high level of professional competence and ethical behaviour on the part of the goods/services provider which is, so Bailey (2000) argues, the key difference between the two, as outlined in Table 1. Hence, he favours the student-as-client metaphor.

Nevertheless, it should be recognised that the learning experience offered in both cases is firmly grounded in traditional relationships between the expert (the teacher) and the novice (the learner) and represents classical transmission pedagogies. This view of higher learning received is quite different in a non-traditional relationship between teachers and students, when students are asked to become "producers" of knowledge and goods, which results not simply in knowledge acquisition, but should have a transformative effect, enabling the demonstration of deep commitment to learning and the development of civic responsibility vital for successful 21st-century life and work (Trilling & Fadel, 2009).

A recent objection to the student-as-customer view (Lambert *et al.*, 2007; McCulloch, 2009; Neary, 2009), which is said to be based on a *"neo-liberal market model of corporate governance"* (Neary, 2009:6), is concerned with involving students in quality assurance processes (such as rating lecturer performance based on students' satisfaction) at the expense of deep engagement with learning. Little & Williams (2010) found that there is an over-emphasis on student-as-customer in the (UK) higher education community. They note:

> *"[A] sense of one-directional transactions between the higher education provider and learner ... tends to heighten notions of students as customers or consumers. ... This might lead to students behaving as passive recipients of higher education and restrict their full involvement in a learning community in ways that inform and enhance the collective student learning experience".* (Little & Williams, 2010:125)

Similarly, in a recent speech at a European HE summit, the then UK business Secretary Lord Mandelson explained pragmatically:

> *"As students who go into higher education pay more, they will expect more and are entitled to receive more in terms, not just of the range of courses, but in the quality of experience they receive during their time in the higher education system".* (Mandelson, 2009)

How is the quality of experience related to the quality of product and service rendered? Is it implied that students go on an enjoyable, stress-free journey to be pampered and looked after to somehow finish the journey with a degree after four years, or is the quality of experience related to how transformational the education rendered is?

What Is and What Is Not "Quality" Education?

In his rather one-sided and unflattering account of the effect of student satisfaction ratings on his teaching, Peter Sacks is able to demonstrate eloquently the tension between lecturer and student and the significance of the current debate. As Sacks (1986) explains:

> *"And so, in my mind, I became a teaching teddy bear. In the metaphorical sandbox I created, students could do no wrong, and I did almost anything possible to keep all of them happy, all of the time, no matter how childish or rude their behavior, no matter how poorly they performed in the course, no matter how little effort they gave. If they wanted their hands held, I would hold them. If they wanted a stapler (or a Kleenex) and I didn't have one, I'd apologize. If they wanted to read the newspaper while I was addressing the class or if they wanted to get up and leave in the middle of a lecture, go for it. Call me spineless. I confess. But in the excessively accommodative culture that I found myself in, "our*

> *students" as many of my colleagues called them, had too much power for me to afford irritating them with demands and challenges I had previously thought were part and parcel of the collegiate experience".* (cited in Haskel, 1997:37)

Subsequent studies reported in the education literature confirm the dilemma posed by Sacks; some of these studies even point to an inverse relationship between student satisfaction and academic attainment. For example, Yunker and Yunker (2003) found that first-year students who attended an introductory accounting class that received high ratings for student satisfaction tended to perform markedly less well in subsequent accounting classes than students who were taught by lecturers who received less favourable ratings from students.

What are unintended outcomes of conflicting role conceptions of students (as learners as well as evaluators of teaching effectiveness) in an increasingly diverse and competitive, globalised, HE marketplace? Current practices of student evaluation of teaching have been shown to reinforce stereotypical views and perceptions: i.e. in student satisfaction ratings minority faculty has been rated markedly lower compared with non-ethnic lecturers (Pourmand Nordick, 2005).

Nevertheless, it needs to be stated that no consensus has been reached on the validity of student satisfaction ratings; findings have been varied and controversial. With the availability of the research findings I have reported above and many more, it is relatively easy for antagonists to pick those that support their view. The most recent meta-analysis of studies about this issue was conducted by Clayson (2009:16). He was unable to settle the debate and concluded that *"the more objective learning is measured, the less likely it is to relate to the [student] evaluation [of teaching]"*. Moreover, he finishes his paper with a rather dark statement about human behaviour:

> *"If you make people think they're thinking, they'll love you. If you really make them think, they'll hate you".* (Marquis, cited in Clayson, 2009:27)

In the section to follow, an example of the incorporation of inquiry learning approaches in teacher education is provided to illustrate the evolution of views and the emergence of a new metaphor, namely, student-as-producer.

Inquiry Learning and the Out-of-the-Comfort-Zone Reaction of Students

Henry Giroux (1988, 1994) and Paulo Freire (1970), two of the more prominent critical pedagogy scholars, alerted at the end of the last century to the need to create opportunities for transformative experiences in education at all levels. Giroux (1994:280) noted that *"educators will not be able to ignore the hard questions"*, which ultimately *"will play a major role in defining the meaning and purpose of [higher learning]"*. Contemporary researchers in the field of education renewal argue that inquiry-learning experiences are essential for the preparation of workers in a networked and knowledge-based society that is faced with increasingly unequal distribution of resources (Levy *et al.*, 2010; McKinsey, 2007; Nygaard *et al.*, 2008; World Bank, 2008). Such a call for renewal of education practices in the service of a globalised world and socially aware cultural practices emphasises the development of soft skills, such as critical and creative thinking, communication, collaboration and networking. This has been referred to by Reynolds (2006:55) as *"learning-centredness"*. Although researchers advocate a variety of inquiry learning models, they all acknowledge the active and independent role of students. This is a distinct departure from the student-as-customer and student-as-client models, both of which imply that students are passive recipients of education goods and services from lecturers and teachers. In the case of student-as-customer, the lecturer or teacher is primarily concerned to satisfy the student-customer. As was outlined above, this view is contrasted with the student-client, who receives educational products (learning content) of high standard, and the lecturer or teacher who has the best interest of the client in mind even when this takes precedence over the wishes of the client. Hence, in a "client relationship" the roles of the lecturer/teacher and students are somewhat altered: the lecturer/teacher is not expected to provide an easily digestible education (often through fulfilling the role of "sage on the stage"), transmitting knowledge to the student through a banking system of education where lecturers/teachers *"make knowledge deposits"* (Freire, 1970:27). Although still utilising traditional pedagogies, the role of standards and quality control supersedes the need for student satisfaction, hence the lecturers/tutors are moving towards a more educative mode of teaching with the aim of inducing deep learning, employing social constructivist pedagogies such as class discussions and debates, cooperative learning and peer mentoring to ensure maximum learning.

In a complex learning environment (Rupp *et al.*, 2010), where teachers are no longer asked to be primarily information transmitters but rather learning managers, students are active learners, effectively becoming knowledge and goods producers; hence student-producers. Active learning includes asking questions, determining problems, engaging in deep and independent thinking, investigating, inquiring, testing explanations, and dialogue in the search for possible solutions (Trilling & Fadel, 2009). The demands placed on students in such an environment are very different, requiring a willingness and ability on the part of the student to be proactive in the learning of skills as well as content-specific understanding (Ringleb & Rock, 2009). Moreover, students need to be willing risk-takers, learn to cope with ambiguity and embrace the possibility of mistake-making as a necessary learning step. In this way they develop and practice a collection of skills and knowledge, assume identities and test personal values that form the transformative framework of the student-producer. Rupp *et al.*, (2010:17) refer to this collection as *"SKIVE (skills, knowledge, values, and epistemology)"*.

The metaphors of "swamp" and "mess" provide useful images to illustrate possible emotional responses to necessary engagement levels of students when they are presented with ill-structured problems that demand active participation and the application of SKIVE. As Schön (1987:28) noted: *"In the swampy lowland, messy, confusing problems defy [easily transmitted] technical solutions"*. Similarly, Russell Ackoff (1974:21) acknowledges that *"a mess is a set of external conditions that produces dissatisfaction; alternatively a system of problems"*. When it comes to learning, complexity acts as a barrier to understanding. It requires of the learner strategic skills in "mess management", especially a willingness and ability to engage in deep thinking and problem solving (Little & Williams, 2010; Piihl & Philipsen, this volume). In other words, it is argued here that active learning processes demand collaboration, inquiry, a commitment to understanding, and a tolerance for ambiguity in the name of new knowledge, goods and identity production.

Arguably, if the student is to embrace inquiry learning it means agreeing to become a student-producer rather than demanding a consumer/client relationship with the lecturer/teacher. In particular this applies when the lecturer/teacher is able to satisfy the need of a student to gain narrow technical knowledge in a particular field (which will be outdated very soon) even though they have not yet learned to value and perform critical and creative problem-solving on the job. Through active participation, collaboration and the testing of ideas, the student-producer becomes engaged in deep transformative learning by the active production of knowledge (Neary, 2009) and self (Giroux, 2010; Rupp *et al.*, 2010). Hence, a willingness to engage, to choose to be an active participant in a learning/working situation, is increasingly perceived as a lynch pin in successful outcomes, because it signals *"the degree of positive emotion"* a student is willing to exert towards the learning situation. In short, *"they are attracted to, inspired by, committed to, and even fascinated by their work or their input to the work relationship"* (Ringleb & Rock, 2009:4).

Similarly, Neary (2009:6) advises that:

> *"[The] process of turning the student as consumer into the student as producer can be achieved by providing more research or research-like experiences as an integral part of the undergraduate experience. ... This is particularly important in a context within which students have been forced into the position of consumers in a service culture that many academics regard as antithetical to the academic project of the university".*

However, inquiry learning models, such as problem-based learning and collaborative project work, place great demands on students and require them to show willingness and ability to embrace their roles as producers rather than consumers. For students to actively resist such a challenge is an understandable reaction to novel teaching models. But the reward for perseverance is what Dewey (1910) referred to as *"the formation of wide-awake, careful, thorough habits of thinking"* and a thirst for understanding (cited in Hickman & Alexander, 1981:274). Moreover, an ability to assess risk is the first step in switching from a passive learning mode to one that is more active and directive (Papastephanou, 2006).

Changing educational experiences that are geared less towards pandering to student satisfaction ratings and more towards the students pushing through their personal "risk barrier" should be seen as the key to quality teaching and learning. Hence, making available experiences of inquiry learning may become a personal catalyst for unsettling taken-for-granted views and practices, opening up possibilities for localised educational transformation (Robinson *et al.*, 2008).

I argue that teacher education and school education have for too long been dominated by didactic approaches to learning and teaching, where students have been viewed as empty vessels to be filled with pre-programmed content knowledge (Dobozy, 2007). One of the main aims of traditional school education was to produce students who demonstrated basic factual knowledge and basic functional skills in the key learning areas of English (reading and writing) and mathematics. These basics were deemed sufficient for most people to participate successfully in an industrial society (Cazden *et al.*, 1996). But as outlined by the Australian Curriculum Assessment and Reporting Authority (formerly known as the National Curriculum Board), there is a need to move away from traditional views and practices in education to a system that accommodates the needs of a knowledge economy and a rapidly changing globalised world. *"However dimly the demands of societies in the mid-2020s can now be seen, some serious attempt must be made to envisage those demands and to ensure they are taken into account in present-day curriculum development"* (National Curriculum Board, 2009:5).

Nonetheless, student satisfaction ratings are not conducive to nurturing teacher education students' critical thinking and creative problem-solving. It is vital to provide learning experiences in teacher education that enable students to practise and extend reflective abilities. As Snowman *et al.*, 2009:588) note:

> *"Although reflection will feature in more and more pre-service teacher education, the available evidence suggests that pre-service teachers are severely limited in their ability to step back from and critically reflect upon their actions in university study, practicum tasks and learning activities".*

In a somewhat humorous way, Semler (2007) has referred to the paradigm shift from traditional teacher-centric, content-driven didactic approaches to learning-centred models in education as "the James Bond effect" – where students come to wonder what just happened. Moving from one paradigm to another leaves, so he argues, too many *"shaken, not stirred"*. Moreover, he notes that:

> *"[when an] individual has been deeply drilled (consciously and unconsciously) in the methods and ideas of an enormously powerful pedagogical system* [student-as-consumer] *and then finds herself in the grip of another quite different system* [student-as-producer] *... [it] requires no less than submission of the student mind to a paradigm of pedagogy and scholarship that from the student's perspective comes out of the blue"* (Semler, 2007) with my explanatory insertions.

The discrepancy in expectations of what is perceived to be good teaching presents real obstacles and increases anxiety levels of many students who encounter inquiry learning, more often than not by chance rather than strategic planning in HE which, in many parts of the Western world, is still dominated largely by transmission-style lecturing.

Students-as-Producers and Transformational Learning

As student-producers progress in their learning, their understanding of the interplay between learning goals, learning design and learning output grows. Inquiry-based learning and teaching enables students to have substantial decision-making powers, co-directing their learning with their teacher and with each other. Learning goals are typically stipulated in advance by external bodies, such as transnational curriculum organisations (e.g. the OECD Directorate for Education) or political and/or professional associations and agencies (e.g. The Australian Tertiary Education Quality Standards Agency; The Association of European Universities). However, the learning design and learning output is regulated to a lesser extent if at all (Dow *et al.*, 2009). After learning goals have been explained to student-producers, working through an inquiry-learning process, they set out to design the product plan, thinking through individual steps and strategies. There comes a time where student-producers encounter unanticipated problems and hurdles that need to be addressed and a solution found in order to proceed. This particularly demands stamina and coping skills in addition to technical knowledge and skills (Spronken-Smith, *et al.*, 2011). As student-producers work towards the completion of their product, they enjoy learning successes and challenges. This type of learning has been deemed transformational because the students bring their own ideas, deep-seated values, skills and knowledge, and a variation of constructs and domain-specific expertise to the learning endeavour. In grappling with the complex learning tasks they are become engaged in building new metal models, values and attitudes; in other words, SKIVE (Rudd, *et al.*, 2010). Moreover, in doing so, they learn to *"appreciate the difficulties and values of 'getting stuck'"* (Whitehouse, 2011:158) as they mobilise their collective wisdom and find innovative solutions to emerging problems. Both the problems and solutions were previously hidden from students' views. This learning has been described by various scholars (Dobozy, 2007; Giroux, 2010; Hayes, 2008; Rudd *et al.*, 2010; Spronken-Smith, *et al.*, 2010) as transformational, implying a fundamental change in the student, a shift in thinking and acting as they perceive their reality and their role as learners differently than they did prior to the learning experience. The student-producer comes to appreciate the learning journey and their role in it. Hence, transformation is more than simply a new way of thinking. It is, so Hayes (2008:28) argues, *"evidenced in behaviour, felt and manifested in emotions"* as students are willingly rejecting the role of student-as-consumer/client and appreciating the opportunities that student-as-producer roles are offering to them, individually and collectively, they are acquiring a mindset that is accommodating the changed reality.

Conclusion

At a time when competition for HE students is intensifying, awareness of competing demands and tensions concerning student satisfaction on the one hand, and academic standards concerning student learning engagement and learning outcomes on the other hand, need to be addressed. The aim of this chapter has been to alert the reader firstly to some common pitfalls in conception and metaphoric speech patterns and, secondly, to tensions that exist between student-as-customer satisfaction goals and quality assurance measures. The goods and services that universities (ought to) provide is education; a process in which students are developing a collection of knowledge, skills, and values that are transformative in nature, enabling the development of a deep commitment to learning and personal agency. There is an inherent danger in viewing students as higher education customers because it is simply not enough for students to passively acquire technical skills and knowledge; they need to become competent in the production of SKIVE (skills, knowledge, identity, values and epistemology), enabled through active learning processes. The student-as-producer metaphor makes provision for students to embrace the swampy lowland and messy, confusing problems in appreciation of transformative education (Schön, 1987). But for this metaphor to gain credence, students, lecturers, education administrators and corporate business will need to buy into the changed conception and see its value. Students are not, and should not be, referred to as customers, they are active and productive participants in their learning endeavours. Hence, the societal and individual cost of the businessification of HE will need to be acknowledged in order to increase the willingness of university teachers and learners to explore alternatives to transmission education.

About the Author

Eva Dobozy is a Senior Lecturer in the School of Education at Edith Cowan University, Australia. She can be contacted at this email: e.dobozy@ecu.edu.au

Chapter Three

A Research-based Approach to University Curriculum Development that Prepares Students for Subsequent Practice

Jesper Piihl and Kristian Philipsen

Introduction

The quest in higher education to go beyond transmission involves creating student-producers (Dobozy, this volume). But in what way should we create student-producers in the research-based setting of universities which at the same time strive for practical relevance for professionals after graduation? Donald A. Schön suggests that after graduation many professionals are faced with a dilemma:

> *"Shall he remain on the high ground where he can solve relatively unimportant problems according to his standards of rigour, or shall he descend to the swamp of important problems where he cannot be rigorous in any way he knows how to describe?"* (1995:28)

Schön describes this as a dilemma between rigour and relevance. University-based educational programmes can easily find themselves in the same dilemma. The universities have a special task in delivering teaching based on research which can be interpreted as teaching with a strong and dominant element of rigour. In contrast, the quest for relevance tends to focus on important and practical challenges which demand competence to act in enterprising ways in professional situations.

If we follow Schön's argument, educational programmes based on research and enterprising behaviour in professional situations would appear to be mutually exclusive.

One way to overcome the dilemma between rigour and relevance is to make sure that students are presented with research-based knowledge and methods as well as being faced with the need to solve practical challenges during their study. Our experience from a bachelor degree programme in business administration, innovation and entrepreneurship shows that many students do not recognise the dilemma between rigour and relevance; instead they experience two separate worlds that have very little in common!

Our efforts with teaching entrepreneurship and innovation courses and being responsible for developing the curriculum of the entire bachelor study programme have made us curious to understand the theory underpinning the mix of research and practice in curriculum development. Within business disciplines the research-practice gap has been discussed in the literature (Syed *et al.*, 2010), and some authors see teaching as one way to bridge this gap (Burke & Rau, 2010). The literature tends to divide the research-practice gap into two separate gaps and deal with them in isolation: one gap between research and teaching, focusing on how to bring research-based knowledge into the classroom and another gap between teaching and practice which is focused on developing informed and thoughtful managers.

Instead of treating this issue as two separate debates we will, in this chapter, view it as one debate concerned with interpreting research-based teaching that develops students as knowledge producers through working with and like researchers (Fibæk-Laursen, 1998). However, since most of our students are not going to stay on the high hard ground by turning into researchers in their future career, we need to resolve the dilemma suggested by Schön. In this chapter we therefore expand our image of knowledge production by building on the distinction between knowledge production in the two Modes defined by Gibbons *et al.* (1994).

"Mode 1" describes a classical idea in which knowledge production takes place in research institutions working with defined disciplines that because of their delimitations are relatively homogenous across academic fields. Mode 1 has a hierarchical structure in which quality control follows logics of objectivity and independence and is checked by peer reviews. Mode 1 can be said to correspond to Schön's demand for rigour.

Unlike the knowledge production of Mode 1, "Mode 2" examines the idea that knowledge production is not confined to only one place and is closely connected to application contexts. Knowledge production in Mode 2 is dispersed among a number of parties including universities, customers, firms, institutions, organisations, single persons etc. Mode 2 delimits its problems on the basis of the application context in contrast to the way in which the disciplines are divided in Mode 1. This makes the knowledge of Mode 2 seem more heterogeneous. In Mode 2 the quality control consists of a so-called reality check in which the quality is judged by the actors of the specific application contexts in which knowledge is produced and unfolds during specific actions. In this respect, Mode 2 can be said to correspond to Schön's demand for relevance.

Within curriculum development theory, relevant theoretical concepts like competence-in-practice (Nygaard & Holtham, 2008) can contribute to explaining the practical part of knowledge. However, Nygaard and Holtham (2008) primarily examine *learning* competence-in-practice and do not reflect on what it means to be competent-in-practice and how this links to curriculum development and research-based teaching.

Following the arguments above, the question we ask is: how do we develop university curricula, emphasising research-based teaching in which the students are seen as producers, in ways that make better practitioners?

These issues are investigated through the development of a theoretical frame of reference in which the question is discussed in relation to knowledge production in Mode 1 and Mode 2 (Gibbons *et al.*, 1994). The contribution of this theoretical frame of reference is a broad typological description of how theoretical fields of knowledge relate to different perspectives on how a competent practitioner makes use of different areas of scientific knowledge in subsequent practice – or what we term "theory-of-application". The investigation of theory-of-application is related to students' learning situation and, in particular, to curriculum developers' perspectives on how to develop a curriculum to match theory-of application.

This chapter is structured into the following sections. Firstly, we briefly sketch central themes in overall curriculum theory in order to position our contribution in relation to the overall theme of this anthology. Our starting point for discussing issues regarding curriculum development is our personal journey from teaching and researching entrepreneurship and innovation to being responsible for entire study programmes. The second section dwells on two challenges emerging from the clashes between pedagogical developments within the specific field of entrepreneurship to the broader fields of business economics and social sciences. In the third section these building blocks are combined into a theoretical framework for discussing curriculum development which balances different conceptions of the relationship between rigour and relevance. The final section illustrates how this theoretical framework relates to different lines of study and how application can be built into curriculum in different ways.

Curriculum Theory and the Link to Practice

Nygaard & Holtham (2008) distinguish between content and process perspectives on curriculum development and discuss five concepts to be taken into account when developing a learning centred curriculum:

- People base their learning on their individual experiences and expectations;
- Learning is an individual as well as a social process;
- Learning is contextual and tied to specific situations;
- Learning is affected by the identity of the learner;
- Learning is affected by the learner's social position and the learner's embeddedness in social collectives.

Following Schön's ideas introduced above, teaching aiming at knowledge with a high degree of rigour does not in itself develop the competences needed to deal with problems of high relevance. Instead Nygaard & Holtham (2008) discuss the idea of competence-in-practice as *"the ability to apply one's knowledge and skills so the* ***task at hand*** *is solved in a way which is recognized by relevant peers as being competent"* (our emphasis added).

The literature on curriculum theory views the relationship between educational programmes and practice from different angles. Several studies discuss the expectations of students about the link between formal education and professional working life (Abrandt Dahlgren *et al.*, 2008; Dahlgren *et al.*, 2005). Tynjälä *et al.* (2006) examine the long term effects of university education by making graduates reflect on what aspects from their formal education they use in their professional career. They report that 64% of the respondents said that the most important skills they needed in their job were learnt at work while only 14% reported that these skills were learnt during their university education. In short, empirical evidence that supports Schön's conjecture.

A common theme in the literature on the relationship between university education and practice is that students are held to be the focal point of interest. The perspective on the students as the "journey men" between different contexts (Dahlgren *et al.*, 2005) comes in different ways. Firstly, in discussing learning-centred curriculum development the focus is the learning of the students. Secondly, in discussing the expectations of the students, the link between education and professional life is the main concern. Thirdly, when studying graduated students' experience of the relationship between education and practice, the retrospective reflections must be dealt with. The final perspective is concerned with targeting students' perceptions about what it means to be a professional.

Challenges to Curriculum Theory from the Field of Entrepreneurship Teaching

Having our professional roots in entrepreneurship and innovation research and teaching, and now targeting curriculum development in broader terms, we perceive two chief challenges:

- Challenge 1: How do we develop competence-in-practice?
- Challenge 2: Does real life professional work match the implicit assumptions about practice which are built into the content and processes of our teaching and what is the theory-of-application in different academic fields?

Concentrating on the first challenge, entrepreneurship and innovation is seen in many countries as a way to assure economic growth and prosperity in society (Acs & Szerb, 2007; Thurik & Wennekers, 2004). As a result there is strong political interest in developing entrepreneurial skills among university students. However, it quickly becomes difficult to explain how reading entrepreneurship literature would develop the skills for actually being an entrepreneur. Management researchers like Drucker (1985) argue that *"entrepreneurship is neither a science nor an art. It is practice. ...what constitutes knowledge in practice is largely defined by the ends; that is, by practice"*. Although Drucker it is not offering a how-to book his argument is concerned with the practice both of innovation and of entrepreneurship. He views the practice as dealing with what, when and why (Drucker, 1985:vii-viii). Though Drucker defines innovation and entrepreneurship practice he does not explain how students are going to learn it. From our own teaching practice we have seen that internship (the situation in which students are temporarily affiliated by a firm or an organisation) raises questions about the relationship between both forms of knowledge, theoretical and practical, because both types are present simultaneously for the students.

There is a need to ask how the knowledge developed through the curriculum is supposed to be employed and create value in practical situations. In the literature this is certainly not a new question or challenge (Biggs & Tang, 2007); however, in contemporary universities it is easy to find course descriptions in which this link is not necessarily obvious.

The second challenge might not be obvious to the same degree. It is concerned with the idea that the nature of practice does not always match the implicit assumptions regarding practice which can be said to be implied by the traditional research-based knowledge communicated through a traditional transmission model. Tynjälä *et al.* argue that:

> *"Paradoxically, expertise being collective poses challenges to individuals. Sharing knowledge, working in networks, communicating with professionals from other fields, all these require social interaction and interpersonal skills of individuals. Thus, professional expertise is much more than having a strong domain-specific knowledge base".* (Tynjälä *et al.* 2006:75)

This concern about expertise as a collective and not an individual element poses challenges to the content-focused transmission model.

Furthermore, these authors argue that the conditions for knowledge production have also changed:

> *"New kinds of industrial production are dependent not only on new information technology but also on new kinds of expertise. Knowledge production has extended from universities to the areas of application. The dichotomy of basic and applied research is fading. Work organisations are not only using and applying knowledge produced in the university but they are also producing, transforming and managing knowledge by themselves to create innovations. In other words, many organisations have become knowledge intensive innovation centres in which collaborative work, networking, and transformative and creative learning have become key concepts in organisational development. And this applies not only to large private sector production."* (Tynjälä *et al.*, 2006, p. 74)

These ideas suggest that developing a learning centred curriculum with emphasis on building competence-in-practice needs to be based on relevant conceptual and theoretical understanding regarding the nature of practice and specifically how the competent practitioner is expected to make use of their professional training in practical situations. In their work, Biggs & Tang (2007) do make connections between learning and the context of application in arguing that intended learning outcomes should be formulated in the form of "*verbs that the students have to enact as appropriate to the context of the content discipline*" (Biggs & Tang, 2007:59). However, they do not link their discussions to different forms of knowledge production within different academic disciplines.

Therefore, we see a need for contributions linking curriculum and practice; not in terms of "student as journey man" connecting two different worlds but in terms of a form of theory-of-application related to various scientific knowledge areas in the curriculum. Taking any specific domain of knowledge, we need to start asking for an explication of that knowledge area's implicit assumptions about how this knowledge is expected to produce value in real life professional applications.

Furthermore, while recognising the definition of competence-in-practice presented above, we see a need to examine it in the context of a task in hand. When the practitioner has a clear and mutually accepted definition of the task in hand it might be possible to deal with it in ways that peers will recognise to be competent. However, in many practical situations, the professional practitioner will be confronted by important problems but task in hand may not be obvious – especially in situations where s/he is expected to drive innovative processes. The primary concern will be to identify, frame, legitimise and communicate the task in hand.

Therefore the theoretical framework developed in this chapter intends to open a discussion of implicit assumptions regarding application in different theoretical fields and forms of knowledge production.

Development of a Theoretical Frame of Reference

Lave and Wenger (1999) distinguish between teaching curriculum and learning curriculum. Teaching curriculum refers to the ideas put into the curriculum by the persons developing it, i.e. intended learning outcomes, intended types of teaching, intended learning behaviour etc. Learning curriculum on the other hand refers to the curriculum seen from the perspective of the learner/student and thereby refers to the personal objectives of a given learner with his/her particular background and intentions.

The specific purpose of this section is to develop a theoretical framework in which we can, in a structured manner, describe, analyse and clarify the challenges of developing university curricula aiming to achieve both rigour and relevance. Therefore this section deals with teaching curriculum and we also address how the concept of learning curriculum can be utilised to address the issues discussed.

The need for relevance and competences to act in enterprising ways makes it clear that we need to relate our curricula to the ways of working in the communities to which the students are expected to contribute after graduation.

To address this we have developed a two-dimensional, theoretical frame of reference with the following axes:

- A vertical spectrum spanning from scientific knowledge areas to the graduate's professional behaviour in the context of application. In the centre of this spectrum is the intended student learning behaviour. Above the centre line are the elements bridging between scientific knowledge areas and intended student learning, which are the elements included in the teaching curriculum. Below the centre line are ideas regarding the elements bridging between the intended student learning and expected behaviour as a competent professional – which is what we term theory-of-application.

- The horizontal spectrum spans two institutionalised impressions of knowledge production. On the left side, Mode 1 theory of knowledge production, and Mode 2 on the right.

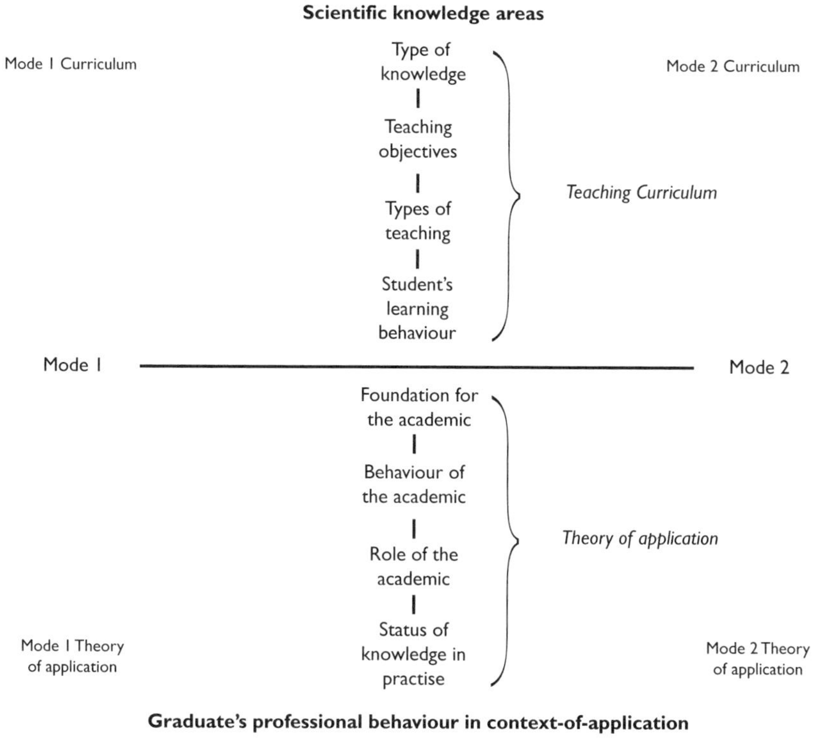

Figure 1: Linking Teaching Curriculum to Theory-of-Application.

The Vertical Dimension Depicted in Figure 1

On the vertical dimension, the upper part relates to what is going on during the programme of study, while the lower part is related to theories-of-application regarding the role expected to be fulfilled by the trained academic in his/her career following graduation. In developing a traditional research-based teaching curriculum, the focus is on the elements above the line – ranging from types of knowledge to students' learning behaviour. But, because of the challenges we have described, it is necessary to do this with an eye on the elements below the line – the roles that the trained academic has to fulfil after graduation. In short, on theory-of-application. Therefore, the vertical axis spans from "scientific knowledge areas" to "graduates professional behaviour in context-of-application".

Concentrating first on the upper part of the vertical dimension, scientific knowledge areas are linked to students' intended learning by the way in which the curriculum is designed. If the idea of alignment is followed (Biggs & Tang, 2007) this dimension starts by scoping the types of knowledge to be dealt with in a particular educational programme. This results in a set of teaching objectives, course descriptions, and the subjects to be addressed. When the teaching objectives are established, relevant types of teaching must be developed, based on impressions of student behaviour during the educational programme. In Figure 1 this is labelled "students' learning behaviour".

If we turn to theory-of-application – the zone below the horizontal, mirror axis – we can also differentiate between the different levels. For example: how knowledge relates to practice, which role the academic is expected to fulfil, and which academic competence this rests upon.

The vertical mirror axis thus provides a coherent linking mechanism between curriculum development and theory-of-application.

The Horizontal Dimension in Figure 1

Horizontally, the discussion spans different perceptions of knowledge production, as they can be seen as having different theories-of-application. This dimension is developed in response to the second challenge we have identified, namely; that the theory-of-application in traditional research-based teaching does not necessarily match the world as encountered by professionals.

Following the advice of Tynjäla *et al.* (2006) we propose more varied reflections on practice by distinguishing between two alternative theories-of-application built on the distinction between Mode 1 and Mode 2 knowledge (Gibbons, 1997; Gibbons *et al.*, 1994). To a large extent this debate concerns the university and the interaction of research with the surrounding society and is rooted in both university history and theory of science. However, if the concern shifts towards curriculum development and theory-of-application it will have massive consequences whether Mode 1 or Mode 2 is considered.

We unfold the typology by discussing the content of the two pairs of opposite dimensions: Vertically, by the play between scientific knowledge areas/curriculum development on one side and theory-of-application/competent professional on the other, and horizontally, between the two perspectives of knowledge production – Mode 1 and Mode 2.

By elaborating the content of the four quadrants in the framework, Figure 2 emerges:

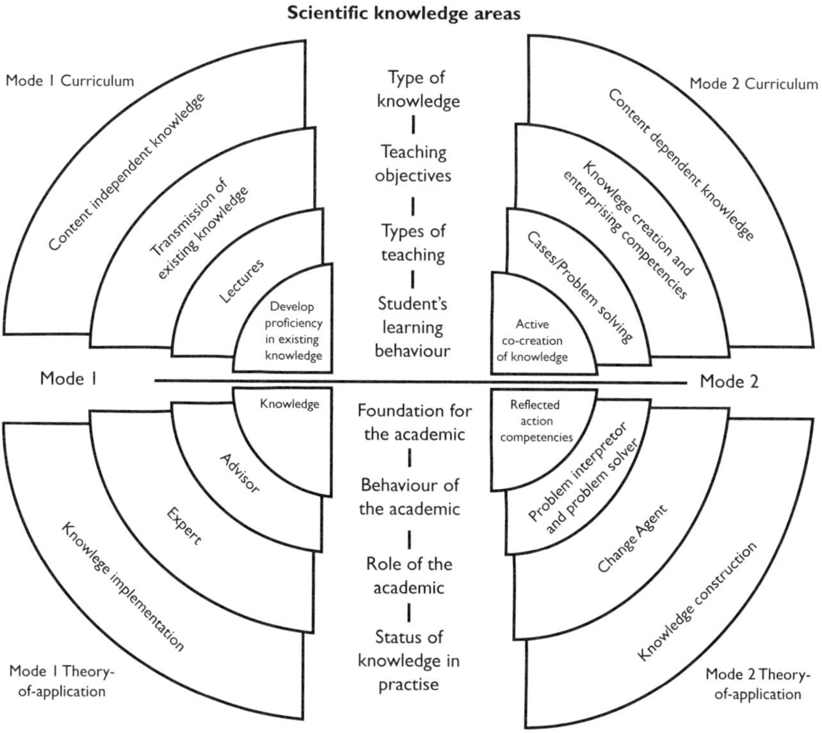

Figure 2: Specific Examples Linking Teaching Curriculum and Theory-of-Application.

Mode 1 curriculum. In the top left quadrant – in Mode 1 and concentrating on curriculum – the starting point is that research produces general knowledge that is independent of specific contexts. The objective of the teaching is to make students proficient regarding existing knowledge. This is typically done through lectures aiming at making the students learn facts through various kinds of learning behaviour.

Mode 1 theory-of-application. Looking at the bottom left quadrant – in the theory-of-application section – this is mirrored by the idea that context independent knowledge should be useful through implementation in specific contexts. Here the academic functions as an expert, based on academic skills applied in the role of advisor and on the fact that they have obtained a given knowledge base through their study.

Mode 2 theory-of-application. Here the idea is that academics entering the world of the professional practitioner need to be capable of constructing the knowledge necessary in a given situation. The role of the academic is no longer to be an expert, giving advice from a position outside ongoing processes but to be a change agent actively participating in processes in a manner that deals with problem identification, interpretation, analysis, and solution. The academics ought to be able to do so because their education has provided them with the necessary competences – which we label "reflected action competences" in Figure 2.

Looking at the top half of Figure 2, this Mode 2 theory-of-application must be supplemented with activities that animate the spectrum from scientific knowledge areas to student learning.

Mode 2 curriculum. Beginning at the top right quadrant of the figure our perspective is that knowledge depends on context. Thus, the teaching objective should be to teach enterprising students knowledge creation competences. This can be done through case and problem oriented types of teaching, for example, in which the students learn through active co-creation of context dependent knowledge – and this requires training.

Thus, in Mode 2 our argument is that it is not the knowledge content alone that gives the academic practitioner their foundation. The foundation also consists of the ability to work with knowledge construction principles and to act as a local change agent by having the action competences to intervene in the processes that unfold in specific contexts.

Application of the Framework

Our theoretical framework for curriculum development that balances rigour and relevance can inspire a clear-cut route beyond transmission. We will illustrate this by describing how two study programmes in our own department have used the framework to develop curricula capable of resolving the challenges we have identified. First, we review how competence-in-practice varies across different lines of study. Then, we present three ways of integrating theory and contexts of application into students learning by taking advantage of the distinction between teaching and learning curriculum.

Our department primarily focuses on offering programmes of study in the area of management and business administration. The two specific programmes of study to be discussed here are a Bachelor in Business Administration degree emphasising Entrepreneurship and Innovation and a Master of Science in Business Administration and Auditing. These lines of study present two extremes in relation to the application contexts to which the students are expected to contribute after graduation. Furthermore these differences mean that, typically, the students taking each programme tend to approach contexts of application in rather different ways.

One way in which to distinguish between different contexts of application is to distinguish between the degrees to which the environment is governed by technical and institutional controls (Scott, 1998). Technically strong environments allow the use of output controls to evaluate the quality of a given piece of professional delivery. In technically weaker environments it is more difficult to evaluate the quality of a given output. On the other hand, environments with strong institutional controls rely heavily on the degree to which a professional delivery is produced according to appropriate procedures.

		Institutional controls	
		Stronger	Weaker
Technical Controls	Stronger	*Auditing programme*	
	Weaker		*Entrepreneurship & innovation programme*

Figure 3: Examples of Programmes of Study Approaching Different Contexts of Application.

The Auditing programme and the Entrepreneurship & Innovation programme relate to different contexts of application, as reflected in Figure 3. Auditors are expected to work in an environment with strong technical and institutional controls. Graduates from Entrepreneurship & Innovation are expected to be able to contribute professionally to environments in which it is much more difficult to evaluate the quality of output of a given piece of professional work and in which the procedures for developing and evaluating professional work are much more ill-defined. Similarly, the nature of practitioners tasks in hand differ markedly in the two contexts. Therefore the competence-in-practice to be developed is significantly different.

In terms of our theoretical framework, the two programmes of study balance the knowledge production in Mode 1 and Mode 2 in different ways. The Auditing programme will have an emphasis on Mode 1 and the Entrepreneurship and Innovation programme will tend to tip towards Mode 2.

Our theoretical framework indicates why curriculum development must take the context of application into consideration in designing learning activities. We suggest three different ways of integrating the context of application into the learning activities.

Planned teacher-driven:

- This means that the developers of lines of study and specific courses develop an explicit theory-of-application and strive to design a teaching curriculum related to this theory-of-application. In this way, the course developers take responsibility for developing specific learning goals and take the opportunity to design an alignment between learning goals, forms of examination and specific learning activities. However, as with any theory the theory-of-application might be contested and the students on the course might not want to accept the proposed theory-of-application.

Planned student-driven:

- This approach is well suited to the study of entrepreneurship and innovation. As a planned part of the curriculum in this line of study, the students are obliged to work as an intern in a company concurrently with the formal study activities. The formal study activities are linked to the internship by integrating the project carried out in the company to the examinations in specific courses. Through this internship the students act as legitimate peripheral participants (Lave & Wenger, 1999) in the context of application. It is notable that, because of their firsthand experience with the context of application, the internship students very often confront formal teaching in much more critical ways than other students. This means that the internship students tend to develop their own personal learning objectives – or what Lave & Wenger (1999) term learning curriculum. As a consequence these students often have a more critical attitude and will challenge the teaching curriculum – that is, the way in which course designers intended to design alignment into specific courses. In this way, learning is beyond transmission-mode because the students are put into a situation in which they tend to develop their own learning objectives based on experience with the context-of-application.

Practitioner driven:

- This method is exemplified by our Master of Science in Business Administration and Auditing. Two-thirds of these students already have a career in an auditing company, concurrent with their studies, and the Masters degree is a prerequisite for further career advancement. In this case many students are highly aware of their personal learning goals and several teachers report difficulties in maintaining their students' interest in subjects which they perceive to have no immediate application.

To sum up, the relationship between the theory-of-application and the learning situation of the students at the university will shape how the curriculum development should be framed. In both programmes of study we have described, the theory-of-application is relevant for curriculum development even though the studies differ according to the technical and institutional control described in Figure 3. The Auditing programme is considered to encompass most of the Mode 1 knowledge production and elements of Mode 2 knowledge production. The Entrepreneurship and Innovation programme includes elements of both forms of knowledge production but with a more significant element of Mode 2 compared to the Auditing study. Consequently, both types of knowledge need to be present and co-exist in Higher Education programmes. Furthermore, curriculum developers must focus on ways in which to make an explicit and deliberate use of these types of knowledge in developing studies and courses.

Conclusion

The literature about differences between research and practice tends to consider two gaps in isolation: one gap between research and teaching and another gap between teaching and practice.

In this chapter we have asked the question: how do we develop university curricula emphasising research-based teaching, where the students are seen as producers, in ways that make better practitioners?

This question challenges the literature on the research-practice gap by addressing both gaps together and emphasising research-based teaching for subsequent practice. The question led us to identify two challenges: how do we develop competence-in-practice in situations where the task in hand is not obvious?, and what are the implicit assumptions regarding application in practice within different academic disciplines?

In answer to the challenges we have suggested that we must be explicit about our theory-of-application. What is our theory about how the student is expected to be a better practitioner as a result of a given study programme? And how is this reflected in the curriculum design?

To broaden the debate in research-based teaching about how to develop "student-producers", we made a distinction between Mode 1 and Mode 2 knowledge production. This enabled us to produce a theoretical frame of reference suggesting that different forms of knowledge production have different theories of application and therefore demand different forms of teaching.

The Mode 1 approach is based on a hierarchical understanding of how knowledge is produced and has as an ambition to make students proficient in existing knowledge. This corresponds to a theory-of-application that positions the practitioner as an expert who can apply generalisable knowledge in specific contexts.

The Mode 2 approach differs in the sense that knowledge may be produced in many different places. It can be context independent knowledge as developed in universities and it can be context specific knowledge in particular contexts-of-application where solutions to messy problems call for problem definition skills crossing traditional disciplinary boundaries. Mode 2 knowledge production is mirrored by a theory-of-application where the practitioner is expected to be able to construct knowledge and to act as a change agent in situations where problems are not easily defined in ways that can be handled through existing methods and procedures.

Although the specific competences to be practiced for Mode 1 and Mode 2 knowledge production differ significantly, both approaches call for teaching methods that go beyond transmission.

Schön suggests that rigour and relevance represent a dilemma for the practitioner. These two aspects of knowledge do not only exist as two separate worlds for students – teachers also often regard them as mutually exclusive. However, we do not find that this is a productive separation to be made in developing university curricula in which the bulk of students are not expected to enter a research career.

By explicating different relationships between scientific knowledge areas and graduates' professional behaviour, we describe two types of knowledge production underpinning the relationship between theory and practice. Both types must co-exist in university curricula and our framework shows that they can be supplementary to one another rather than opposites.

We conclude that the balance between the different forms of knowledge production should be developed with an eye fixed on what is expected of practitioners in the context of application, to which today's students will be expected to contribute in their subsequent practice.

About the Authors

Jesper Piihl is associate professor and head of studies at the Department of Entrepreneurship and Relationship Management, University of Southern Denmark. He can be contacted at this email: jpi@sam.sdu.dk

Kristian Philipsen is associate professor at the Department of Entrepreneurship and Relationship Management, University of Southern Denmark. He can be contacted at this email: kp@sam.sdu.dk

Chapter Four

Innovation and Student Learning: ePortfolios for Music Education

Jennifer Rowley

Introduction

This chapter describes the introduction of ePortfolios into a music teacher preparation program and discusses the effect this has had on students' learning as lifelong learners. I investigate the advantages of ePortfolios for student engagement and learning and the benefits of assisting students to think about collective learning objectives, processes and outcomes of their four-year degree program as an innovation beyond transmission.

In the examples I will describe, students learnt independence, took ownership for their own learning, engaged in learning journeys of others and developed their musical and teacher identity through the process of creating an electronic folio. The advantage of this style of engagement with learning is that it enables students to make links between discreet units of study within the degree program – thus taking a holistic approach to their learning. They sort, classify, select and collate evidence to demonstrate their holistic degree learning achievement – skills, competencies and knowledge. The role of the student morphs into the role of learner (and peer mentor) by expanding their technology and learning skills and by exploring different ways of expressing themselves, their discipline and their learning achievements. This is innovative teaching because it is student focused, independently driven and evaluative, because students assume responsibility for their own learning.

What is an ePortfolio?

The use of ePortfolios is well documented in various forms of professional training, notably that for nursing (Garrrett & Jackson, 2006; McCready, 2007) and teaching (Wertzel, 2005; Ackil & Arap, 2009; Adamy & Milman, 2009). Their use in the training of music educators is less well documented, so the introduction of ePortfolio to a music degree was seen as innovatory and a suitable site for research into the potential of ePortfolios to implement change in music teacher preparation (Rowley & Dunbar-Hall, 2009; Dunbar-Hall *et al.*, 2010; Rowley & Dunbar-Hall, 2010).

The initial aim of the project was to devise a suitable way of adapting ePortfolios to the professional needs of music teachers. That is, the ability to demonstrate skills across a wide range of musical and pedagogic fields including, performing, composing and arranging music and conducting ensembles. And it would give the student teachers a way to show skills such as teaching in both one-to-one and group situations, working with community music groups, producing and directing stage works, managing performance programs, and recording and producing CDs/DVDs of their own and their students' work. The ability of ePortfolios to use different forms of electronic media such as text documents, graphics, and sound and visual files to show these aspects of the professional expectations placed on a music teacher was seen as a rich field for their introduction into music teacher training. In addition to this was the ePortfolio's ability to provide hyperlinks to websites such as YouTube on which music educators could place files. Willingness to innovate and participate in technology-supported student learning has been shown to be successful in promoting student autonomy (Bartholomew, this volume).

Use of ePortfolios in HE

The use of ePortfolios in Higher Education (HE) is part of a growing trend among HE institutions to talk in terms of deliverables, client accountability and graduate employability. Recently, two Universities in

Australia introduced ePortfolios into tertiary students' programs across the whole institution and this demonstrates how the learning community could adapt to an innovation centred on students and enhancement of their learning.

The "iPortfolio" at Curtin University of Technology in Western Australia was a purpose built platform intended to store all material showcasing a student's achievement across their degree program (with a focus on the attainment of graduate attributes). It was designed as *"an online space for students and staff to create, share and publish evidence of their learning achievements and professional development"* (Curtin University, 2010). The decision to use "i" instead of "e" highlights the reference to the personal ownership of the electronic folio. It was also intended that staff should engage in online pedagogical practices.

> *"The iPortfolio facilitates social learning and encourages feedback and collaboration with peers and mentors… [and] is intended to be both life-wide and lifelong, encouraging and enabling iPortfolio owners to collect evidence of learning arising from formal coursework and complementary extracurricular activities".* (Oliver *et al.*, 2009:717)

Queensland University of Technology's ePortfolio is designed for students to document their academic, professional and personal development:*"[It] is a university-wide, online tool designed to enhance the learning process and to assist students with the transition from university to graduate employment"* (QUT, 2009). It is intended as a repository of a student's achievements with examples and evidence related to their skills, interests and personal attributes to use when applying for jobs. The AeP (Australian ePortfolio) project at QUT focused on developing a community of practice and encouraged staff to engage in professional development so they could support student use of the platform and share and interact with other teachers who were utilising ePortfolios (AeP.2, 2009). A key factor in the success of these two projects was the support given to staff in implementing the university-wide initiative and in providing professional development about pedagogy surrounding electronic portfolios.

Although many believe that the innovative use of technology can enhance student learning, the introduction of eLearning into HE has been a dynamic but ill-structured undertaking. In fact, teachers in HE could do well to focus on the modelling of that pedagogy in preparation for embedding technology into their professional practice. An example of this is through widely-used virtual learning management systems (e.g. Blackboard®) that manage different levels of online learning, from informational sites to blended learning, and beyond that to distance education. Today's students are "iTool- ready" with suitable and usable technology already carried in their pockets. Learning can be enriched by embedding technology into curriculum appropriately; experiencing technology as an authentic pedagogical practice, rather than an "add on" effect, has true significance to learning.

ePortfolios in Music Education

Specifically in the area of Music Education, students training to be teachers are expected to integrate technology into their teaching practice. As musicians they will already have both training and experience in a range of technologies for producing and documenting music. This expectation of teacher training responds to current curriculum requirements that teachers entering the workforce are technologically literate and that they can model best practice in the critique and adaptation of technologies relevant to music as a pedagogical area. Concern about how to integrate evidence of professional teaching standards with evidence of being an accomplished musician has led to much discussion about interdependence of one professional practice on the other. This in addition to the requirement to demonstrate that university graduate attributes have been accomplished within students' academic work. The result has been that

> "*... balancing these criteria along with mandatory teacher preparation curriculum was posing a challenge for teacher educators as both required students to engage in a technology rich learning environment. It was clear, therefore, that the e-portfolio potentially had many masters to serve.*" (Rowley & Dunbar-Hall, 2009:898)

Initially, the focus of the ePortfolio was on students' understandings of their own learning through graduate attributes and professional standards for graduate employability. The ePortfolio encouraged the students involved to select evidence and match it to these professional standards as a measure of achievement. The final product, the web folio (or web page) provided a standard where student centred learning could be measured as it becomes a practical application of theory. As Rowley and Dunbar-Hall (2009) have noted

> *"While the concept of portfolio-based evidence and demonstration of students' work is not new, in this case the transfer of this to an electronic site raises issues through which the intentions of this degree program can be critiqued. Specifically, ways in which electronic modes of learning are utilised; the longitudinal, and thus incremental, nature of teacher preparation; the interface between staff input and student uptake of teaching material; and how students can address expectations of official teacher accreditation are all scrutinised when they are assessed for their contributions to an ePortfolio platform. In this way, the use of ePortfolios becomes a way of evaluating this degree program, its aims across numerous criteria, its outcomes, and the teaching and learning that occur within it".* (Rowley & Dunbar-Hall, 2009:898)

To flesh out these ideas, this chapter discusses the embedding of ePortfolios into curricula as a means of showcasing students' achievements and tracking their development of a personal philosophy of beliefs about teaching music in schools. It also looks at measuring students' engagement with music in learning communities and at documenting, with relevant artefacts, their abilities as teachers, composers, performers, conductors and reflective pedagogues. This list implies that an ePortfolio will be in a multi-media format and include original evidence, such as student-created sound and video recordings. One purpose of the ePortfolio is for students to engage actively with a variety of technologies and to demonstrate skills in that area. Another is a medium for applying for a job at the end of their degree, by demonstrating evidence in accordance with set application processes where they show accomplishment of graduate teacher professional standards as mandated by a government accreditation body. Finally, and most importantly, ePortfolios are seen as a form of pedagogical development for both teachers and students that demonstrate innovation in teaching and learning.

Staff Expectations

In cases I have observed, the learning benefit tended to differ from the intentions of staff managing ePortfolio introduction. The role of the teacher was to integrate the ePortfolio into curriculum in a meaningful way that would support and guide the student through the learning process whilst also meeting specific outcomes of the program. Initially, staff saw the ePortfolio as a series of individual assessment tasks that sat independently of each other. Students, however, managed to go beyond the individual requirements of the assessment and created a personal folio with each one being unique in its design and purpose. Despite these conceptual differences, both students and staff agreed that ePortfolios had helped create a site of learning through an adaptation of technology to the specific academic and professional needs of music education students.

Student reactions to the embedding of an ePortfolio into curricula revealed aspects not considered by teachers. Notably that this empowering of student learning by staff contributed to deeper student learning (Winka & Grysell, this volume). This led to a better understanding by their teachers of how students need to "story" their learning journey. But it also revealed discrepancies between staff intentions for learning through ePortfolios and student responses to them. Reflection by both students and teachers was paramount to the success of the ePortfolio and gave substantial information and insights about the challenges faced in the transmission of learning through this medium.

Embedding the Technology

Well-planned, innovative curricula in HE that utilise technology, eLearning and types of blended learning, assist teachers to develop good learning and teaching practices. The use of ePortfolios can be viewed in relation to contemporary learning and curriculum theory. Curriculum renewal is a mandatory component of a teacher's role in HE and often it is misinterpreted as the need to replace the course textbook! Indeed, specific training and staff professional development is often a low priority in HE because many regarded as "expert" in their field are assumed already to be an expert in pedagogy. Essentially the teacher in HE must prepare and plan curriculum which is relevant to their discipline and also meets appropriate learning and teaching practices for adult learners. Darling-Hammond *et al.* (1995) noted that the use of aspects of authentic pedagogical practices encourages teachers to engage in student-focused teaching. However, it is often noted that the intellectual dimension is highlighted at the expense of the learning environment and the significance of the learning (Gore, Griffiths & Ladwig, 2004). The fact is that students need to understand the significance of the learning because this takes them beyond the transmission of the learning and the technology aspect of it.

The technology can be embedded once the curriculum is aligned with course learning outcomes, learning and teaching activities, assessment, graduate attributes and professional standards. The curriculum needs to be student focused, research led, and able to accommodate regular input by students. An important reason for introducing the ePortfolio was that it creates a foundation for ongoing student input.

An action research approach (Revans, 1980) was used to drive developments as the project unfolded. In common with action research as a style of inquiry, this project simultaneously converts research into practice while it observes practice as a topic of research. This process of empowering student learning through research-based teaching contributes to improved professional practice (Piihl & Philipsen, this volume). It proceeds as a series of overlapping stages in which findings of earlier stages are seen as influencing the directions, objectives and processes of subsequent findings. Therefore, the project addressed a problem in a specific context, namely; how to integrate ePortfolios into a music education degree program. It is collaborative, involving student practitioners and staff researchers; its team members contribute to implementing stages of the research and to its outcomes; and it is evaluative in an ongoing manner, making it open-ended in its potential (Cohen & Manion, 1996:186). It relies on and draws from relationships between researchers and research not only to understand an issue, but also to produce ways of addressing it. In their study of action research, Denzin and Lincoln (2000) observed that:

> *"[through] collaborative dialogue, participatory decision making, inclusive democratic deliberation, and the maximal participation and representation of all relevant parties ... research subjects become co-participants and stakeholders in the process of inquiry".* (Denzin & Lincoln, 2000:32)

All of these common attributes can be seen to have been part of the development of the ePortfolio and the embedding of it in ways that the students involved could be engaged in thinking about their learning.

Reinvigorating Student Learning

High quality teaching and learning experiences in HE need to include ways to measure the degree to which competencies of the discipline are achievable and achieved. The development of reflective practice, for example by creating a learning journal, can complement and assist students and teachers in understanding the world of professional practitioner in a given discipline. This is where reflection activities established through blended learning – the ePortfolio for example – are valuable learning tools both for teachers and for students. The use of a blog housed within the ePortfolio also allows students to express personal growth, alongside their fears and anxieties about becoming a professional practitioner, because it is designed as a "space" free of ridicule (Hughes, 2011). This innovative teaching method is learner centred and impacts students' learning outcomes by allowing students to take ownership of their learning.

The blog is used by both students and teachers, who will be able to co-learn as learners in the group, which in turn creates another avenue for teachers to engage in professional development and model good pedagogical practices. By investigating the threads of both students' and teachers' arguments and reflections, learning can be truly collaborative as it is ongoing and continual (Hughes, 2011). Through these avenues, an ePortfolio can be seen as a tool that will enhance learning, and the reflection allowed through its processes as contributions to the enjoyment of learning (Rowley & Dunbar-Hall, 2010). The student's "story" of learning (or their learning "autobiography") can be used as a model for staff to engage in creating their own autobiography (Hughes, 2011). This practice in turn will allow the staff to model to students some good, productive pedagogy and allow the teachers to contribute to and participate in the learning with the students.

Innovative teaching in HE is a dialogue between teachers and students by being collective, reflective, reciprocal, purposeful and supportive (Coffield, 2008). Ideally it should resemble a meeting of minds in academic discussion and not be solely a participatory activity where students are talked at for an hour in a lecture, seminar, demonstration, laboratory or tutorial setting. There is no simple solution for improving the student learning experience. The approach to teaching and learning through the embedding of ePortfolio into curricula described in this chapter is informed by research that has demonstrated the importance of understanding pedagogy to improve teaching in HE. Teachers must engage in the professional development of appropriate pedagogical practices to maintain a discreet understanding of learners. One way to do this is to understand the power of reflection and to engage in reflective practice in their professional pursuits. As a result, ePortfolio is recommended as "essential" for use also by the teacher:

> *"The main problem with preparing learners for the complexities of the world ahead is that HE seems to take such a narrow view of what learning and knowledge are".* (Jackson, 2010:xii)

The Dilemma of Musician versus Teacher: a Case Study

I will now describe a particular implementation of the ePortfolio approach that allowed staff to observe students transitioning from being musicians to being music teachers. As this progressed, the students experienced a challenge to their identity and they questioned where they were really positioned for the future: their career choice, professional identity etc. This tension in the students' perspectives of themselves was manifested in their approach to the ePortfolio. At times, they were undecided about how to portray themselves in the portfolio and often would change pictorial themes in their profile to show a new taste in music or advancement in their musical development. For example, one student started with a picture of himself as a percussionist; after a few months engaging with the ePortfolio he amended it to a picture of his favourite characters on a TV show.

Typical of the 3rd year students observed at the case institution, Hugo and Katia [pseudonyms in both cases] developed their ePortfolios beyond assessment tasks and into a personal reflection and "story" – not just about their tertiary music study but also about their performances and experiences as a musician. Katia included video footage of her sabbatical study in an American University where she performed regularly in a Marching Band as part of her studies. Hugo included his work as a music teacher to children in disadvantaged schools as a demonstration of skills learnt and competencies developed in music teaching.

The Discrepancy between Staff and Student Expectations

In the case study example I observed a discrepancy between staff and student expectations that was concerned with the nature of the students' "musician versus teacher" identity dilemma. While the two sets of perceptions diverge along a theoretical versus active engagement division, they concur on the advantage of ePortfolios in leading students to think about their studies, and to view their degree program, as a unified event. This advantage allows students to create a site of personal value and to evaluate their own learning and its methods. The teaching staff were realistic in their expectations of the competence of their students to complete the carefully planned ePortfolio tasks and they were relatively comfortable that the students would have the required technology skills to undertake the tasks.

Specifically, staff planned implementation of ePortfolios to address the:

- Creation of a digital product for students to use in job applications,
- Acknowledgement and utilisation of current students' identities as "digital natives", that is, young people "immersed in technology . . . With sophisticated technical skills and learning preferences" (Bennett, Maton & Kervin 2008: 775), and adaptation of this into their studies,
- Demonstration in a summative outcome of how each student has addressed the university's generic skills/graduate attributes throughout the four years of the degree program,
- Demonstrating ability to teach according to the professional standards of the NSW institute of teachers, and thus receive government accreditation as qualified school teachers,

- Integration of digital tasks throughout the four year degree program, and
- Creation of a site of learning and teaching of pedagogic benefit to students and the Music Education staff involved in the project.

These intentions for the project represent staff conceptualisation of ePortfolios as primarily a product through which aspects of the degree program could be developed and demonstrated. Among these expected developments was the necessity to raise students' technological skills to the level at which they could confidently design and produce content for an ePortfolio that included their own edited and produced sound and film files. Selection of ePortfolio components from all possible inclusions across four years of university study was another area that would require consideration. In addition to this was student ability to treat an ePortfolio as a longitudinal artefact – one that represented four years of study and could show progress over that time span.

The discrepancy between staff expectations of ePortfolios and students' reactions to ePortfolios can be summed up as the difference between theorisation in relation to a planned curriculum outcome on the one hand and reactions to ePortfolios resulting from active engagement with them on the other. In this space and through this interpretation of the project, the introduction of ePortfolios became a site of learning-centred education rather than a product-related activity. By placing students in the position of solving problems and making decisions about content and use of ePortfolios, the project required students to understand the design, content, processes, outcomes and official status of their degree program; to critique it and their own learning within it.

The tension that existed between staff expectations and student adaptation to the ePortfolio did not affect the original foundation of the innovation. In fact, students' comments during focus group interviews in 2009 and 2010 revealed aspects of the innovation that had not been predicted. Among some of the surprises were the ability of the students to "go beyond" the technology and the students' growth in conceptualising ideas for pedagogical practices for use with their own students. This transfer of learning into their teaching practice demonstrated an understanding of allowing students to engage in independent learning – going beyond the transmission.

Students' Views After Implementation of ePortfolios

Here I present material from focus group interviews with students to demonstrate changes ePortfolios brought about in students' perspectives on learning, the nature of their degree program, their understanding of learning outcomes and their critique of technology as a support to their learning. These student opinions differ from staff intentions for the project, which alongside the ability of ePortfolios to demonstrate professional skills, were based on institutional requirements for the development of academic skills. As HE teachers we need to understand that the learner "stories" his/her experience rather than "storing" these experiences; the ePortfolio allows evidence to be stored so that they can tell their story. Examples of how the music education students have responded to the implementation of ePortfolio is in the story they have created about themselves and their learning. This story-telling about how the ePortfolio has been embedded into the program through good curriculum modelling provides evidence that the portfolio has enhanced the student learning experience. In understanding the role of ePortfolio in a music students' program, the students reported that they believed an ePortfolio should be a representation of themselves in their professional practice role as both a musician and a music teacher:

> *"It's pretty much a documentation of us in our music career … what's happening in our music education course, where we provide evidence of us teaching, either in a school or privately"* (Student Angi, 2009).

So, in the early days of embedding ePortfolio into the course, the students viewed it as a means of presenting themselves in a professional manner. They mentioned that it could be a way of telling their story "formally" in a Curriculum Vitae. Student "Bev" reported that it gave her the perfect place to voice her personal belief about teaching and learning:

> *"I think it can also say your beliefs of teaching and learning basically, or behaviour management and things like that. Not just your CV. Your CV could be part of it … you can have where you've worked previously, what experiences you've had in different schools or that kind of thing, but also some of your beliefs about teaching"* (Student Bev, 2009).

This student is beginning to articulate her story and realises that it is valuable. Here, for the students, the real value is that the ePortfolio provides a place where their story can be told and stored and it provides a range of possibilities for collection of evidence to support the student's story – or learning journey. Students mention that they were not always sure what they could place in the ePortfolio as evidence of their learning and were concerned, at first, that they may be "stuck" with that piece of evidence "forever". They took some time to understand the flexibility of the ePortfolio and the tailoring capacity it contained to make it their own:

> *"I think the scope is just so big with an ePortfolio because you could really put in whatever you like. .... With video, as we're discovering now, there's so much that you can video because being a musician means we're a performer, we're a learner we're a teacher, we're all those different things"* (Student Julie, 2009).

An ePortfolio, therefore, has a "philosophy of learning" embedded in it, as the students are able to create their individual development as a teacher and a musician and to engage in the dialogues of both theory and practice. This is reflection-in-action and it brings the curriculum alive. The ePortfolio will impact assessment strategies in HE because it will include how students reflect on future professional practice.

Student Autonomy

Students and staff had access to one-to-one tuition with an expert on how to use the ePortfolio and the potential of its use. Each was treated as an individual learner allowing them (in partnership with the expert) to customise their learning to meet individual needs.

There are implications in using ePortfolio both for staff and for students. The first implication is the enhancement of the student's learning experience through enjoyment of his/her own journey for life-long learning. This generic graduate attribute will contribute to the student's understanding of leaving tertiary study and operating in the world of non-student – that is, in employment, business creation, travel, partnering etc. Students had to include a personal statement on their philosophy of teaching and also on being a musician. The student's perception of his/her identity is enhanced by creating this description of who they are, what they see themselves as undertaking in the future, and of "becoming" a music teacher. This "autobiography" is the web folio and, as a one page "coversheet" to the ePortfolio, it allows students to massage and modify the story according to the reader being targeted.

Secondly, each ePortfolio is different and, as the student is creator of the individual ePortfolio, the portrayal of their image, identity and perception of themselves as teacher and musician had to be clearly articulated. Students were free to choose how they would like to be seen. This, and the options inside the ePortfolio to design and personalise, engage the student in a reflection of him/herself beyond the image of a student. So, as the ePortfolio requires independence and thinking about design, look and contents, the students are engaged in selecting appropriately how others should perceive them.

In addition to this, each ePortfolio activity embedded into the curriculum is a problem-solving exercise. This is not just through the skills required to manipulate the technology but also in the selection of evidence or artefacts to match and demonstrate the meeting of the professional teaching standard or skill. Being dynamic in its format the ePortfolio engages the student in an evaluation process of what to showcase and what to select for each particular use. For example, each student will have different experiences in music – exams, groups of musicians they work with, compositions, conducting etc. – and so they need to analyse evidence in the ePortfolio required for the particular purpose. For example, for releasing components to potential employers or to teachers. The ePortfolio allows them to make connections of non-associated learning within an expected context. This truly is going beyond the transmission of the learning and shows how innovative the ePortfolio can be when accurately explained and supported.

Becoming eTeachers

The adoption of eLearning practices by teachers in HE for eReady students through the ePortfolio platform has broad implications. These include the preparation of students for operating in today's environment of an ever emerging technology revolution. This, in itself, has implications inside and outside the tertiary environment for ensuring a quality student learning experience. There are many examples but this chapter has focused on the emergence and adoption of the ePortfolio within tertiary teaching. Portfolios have been used for some time for gathering evidence of what a learner has accomplished. The ePortfolio, however, extends this traditional approach because the concept is really about students taking ownership of their own learning journey instead of being dictated to and obliged to use mandatory components of the portfolio.

The stakeholders in this process include the students, the teachers, and employers. All of these stakeholders engage in the learning through the design, implementation, use, and future implications for the ePortfolio. The learner is positioned appropriately at the centre of the pedagogy but a premise of the ePortfolio is that students engage in academic discourse with all stakeholders. The ePortfolio has moved beyond assessment to empowering the individual students' learning landscape, as the key factor here in its design is student ownership.

The ePortfolio encourages students to form judgements about their own learning, which contributes to their achievement of the prescribed graduate attributes, skills, competencies and learning outcomes. How do you ensure that learning has occurred through the implementation of the ePortfolio into curricula? The ePortfolio goes beyond proving knowledge of and understanding of the information contained within a course. It allows students to analyse, synthesise and evaluate their learning in terms of their own learning journey. It also allows the students to map the learning journey themselves because measures of achievement have traditionally been subjective. Finally, it allows for different approaches to documenting a student's profile as they build incrementally a learning autobiography over the three, four or more years of their tertiary education.

Graduate employability is a priority for tertiary institutions and this is why the capstone experience is prioritised in their learning and teaching strategic plans. Employers want evidence of the capstone experience and an ePortfolio provides an organised collection of evidence of a student's tertiary learning journey (Rowley & Dunbar-Hall, 2010). The ePortfolio allows students to select what they want to showcase depending on who the reader is and how the evidence can be deployed to tell their story effectively. So, in a sense, ePortfolios can be the product of a set of practices students learn through the careful curriculum planning of their teachers. The capstone experience should expect students to demonstrate that they have developed higher order thinking skills and can evaluate what it means to become a practicing professional in their chosen field. Accordingly, the capstone experience is an assurance of learning and this defends the embedding of graduate attributes into curricula throughout the degree program.

Conclusion

The potential for an enhanced transmission of learning resulting from the embedding of ePortfolios into a music student's degree program is positive. The ePortfolio is an innovation in the transmission of learning for both students and staff and, through the student voice, we have heard what it means to them as musicians and teachers. The recent introduction of ePortfolios at Queensland University of Technology and at Curtin University is an innovation that empowers our pathway to improving students' eLearning experiences. The projects did raise questions, however, about future innovations in student learning and how curriculum renewal should include a stronger student voice. Other questions raised were the "after-life" of the ePortfolio once graduating; the logistics of maintaining staff professional development to continue developing skills and competencies in teaching with technology; and the germination of the project to other discipline areas. This provides some thought for future inquiry about collaboration, blended learning experiences to enhance student learning, student autonomy, the role of the eTeacher and how the relationship between teachers and students in future will be manifested in HE.

The evidence from teachers reveals that the nature of innovation described in this chapter lies in the way that the technology was embedded into curricula to meet teacher professional standards as part of an accreditation process for the degree program. This relationship to other approaches (such as blended learning activities in the individual courses making up a degree program) has the potential to increase the student's own embedding of technology into their teaching. Staff interaction through this type of curriculum renewal, and their personal use of ePortfolio, contributes to the teacher's own professional development and reinvigorates the student learning experience. Tensions and surprises that emerged as a result of the introduction of the innovation led staff and students to understand more about the dilemma of musician versus teacher identity and encouraged all to engage in individual tuition to meet student and staff needs appropriately in creating a personal ePortfolio product.

Allowing the student voice to be heard before and after the introduction of the innovation allowed subsequent stages of this research-led project to develop. The way in which both staff and students become eTeachers is evidence of the use of good pedagogy in HE. The development of student autonomy in their interaction with technology and its pedagogy revealed implications for using ePortfolio –including the students' engagement in their futures as music teachers.

The use of technology, in both staff and students' learning and teaching spaces, can improve learning and can improve and change existing teaching practices because it creates the need to rethink curriculum for the 21st century.

About the Author

Jennifer Rowley is a Lecturer in Music Education at the Sydney Conservatorium of Music at the University of Sydney, Australia. She can be contacted at this email: jennifer.rowley@sydney.edu.au

Chapter Five

The Sequence of Educational Innovation from University to Working Life

Pekka Räihä, Marja Mäensivu, Matti Rautiainen and Tiina Nikkola

Introduction

Nowadays there is a straightforward demand for innovations, but innovations seldom become part of or change the basic operations of institutions. It is more typical that renewal and reform are born and die with an individual. This also often applies to teaching innovations. Furthermore, even though Higher Education (HE) teaching innovations are constantly being developed, there has nevertheless been a dearth of follow-up studies and assessment of their impact. In this chapter we shall endeavour to make up for this shortcoming.

This chapter takes a practical perspective on the implementation of educational innovation. Since 2003 we have been developing the Critical Integrative Teacher Education (CITE) programme for primary teachers at the University of Jyväskylä's Department of Teacher Education. In CITE education, the aim is to develop teachers' professional skills towards understanding, not controlling. CITE endeavours to find an alternative to the routines of school and education. Education is a holistic totality, and because the world is not structured according to school subjects, school itself should not be based on such artificial divisions.

In this chapter we examine how teachers who have gone through the Critical Integrative Teacher Education (CITE) programme for primary teachers have been affected by the programme. We focus particularly on whether educational innovations have spread with them into working life and whether there has then been a diffusion of innovation.

Innovation

Innovation means the ability to adopt and develop new ideas, processes and products (Lam, 2004; Lam & Lundvall, 2007; Siltala *et al.*, 2009). However, the degree of novelty of an innovation varies. At its lowest level, an innovation's novelty means the improvement of something old and pre-existing, a case of incremental innovation. In contrast, the degree of novelty is greatest when the product developed has not been constructed on top of an earlier one or derived from something old. In such cases the innovation can be called radical (Grupp & Maital, 2001:9–11; Suomala *et al.*, 2005:181–182; Tidd *et al.*, 2005:11–12).

In addition to its novelty, an innovation can be examined in terms of change. Change can take place in an innovation at four different levels: product innovation, process innovation, position innovation and paradigm innovation. Product innovation refers to change in the actual product whereas process innovation affects the product's modes of production and position innovation changes the environment in which the product is made available. The greatest change, however, is paradigm innovation since here the change takes place in the mental models which frame what the organisation does. (Tidd *et al.*, 2005:10–11).

Innovation can also be examined from the viewpoint of benefit. Competitive advantage or economic benefit, for example, can be gained from innovation. Innovation has traditionally been linked to the economy, the capacity of a company to create a product that will in one way or another revolutionise or reshape the markets. According to Joseph Schumpeter's classic work on innovation literature, innovations are the essential foundation of economic growth (Schumpeter, 1934).

In many cases, for example in school history textbooks, innovation means revolutionary, often technological, inventions such as the steam engine, telephone or automobile. However, the concept of social innovation has extended the range of innovations to affect a broader area than merely technical domains (Vidgrén, 2009:16). Increasingly, innovation and innovativeness appear in the discourse on teaching and education. Today, innovation is widely used to describe something new and is often linked to creativity; according to Hautamäki (2006:15–16) innovations are born in creative environments. Hautamäki has developed the term innovationary ecosystem to describe the dynamic interactive environments where enterprises are capable of innovating. The basis of this dynamism is the mobility of ideas and people and especially a ruthlessly risk-taking culture of innovation. Even though Hautamäki talks about extensive networks in describing the innovationary ecosystem in the economy, its basic principles also apply when evaluating the operation of educational culture.

At HE level, innovation in teaching and learning is a relatively recent phenomenon. After the Second World War, a debate began in the United States concerning the rise, alongside lecturing, of small-group teaching. The lecturing paradigm in HE teaching was queried (Hannan & Silver, 2000:3–4). Generally speaking, the object of change in innovations affecting education and training can be the structure, the system or the implementation. (Tella & Tirri, 1999:18). An individual or a team can act as innovators, but the innovation can also derive from a higher level of HE (Silver, 1999:145).

CITE – Educational Innovation

Although innovativeness is often understood in the world of teaching as a technical novelty or as a new teaching method, it can also be a more comprehensive modification of the principles underlying teaching (Siltala *et al.*, 2009:163). The Critical Integrative Teacher Education (CITE) programme that we have developed is a primary school teacher education programme which, in both its theoretical origins and practical implementation, differs from traditional Finnish teacher education.

In CITE we have endeavoured to go beyond transmission and create a culture of doing things differently that offers the opportunity to understand the phenomena of school reality instead of merely having mastery of them.Whereas the traditional teacher tries to control pupils and "cast them in the same mould", the role of the teacher in the CITE culture is to allow room for difference.

Instead of being organized along traditional school subject lines, the programme is constructed around the experience of research-based and long-term study involving examination of extensive modules related to teaching and education. In addition, we have developed a structure (two to four regular sessions per month) that allows students time to reflect, in a supervised manner, on questions and emotions arising from their studies and thus increase their ability to reflect on their own activity. In practice this requires not only that students study together over the term and in a stable group, but also that teacher educators cooperate, from planning the programme right through to its teaching. (Nikkola *et al.*, 2008; Rautiainen *et al.*, 2010; CITE, 2011).

Since the change in teaching culture brought about by the CITE programme is huge, it can justifiably be termed a radical innovation. The change has taken place not only in the actual product, i.e., the training programme, but also in the process; in other words, in how the programme is produced – for example by means of cooperation amongst the instructors. Even more important than this, however, is the change in the programme's mental models. This is because the paradigm innovation (Tidd *et al.*, 2005) in CITE means that learning and teacher education are seen differently from that under the old training system.

The first teachers to undergo our programme have now had a few years in working life. In this chapter we examine how the innovative studying and teaching methods used in the CITE programme have affected those teachers who experienced it and if innovation has spread with them into schools.

Research Data and Analysis

This chapter is based on a group interview of ten teachers who commenced their CITE studies in 2003, and who, at the time of the interview, had been teaching for two to four years. The interview was conducted at the University of Jyväskylä in December 2010 by five teacher educators. The aim was to collect data on how well the CITE programme had equipped them to cope with working life, especially at the outset of their careers. At the same time as the alumni got the chance to meet and talk about their work, the CITE educators obtained data which can be used to assess which areas of the programme need improvement in order to achieve a better fit between teachers' work and their training. The interview was videoed and recorded. A total of four hours of interview material was produced. The extracted quotations have been translated from the original Finnish.

A month or so after the meeting the teachers were contacted by e-mail and asked to describe what the occasion had given them. Eight interviewees responded. Thematic analysis was used to analyse the collected data (Braun & Clarke, 2006).

The Sequence of Innovations

CITE as a Microcosm

Innovation is about the creation of a microcosm, about creative interaction between human beings (eg. Hannan & Silver, 2000:12) that takes place in particular structures and educational cultures.

CITE is a "grassroots-driven" innovation (see Tella & Tirri 1999:20). Since the reseach and our own observations have demonstrated that there is a wide gulf separating teacher education and school reality, steps were taken to develop a new teacher education (see Suomala *et al.*, 2005:184). The initiation of the CITE programme in 2003 can be described using the term "new creative microcosm". The innovation evolved out of the long-term teaching development work done by one teacher educator, Kai Kallas, and it was this work that aroused the interest of other educators. A microcosm was born with the intention of turning ideas into an innovative training model that was tried out in practice and further developed in a new group. As is typical of innovations, the early stages meant existing in a state of uncertainty, and this in turn demanded long-term commitment from the educators (see Suomala *et al.*, 2005:185). It is rare for innovations in educational cultures to reach this stage because the structures seldom allow teachers the time to spend creatively together for the purposes of developing their teaching. The real test of the innovation was Kallas's retirement. Nevertheless the experiment was continued and developed without its progenitor.

Currently the fifth intake of students is taking part in the CITE programme. Throughout its existence, the programme has been studied and reported on; however, no information had been produced to show on how well it equips students for working life. Now that the first CITE graduates have spent a considerable time at work, it is possible to begin collecting and interpreting the missing data.

Transferring Innovation from Training to Working Life

We have described how a shared educational innovation can evolve from one person's idea. In the following section we examine what happens when the innovation has transferred to the next stage, i.e., to the teachers who have undergone the training.

In the interview, the teachers described how the CITE programme has aroused the idea of the possibility of doing things differently from the way they are presently done at their schools.

> *"When you've been doing that work and had a look at the system, then perhaps you think more about what school could be. What it isn't yet, but what it hopefully could be sometime. Then you try to look at it, thinking about what could be done with this system. Some things really do annoy me, well, not just some but quite a lot. The idea of how you could set about changing it somehow, when you're just a rank-and-file teacher doing her basic work and trying to manage from one day to the next. And even though you might not have the chance or courage to set about changing it, I reckon it's important for me to notice … that I notice that there's something wrong here and something should be done about it. Because then at least you won't be spending your next 40 years wearing blinkers and be like the one who mutters to herself."* (Teacher 8)

The possibility of doing things differently has also partly carried over into practice. In the interview teachers talked about quite concrete applications that they had developed in their work.

> *"Perhaps the neatest thing I've thought of for teaching Finnish (mother tongue) is something that comes from this place [the CITE programme]. We've got this notebook that they've been keeping since class 4. It's a notebook that I'll never read. I make the pupils use the notebook to write down their feelings at that moment. And then they ask if they can use swear words and I said that as I'm not going to read it, then you can write them. I bet someone has written shit, shit, shit. Now we've been*

doing it for so long, you're not going to want to just write fuck for three years. And you're going to get these notebooks after class 6, and I bet it's not going to be very nice to look at what I've been doing. But I don't know what it produces, what I think about it. They've really enjoyed writing and I watch them scribbling away. (...) I don't know what's in the notebooks, but I'm confident that it's helping them develop in some direction. That's perhaps the sort of thing that's my first bold move. I really thought about changing the school's traditions. You can make use of it (the idea) if you dare. I haven't been making a big fuss about it with my other colleagues; that it's against traditional teaching. But then otherwise it's terribly difficult to think of ways I could arrange this teaching another way." (Teacher 5)

Personal experiences are the starting point for the CITE programme. The male teacher (5) offered his pupils the chance to write about their feelings at any given time in a notebook. The notebooks were private and their use can be seen as an attempt by the teacher to extend the pupil's autonomous space, which the teacher neither controls nor rules on its contents. This method also allowed space for pupils to express their experiences and emotions – something that had not been self-evident in the school.

The notebook work described above reveals several of the CITE programme's central principles as applied in practice – for example, understanding instead of controlling. The teachers, however, reported very few such applications. Instead they said that the training programme had given them the capacity to reflect on and observe their own activity.

"I've picked up here the ability to reflect. No way would I ever examine myself and what I do if I hadn't done this training. And where I really saw this myself was on a course about group supervision. I found it absolutely interesting; for example, we'd been through Bion's ideas again. The teacher gave us a task to examine yourself at work and what is beginning to annoy you... For me it was hard and it was only afterwards that I realized I had done a lot of it. It [self examination] is already my tool. The other people doing the course felt they had been enlightened by that task. I realized that I already have this; in my working life I don't need to look for it in a course like that." (Teacher 8)

The teachers described ways in which they acted that differed from those of other teachers; for example, in sorting out classroom management problems in the school. Instead of solving all the problems alone in the traditional way, they shifted some of the responsibility for solving the problems onto the pupils.

> *"Alerting the group to the problems, this is a problem we all share, and not that the teacher has to bring out the problems that are visible here (...) Couldn't the group start to take care of itself a bit more? Of course I can help them, but it'd be better if they grew and started solving the problems and conflicts themselves."* (Teacher 8)

> *"Yes, I've noticed too that asking for quiet works a lot better if it comes from the pupils, because usually it's the teacher who asks first."* (Teacher 9)

A mode of behaviour different from other teachers was also seen in situations other than those concerning quietness in the classroom. For example, teachers felt that they spent less time using textbooks, and systematically filling in workbooks, than teachers do in general. There has also been a systematic effort to break the traditional habit in school of regarding the teacher as the evaluator of everything.

> *"I've outsourced this [evaluation]. Let the pupils decide on the best letter, not me."* (Teacher 3)

The CITE programme challenged the fragmented structure of the typical school and endeavoured to make room for a model involving a more integrated and holistic structure. To some extent the teachers had found solutions for rebuilding the everyday routines of school life, even though they saw it as a challenging task.

> *"[I've had] some kind of thoughts on what the different disciplines could be and how it would be seen in teaching. But I haven't succeeded in structuring my teaching weeks according to this three-way division (...) I don't think it's very realistic to think that there exists completely holistic teaching that is not tied to a school subject (...) In a way, making the move to everyday teaching is not so easy, but the organizing framework has been valuable for me."* (Teacher 2)

The teachers' observations had proceeded from individual school subject or lesson to larger totalities.

> *"The other thing is, at least partly, the influence of this CITE project; observing school, my own class and the school community from the perspective of school culture or operating culture, which we think about a lot here [in CITE group]."* (Teacher 2)

> *"Studying has helped in not making small things too big. If you have a larger goal that you want to work towards, then I don't get disheartened about spending all day long on it, none too well. I don't see it as a problem but I just realise this isn't working and next week we'll try it a bit differently. But still we're moving towards some larger objective that I've set."* (Teacher 3)

At its most radical the CITE programme seems to have affected working life precisely in the area concerning the structuring and understanding of a teacher's work. For example, the teachers reported that they had developed the capacity to limit questions on working life to those that they might affect and to those that appeared to be beyond their influence.

The interview conveyed the impression that work during the first years had not felt particularly arduous and oppressive. It would seem that a training programme in which the questions and feelings aroused by studying are dealt with under guidance, and which aims at an understanding rather than a mastery of school reality, provides teachers with the equipment needed during their first years of employment to cope with the chaos and oppressiveness of the so-called induction period (Marvel *et al.*, 2007; Scheopner, 2010). A professional skill of this sort – to tolerate chaos and understand reality – would be of crucial importance during a teacher's first years in the profession because in a teacher's job, unlike in many other academic professions, total responsibility lies with the teacher from day one. It is perhaps more typical that responsibility in a job grows with the number of years in it. The first working years have been reported as being surprisingly arduous for teachers to the extent that many of them are considering a change of occupation and some of them will indeed even carry out their intention. (Heikkinen *et al.*, 2010; Ingersoll, 2003; OECD, 2005).

In order to improve the situation, efforts have been made to support young teachers during their first years at work; for example, by means of mentoring and courses aimed at young teachers (Howe, 2006). Our study, however, indicates that through changes in their basic training, teachers could be given some of the resources to help them during their first years. The CITE programme was not always a pleasant experience, as this teacher (4) notes *"the times here weren't always so nice – there are far nicer training programmes – but they were instructive"*. Perhaps this is the very reason why his first years at work were not so exhausting.

The Difficulty of Transferring Innovation

Even though the experiment has developed into CITE, an established educational programme, the regularisation of the programme has not automatically meant the dissemination of the experiment. Many believe that the biggest problem connected with innovations is that an innovation remains within the microcosm that has created it and does not spread. In our case the interview conveyed that an effort was made to spread innovation during the training programme.

> *"It's interesting for me to compare with when I started my studies in sports science. There really was a different way of studying there. Yes, this just woke me up, here we've got some sort of critical attitude and we had some idea what learning could be at its best. Then I had this one mate with a bit of a similar sort of background. Well, we went to see the head of department and everybody to tell them what we thought, that there was no sense in this (...) If you'd gone straight from school to start studying there, you wouldn't have understood a thing but just gone round saying how great it was... It was already then that I noticed I had got something out of this."* (Teacher 4)

In their working life, teachers had promoted innovations mainly in their own class.

> *"When you go into a ready-made structure, you feel there's no way of affecting things except inside your own classroom."* (Teacher 1)

However, the teachers did not give examples where an innovation is promoted more widely in their working community amongst colleagues, even though school is in principle a community where innovation could spread. They had around them a social system where innovations could have been disseminated, such as the school's various communication channels, staff meetings, in-service training days and informal meetings amongst teachers. (Rogers, 2003:12–24).

Explanations can be found for the difficulty of transferring an innovation and Rogers' (2003) innovation diffusion theory offers one suitable approach. Rogers (2003:15–16) has defined five factors influencing the diffusion of innovation: the relative advantage of the innovation, its compatibility with prevailing values and norms, its simplicity and comprehensibility, its ease of testing (trialability) and its observability.

Even though innovation within the CITE programme is in principle comprehensible, transferring it into practice is far from easy. It is a case of having something new for which there are no ready-made models that could be tried out directly – by following an instruction manual, for example. To a large extent, critical integrative training involves the challenging of thought structures, and even changing them. Therefore it cannot be concretely transferred according to the master-and-apprentice principle.

The students clearly find the innovations offered by the CITE programme to be more useful than prevailing school practices but the prevailing social norms of the school inhibit their introduction. School is, after all, traditionally a conservative institution rather than one that creates the new (Siltala *et al.*, 2009). Since the role of school is to uphold tradition, teachers are afraid at the outset of encountering resistance to change (Fullan, 1997). In fact, the interview revealed the fear for their own position felt by teachers if they should ever challenge the school.

Because the CITE programme is a radical innovation, it will be difficult to export it to the world of school, which is more prepared to accept reforms that do not call into question the basic structure of school. Because change in school culture is slow and difficult to achieve it is understandable that an innovation picked up during the CITE programme remains within the class:

> *"I haven't been making a big fuss about it with my other colleagues. That it's against traditional teaching."* (Teacher 5).

The innovation remains within the microcosm of the teacher's own class, especially when there are no other teachers from the CITE programme in the same working community.

In Conclusion

In our study we found that our teacher training innovation appears to be providing teachers with an understanding and reflective approach to their work and to be producing new applications in the school world. At this stage, however, the process of disseminating the innovation remains extremely slow, especially with regard to the community where the teachers work. Althought teachers have adopted new ways of thinking during their training, one reason for slow diffusion is that they have been subjected to the powerful socialising forces of the traditional school (Day, 1999:59–60; Ruohotie-Lyhty & Kaikkonen, 2009). The other reason might be that situations in school where the innovation would be conspicuous do not arise in the school community because teachers do not talk about it or pass it on, thus making it impossible for a new creative microcosm to be created within the school. On the other hand, it is also important to remember the role of the university system as a maintainer of activity, rather than as a structure promoting change (e.g. Ursin, 2011:40). This, too, for its own part slows down the spread of innovations.

It is also a question of the level at which the innovation spreads. Superficial changes are easy to make, but that does not necessarily change the deeper culture of a school. Instead, a shift in perspectives, understandings and values lies at the root of meaningful change (Goodman & Kuzmic, 1997:81). Indeed, it does seem that even though change will be slow and will challenge teachers, our training programme has sown the seed of change:

> *"The meeting gave my work a new boost. The situation has already reached the stage where I noticed I wasn't making my best effort in my work. After the meeting I once again remembered what this job is all about. Next year when I have a new class I will at least try to put into practice the ideas kindled during my studies."* (Teacher 6)

If the goal is to continue advancing the sequence of innovation in a working community, the question arises whether something can be done to make it possible for teachers in that working community to make use of an already existing innovation in their activities. It appears to us that one way of doing this is the one described by the teachers themselves in the messages written after the joint meeting, namely; to arrange and organise in-service training which supports their own professional development.

> *"At a professional level I didn't find one-off meetings like this to be particularly developing, but if it were possible to have this kind of open discussion more regularly, it would definitely help in developing my own professional skill."* (Teacher 3)

> *"I believe that, as CITE alumni, we could greatly support each other's professional growth if we met every now and then to share our ideas and practices. If the topics for discussion were narrower, we could go into them more deeply. A practical challenge facing meetings like this would of course be finding times convenient for everybody, but maybe an annual two-day CITE gathering would allow us to have workshops, discussion and development. At best our employer could pay for travel and accommodation, if the meeting was understood as in-service training."* (Teacher 2)

This kind of method would also simultaneously relieve the in-service training problems facing teacher education. At present, graduate teachers receive additional training in their work through short-term courses. The proposed annual two-day gatherings would mean the group staying together after training and meeting each other regularly for additional training. In-service training would also have reciprocity – from the perspective of developing an innovation, it would allow a counterflow and cross-fertilization of ideas. This also increases the responsibility of the training institution for the impact of initial training. We believe that an innovating educational culture requires these linkages in order to enable the creation of a broader innovative environment.

About the Authors

Pekka Räihä is a Lecturer at the Department of Teacher Education at the University of Tampere, Finland. He can be contacted at this email: pekka.raiha@uta.fi

Marja Mäensivu is a Doctoral Student at the University of Jyväskylä, Finland. She can be contacted at this email: marja.f.maensivu@jyu.fi

Matti Rautiainen is a Lecturer at the University of Jyväskylä, Finland. He can be contacted at this email: matti.rautiainen@jyu.fi

Tiina Nikkola is a Lecturer at the Department of Teacher Education at the University of Jyväskylä, Finland. She can be contacted at this email: tiina.nikkola@jyu.fi

Chapter Six

Introducing a Pedagogy of Optimal Engagement and Transformation (POET)

Sam Elkington

Introduction

As highlighted earlier in this anthology (Dobozy, this volume), the inherent complexity of studying and working within contemporary higher education (HE) has been well documented (see also Barnett, 2004) and is increasingly challenging pedagogues to place peoples' experiences of HE at the centre of their analyses. This shift toward an experiential focus has seen student engagement emerge as a core consideration linked to theories of retention and persistence (Tinto, 1999). Still more recently, attention has been given to the importance of holistic curriculum design for student engagement within the context of what has been termed "transition pedagogy" (Kift, 2009). Transition pedagogy has been defined as a guiding philosophy for intentional curriculum design that attempts to articulate purposeful, integrated, and scaffolded curriculum design to engage more effectively the increasingly diverse student cohorts passing into and through higher education (Kift, 2009) However, work on transition pedagogy has tended to focus on macro-level engagement (Corkill, 2010). In particular, the contexts of systems and institutional transition captured in the movement into HE, and the provision of effective student support, with no indication of the types of mechanisms, activities, or processes required for authentic student engagement and progression in their learning. Changing patterns of student engagement necessitate changes in approaches to and conceptualisation of teaching and learning. Learning is itself regarded as a process of change not only in relation to intellectual re-conceptualisation but also personal, social and practical transformation (Mezirow, 2000). Whilst standards (such as for learning outcomes or assessment criteria) provide a useful list of some core disciplinary formalisms that learners need to know, they provide little guidance on how one should best design and support learning opportunities for students who are "coming to know".

Building upon the close relationship between academic engagement, curriculum development and student learning processes (Nygaard *et al.*, 2008), this chapter introduces an innovative focus for those responsible for curriculum design and facilitating student learning opportunities in HE; one that not only takes in student engagement with and progression through educational programmes, at the macro, systems and institutional level, but also within and between the situated learning activities (e.g. lectures, assessments) that comprise the variety of *lived* transitional experiences had therein. At this micro-level sit the learning transitions that affect individual growth and development more directly. The idea of engagement as presented in current policy, practice and research portrays learning as a series of discrete activities and/or events experienced in a linear sequence of progression through institutional and achievement structures. At the situated level, the idea of engagement is constitutive of subjective learning trajectories as lived; the micro-transitions depicting often non-linear developmental changes and shifts in identity and agency as people journey through and interact with an educational programme (Bridges, 2003).

Like several contributions in this volume (Albergaria Almeida; Enomoto; Herbert & Leigh; Winka & Grysell), this chapter documents the implementation of an experiential perspective of effective teaching and learning. It builds upon recent advances in Flow or Optimal Experience theory (Elkington, 2010; Lutz, 2009) to move beyond traditional transmissive modes of teaching and time-on-task conceptualisations of engagement, shifting focus instead onto the cognitive, motivational, and emotional processes that foster instances of deep engagement for learners.

These are presented hereafter as a pedagogy of optimal engagement and transformation, known by the acronym "POET".

Initially, the chapter outlines the development and core features of a pedagogy of optimal engagement and transformation, before presenting and discussing case examples of how a POET can be implemented and utilised to develop innovative teaching and learning practice through holistic learning-based curriculum design.

Optimal Experience Theory: Thinking Differently about Engagement

Optimal experience theory places positive subjective experience at the centre of developmental processes, more specifically, the "flow" experience (Csikszentmihalyi, 1990). Optimal experience is seen as crucial for healthy development and effective learning for both students and staff (Csikszentmihalyi, 1997). Flow theory is a person-environment interaction theory in which optimal experience is triggered by a good fit between a person's skills in an activity and the challenges afforded by that activity; this creates a very positive state of consciousness and leads to deeply enjoyable and intrinsically motivating experience. Although such a depiction of flow, in terms of what it is, may seem straightforward it is actually quite complex, for though any single activity might engender it, an activity cannot sustain it for long unless both challenges and skills become more complex. Such progressive complexity is integral to every flow activity in that it provides a sense of discovery, pushing the individual to ever-higher levels of performance. Csikszentmihalyi (1997:33) has described flow experience as a *"magnet for learning because continued realisation of flow requires new challenges and the development of new skills"*.

Flow has been shown to be a vehicle for personal creativity and growth through the development of competence through active and subjectively meaningful task engagement (Gammon & Lawrence, 2004; Kahn, 2003; Whitson & Consoli, 2009). Creating challenging activities that require above average skill to complete, increasing the relevancy of tasks, adopting learner-centred methods of teaching, providing timely and appropriate feedback, and constructing positive, enjoyable learning environments are all identified as ways of increasing learner engagement by involving them meaningfully within learning interactions (Whitson & Consoli, 2009).

However, despite its mass appeal, flow theory remains largely undiscovered in the context of higher education.

In recent work I explored the complex holistic experiences of flow from the perspectives of individuals taking part in leisure activities (Elkington, 2010). The core aim of the research was to bring much needed clarity to the experiential, conceptual, and theoretical uncertainty surrounding what goes before and after a state of flow, to provide a more complete, holistic, and systematic understanding of the flow experience. To this effect an experience-process perspective was developed depicting flow as the focal state of mind in a broader, more expansive, multi-phased, and multi-dimensional experiential process. In a separate theoretical extension of flow theory, Lutz (2009) examined flow in relation to Antonovsky's (1987) Sense of Coherence (SOC). Antonovsky identifies comprehensibility, manageability, and meaningfulness as three components of SOC that articulate more broadly into a global orientation that expresses the extent to which one has an enduring yet dynamic feeling of confidence. Confidence that one's internal and external environments in the course of learning are structured and explicable, that the resources are available to one to meet the demands posed by that environment, and that these demands are intrinsically appealing enough to evoke investment and engagement. Lutz suggests that both share core beliefs relating to what makes for effective teaching and learning, namely; both are largely about focusing on bringing to bear of personal resources onto challenging activities. According to Lutz, flow and SOC are not only complementary but represent different dimensions of learning that are mutually reinforcing of one another and would be more useful to practitioners if integrated (Lutz, 2009).

A POET integrates for the first time an experience-process perspective of flow and SOC into a unified pedagogy of optimal engagement capable of dealing with both present or situated perspectives of learning and longer-term perspectives. From this unified perspective, activity and structure cannot be overlooked in favour of articulating some broader learning process; a more nuanced portrayal of the learning process is required – one that embraces the minutiae of situated learning as well as the longer-term layering of student learning experiences.

A Pedagogy of Optimal Engagement and Transformation (POET)

The emergent pedagogy of optimal engagement and transformation (POET) being presented here can be used to focus attention on high levels of involvement in learning activities (eg: lectures, assessments) and the identification of the features of related curriculum structures more broadly (such as module/unit and course design). This can be used to shape and develop teaching and learning so as to set the scene for the kind of deeply involving self-discovery that would allow students to more regularly experience enjoyment and positive feelings about themselves and their learning. Rather than provide a detailed theoretical description of the integral features of a POET here the following discussion explores these features through their relationship to a range of practical ideas for the design of learning activities and environments that have grown to underpin, with relative success, the curriculum and associated learning activities of two 30 week undergraduate units in the third year of a Tourism, Leisure and Sport-related course. In the case of both units, emphasis is placed upon the enhancement of micro learning transitions and student empowerment through guided self-discovery. In contrast with a traditional lecture-seminar format, students using collaborative and interactive approaches are actively involved in subject-mediated, student-centred, learning activities facilitated through an integrated network of workshops.

Such a notion of engagement is founded on the constructivist principle that learning is influenced by participation in "*educationally purposeful activities*" (Coates, 2005:26). Learning as the co-construction of knowledge is most fully exemplified in situations where students are not merely recipients of information and material but are themselves actively involved. This in turn is determined by tutors providing students with the conditions, opportunities, and expectations to become involved. In recent research I have found certain conditions to be a prerequisite for encouraging the kind of deep involvement necessary for flow to occur presently, as well as over time (Elkington, 2010). These conditions are intrinsic to the structure of the curriculum and composite learning activities of each of the undergraduate units discussed in this chapter. I have identified seven such conditions and these are described in more detail under the following subheadings.

Challenges and Skills Must Be in Balance

Learning activities need to include challenging tasks that require skills. Individuals must stand a chance of completing the tasks developed so the ability (ie the skill) of the student must match the challenges of the activity, which in turn must be accomplishable with the skills learned. Learning activities need a clear structure that provides a range of potential challenges, both in a horizontal sense, with progression from easy to difficult or from novice to expert, and in a vertical sense, allowing participants to be involved in the activity on a variety of levels requiring various levels of skill in order to enjoy it. There also needs to be the option of increasing or decreasing the difficulty of the task so that students can match as well as possible their abilities with the requirements for action set by the activity. It holds that if a student is not encouraged to increase his/her challenges continually, by trying new methods and integrating new material, the activity soon becomes boring. Equally, attempting unrealistic tasks can cause anxiety for the student.

The challenge-skill dynamic of flow emphasises the intellectual domain of student learning as they apply skills or learn new ones when faced with challenging activities. While emphasis may be on the intellectual aspects of learning, creating matches between skill and challenge also offers intrinsic motivation to learn, since students are working within an emotional state of well-being, they are neither bored nor anxious. The provision of new challenges when old ones are mastered, and the freedom to model new skills if the challenges become overwhelming, is not new to educators who may well already use the principle of scaffolding in their instructional practice as they try to develop student skills further by creating new challenges in incremental learning steps. Initially such challenges will need to be structured from the outside, by the teacher or some pre-structured task, but eventually individuals must be taught to recognise appropriate challenges and encouraged to structure learning activities in relation to their own perceived skill level.

There Must Be Clear Goals

In a learning activity it is not enough for students and teaching staff to have only a general idea of the purpose of the lecture or the assignment;

the individual must know what has to be done at any one moment and why. Learning activities need to include tasks containing clear, personally meaningful goals or targets so as to convey a sense of task relevancy and personal drive to engage. If students do not see the personal relevance of learning then we are unlikely to engage them in the deep and meaningful learning we value. One way of addressing this is to enable students to understand what motivates them and what they want to achieve, and also recognising that this may change and develop with time and experience. Encouraging progressive learner involvement in the development of short-term personal learning goals that are supported by specific task-related goals helps to make the learning activity – and the broader learning process – more relevant to them. Again, initially such goals will need to be set externally to the individual, from teacher input or pre-set activity, but individuals must be guided in their discovery of how to set goals appropriate to challenging tasks that require skills. This means incorporating activities into learning and assessment which consciously help and support students to explore new possibilities and raise their self-esteem and self-efficacy (Bandura, 1997). This in turn enables them to become more self-confident and self-aware.

There Must Be Timely Feedback

Learning activities need to include the provision of coherent, non-contradictory demands for student action whilst also providing timely and relevant (ie personally meaningful) feedback so as to maintain involvement in the activity. Clear and frequent feedback to students on their progress is integral to any learning activity, allowing for continuous task-involvement. Learning activities need to include mechanisms whereby individuals receive information as quickly and frequently as possible about how well they are doing. At first, feedback will need to come from the outside, from the teacher or some other external source such as peers or grading, but eventually individuals must be encouraged to recognise and administer feedback to themselves about their performance. To develop such an internalised system of learning is to become less dependent on external provision and more independent and self-regulatory as a learner. The aim here needs to be to guide and involve students in their discovery of an internal standard of what is effective, enjoyable and personally meaningful learning; students are then more able to persevere even without formal external recognition – for example, via tutor praise or grades. Without a constant stream of feedback either from their own performance knowledge or from tutors and peers, students' practice can become mechanical, boring, and eventually disengaging.

There Must Be Opportunity to Concentrate

Challenging, appropriate tasks, clear expectations and feedback provide the opportunity to apply skills to challenging activity in such a way that concentration becomes focused in the present. Students must be given the opportunity to concentrate on the task at hand, while distractions in the environment must be eliminated to avoid dissipation of attention; this will enable individuals to recognise feedback and maintain a present focus. Flow refers to an optimal state of immersed concentration in which attention is centred, distractions are minimised, and the individual enjoys an autonomous interaction with the activity. Irrelevant information, a tutor's self-indulgent stories or emphasis on unimportant details, destroy the kind of deep task-involvement that makes the learning activity engaging and enjoyable. A common source of distraction, such as emphasising grades or ridiculing performance, is an unnecessary threat to the learner's self. Creating self-conscious tendencies is a sure way to distract the learner. Whatever can be done to cut out distractions during involvement in the learning activity can only increase concentration and allow for more enjoyable learning experiences. The task is to encourage a present centred focus through clearly structured demands for individual action in the learning activity and by directing concentration on what is happening in the present moment; in short, by focusing attention on the task at hand.

Control Must Be Made Possible

It is critical that students be allowed to exercise a degree of control and choice in the unfolding of their own learning by guiding an active shaping of personally meaningful tasks. Clearly, students cannot be given complete freedom of choice and total control in the learning activity. Yet without a sense of choice, it is impossible for action to be deemed self-determined. And without the possibility of control it is very difficult to become involved in and enjoy what one is doing. Students must be guided in their discovery of ways to eliminate negative thoughts and emotions associated with the learning environment, instead realising the ability to focus with confidence on the task at hand, and in the process of doing so, let go of the conscious controlling tendencies often associated with such learning activities and become freely and creatively engaged in the activity.

Growth and Self-transcendence Must Be Enhanced

Guiding students in the exploration and discovery of personal incremental challenges within learning activities builds a sense of stretching individual capacity to new dimensions of skills and competence. Seeking out personally challenging situations that are repeatedly at the limits of individual capability is thus considered in light of its importance for individual growth and development. As mastery of a given situation is realised, the challenge recedes and the subject's abilities level with or overtake that required to meet the complexity of the task at hand. At this point, the complexity of the activity must be increased by developing new skills and taking on new challenges, thus stretching the individual. It is also important that teachers make students aware that the act of learning is not self-contained, nor is it a matter of simply absorbing information but of becoming part of a "community of learners". There is a need to establish a climate that encourages a positive personal and social affect among students by providing opportunities for learners to deepen their knowledge and understanding through a variety of social interactions. These could include problem-based tasks requiring collaborative participation.

The Autotelic Value of Learning Must Be Highlighted and Supported

No matter how good the formal curriculum, if it does not excite, motivate and engage learners it is unlikely to be effective. In the event that the activity is characterised by a combination of each of the conditions outlined here, it is experienced as worth doing for its own sake; the experience is said to become *autotelic* (meaning having an end or purpose in itself; in other words a "self goal"). The aim is to actively guide students in their discovery of what is intrinsically rewarding and enjoyable to them in the act of learning and how to build this self-knowledge into future learning activities. Activities that are associated with such autotelic experience are important for personal growth in that they are self-sustaining and are typically performed in the absence of extrinsic contingencies. As an individual's self-knowledge deepens they are more likely to seek out and repeat such experiences in subsequent participation.

All meaningful learning stands in relation to, and takes its direction from, a socially defined learning environment or setting that can and should be designed in ways that promote concentration, interest, enjoyment and personal growth, presently as well as over time. Antonovsky's (1987) Sense of Coherence (SOC) identifies comprehensibility, manageability, and meaningfulness as three components that can be used to articulate the conditions outlined here into a global orientation to curriculum design that sets the scene for what is essentially an ecological view of student engagement.

Setting the Scene for Engagement: the Learning Environment

The above conditions, when interpreted through the macro-lens of SOC, translate into three over-arching principles, namely; structure/practice, opportunity/support, and continuity/progression that must be considered in holistic curriculum design to encourage the kind of learning environment or landscape that promotes optimal engagement and transformational learning. The following discussion draws upon comments of participating students derived from individual reflective blogs designed to capture students' experiences and progress. These reflective comments provide a meaningful understanding of the nature and quality of student engagement in relation to each of the units, both of which are underpinned by the over-arching principles.

Structure/Practice

The learning environment must have a clearly recognisable shape that consistently structures action and focuses concentration onto personally meaningful tasks. Tasks only become personally meaningful to the individual when they is are encouraged to actively engage, through their own structured practice, in its unfolding, and whether it is deemed individually (and developmentally) challenging. The challenge for the teacher is to build the sorts of learning environments that offer a wide variety of potential opportunities which will allow students to seek out appropriate challenges commensurate to their ability level. Many traditional courses can be reasonably effective at encouraging students to remember and even understand but are less effective in building students' ability to act. This is often the result of deeper inhibitions and anxieties as well as a mis-match between what is learned and concern about the sort of people students are and want to be. But students must also feel they have the freedom to seek out such personally challenging learning. For example, a Tourism student tells of the approach to introducing new topics adopted on one unit:

> *"I like it when we move onto a new topic in the unit usually every 4–5 weeks that we are given an introductory article or chapter to read and asked to make up our own mind of its key messages... We're also usually asked to find a minimum of one related article that we think is relevant or links to the article we were given. Everybody reports their initial understanding and further reading back at the beginning of the next workshop... we'll usually then explore things in more depth"* (Tourism 2)

The requirement for new ideas and information needs to be met by different means than merely through the formal and didactic input common to traditional courses. We try to meet these needs for new information in rather different ways. Initial orientations in relation to new topics or material are made through background readings rather than through introductory lectures. The subsequent more structured interactive sessions are then used to discuss and explore initial conceptualisations of the reading. The need to discuss new information is addressed by incorporating group-based work to formulate comments and questions to be raised in further in-class discussion:

> *"When we're dealing with new topics we're encouraged to discuss our own understanding of the material we're given – without any input from the tutor. This freedom lets us talk honestly about stuff and not think we have to say things in certain ways. Discussing in groups helps me in this*

> *process – it's like thinking out loud but with people who are at the same level you are"* (Leisure 1)

Presenting material through formal inputs, such as lectures, can be difficult to engage with. Transforming sessions into peer-managed learning activities allows students to find out what is relevant and helpful to their own learning by collaboratively exploring material. Personally relevant information is then discussed within small groups before being reported back to the larger plenary group. This has generated a positive approach to addressing relevant aspects of theory for practice, rather than the previous intellectual detachment of the two, as one Tourism student reveals:

> *"Making sense of theories and applying different theories in small groups has helped me connect my thinking and make my learning more real than doing a lecture and then a seminar where there is a gap in your work and sometimes what you do in one session doesn't support or apply to the other so you're left with a gap in your understanding!?"* (Tourism 1)

In this situation the occasional session labelled as "group-work" may not be particularly effective since individuals need time to establish meaningful relationships to both material and their peers. Unfortunately group work in many instances is often too intermittent to be particularly valuable. It is important to create a learning environment that consistently holds a recognisable shape and structure to allow students to build a sense of familiarity, security and trust in relation to their surroundings:

> *"I like that we work on topics in blocks and break down material into manageable tasks. After repeating this a few times, I feel more confident and free to discuss things because I am familiar with the material and how the sessions work and what is expected of me"* (Sport 6)

Maintaining a recognisable shape and structure over the course of a unit creates a "boundaried" freedom of sorts, wherein intentional student contribution creates a sense of ownership. But ownership can be undermined by the de-skilling of students through empowering emphasis on teacher expertise culminating in disengagement and detachment, as one Sport student reveals:

> *"I've experienced times when lecturers have just lectured us on a topic or subject without any attempt to get us involved in the session or talk about the topic – it gets boring after a while. My best learning happens when I feel I am actively involved and contributing to the session"* (Sport 9)

A trusted learning environment is more likely to encourage freedom in intellectual risk-taking, creative thinking and complete task-involvement. This sense of trust is experienced as a letting go of attempts to control the situation; instead, the student allows him/herself to become completely engaged with what they are doing. In the words of one Leisure student:

> *"When I'm in that space I feel I can throw myself into a topic or session or offer ideas for discussion and not worry what people will think because we are all encouraged to do the same thing. It's quite intense sometimes, but in a good way – I feel strong"* (Leisure 5)

Creating a learning environment with a clearly recognisable shape that functions consistently to structure action and focus concentration onto personally meaningful tasks works towards developing deep approaches and transforming conceptions which emphasise meaning, purpose, seeing in a different way, and relating to students' own experiences and the wider context of the course material.

Opportunity/Support

The intellectual stimulation necessary for deep engagement is never purely intellectual and, with courses which have a more practical (i.e. managerial) orientation, there is need to see that energy is generated to enable the intellectual changes to translate into action. This stresses the importance of the emotional and personal side of learning and is dependent upon giving students a strong sense of identity and confidence, generating an important sense of responsibility and commitment that extends beyond the confines of a discrete educational event. There must be a supportive system of interaction between the person and the learning environment and its associated activities that engenders and sustains attention, keeping the person motivated and involved within learning tasks; there is need for integrated or joined-up thinking. A Leisure student:

> *"Being challenged to contribute to each session using work we have been set to work on between sessions is something that has been really positive for me. It's not set out as individual sessions – it's more like a chain of events. We've covered so much material but instead of losing my way or forgetting stuff I'm seeing how all the work fits together!"* (Leisure 3)

Intellectual stimulation generated on courses may be lost in returning to an environment which is not always supportive of what is being learned. This is addressed on each of the case units through provision of mediating tasks and structured handouts packaged to have a useful shelf-life. These tasks and handouts go beyond what has been covered "in session" and enable students to feel like they are taking away a resource which is designed to help them follow up their often brief acquaintance with complex ideas. The considered use of technology here can also assist personalised learning as a continuous process of knowledge acquisition, transformation and integration, resulting in deep learning rather than mere acquisition of new knowledge (Leadbeater, 2005; Rowley, this volume). The words of one Tourism student best capture this:

> *"Doing THIS... blogging... has helped me when I'm working on tasks between classes as I can record my thoughts or comments and then revisit them again later when I have a better understanding of what has been asked. Tutor comments and feedback on the blogs has also been helpful, though he seems to ask more questions than anything! But I now see that he is trying to get me to think more deeply about what I am saying"* (Tourism 6)

Quality of learning experience can be further enhanced with external supports such as the presence of other learners collaborating and teachers who mindfully model thinking/learning around problem-solving tasks. Too much support, either in the form of being told too much information or required to work within tight and controlling structures, may result in feelings of distance and little ownership. Too little support is likely to cause anxiety and anxious students will be less willing to take risks. Support from tutors (and peers) needs to be matched by challenging tasks, the opportunity to take risks with new ways of working and the opportunity to re-think assumptions. Achieving a better balance of support and independence is often mediated through specific tasks but can be aided by experiencing a wider range of specific roles. For example, a Sport student comments on the value of peer-reviewing of assignment drafts:

> *"Having our draft assignments peer-reviewed and reviewing other peoples' has been new and extremely useful... 1) it really made me think about what I was writing, 2) by commenting on other peoples' work I had to be sure I knew what I was talking about!!"* (Sport 1)

Deep learning requires each learner to develop their own understanding of a topic, building on what they know already, and sometimes requiring the dismantling or re-conceptualisation of existing constructs. Making time for structured reflection and feedback is central to this process, as reflection is the activity which links the personal with the learning (Brockbank & McGill, 2003). Providing regular opportunities to reflect on and make sense of experiences, both inwardly and collaboratively, with significant others is fundamental to any act of learning, allowing students to refine self-knowledge through ongoing exploration and articulation of their own learning processes.

Reflective experience turns on the notion of time and requires a structured system of communication. Within workshop sessions, general reflection on and discussion of the relevance of ideas and concepts is supplemented by frequent personal reflection capturing what is being learned, in relation to the specific learning activity and its outcomes, and how it applies and what it means to the individual. It is from here that students are able to formulate meaning and begin to understand the significance of what was experienced. This is rather eloquently put by one Tourism student:

> *"Whether you're reflecting in your blog or discussing material in a group before presenting something to the class it's all information you can use to help develop you and your learning"* (Tourism 4)

This is further enhanced by providing opportunities for learners to deepen their knowledge and understanding through a variety of social interactions. Supporting the social processes of learning requires not only a change in teaching approach but it also changes how the physical and virtual worlds in which students operate can best support meaningful social interaction. The provision of physical social learning spaces and opportunities for students to use them constructively is important. But in the virtual world provision of safe in-house environments for social interaction (i.e., online discussion forums or group Wikis) enable dialogue to continue and thus extend the parameters of the formal workshop session:

> *"For me the discussion board tasks are good because I can dip in and out when I have something to say or ask a question based on something that I have read during the week... This wouldn't happen in class"* (Sport 2)

One central feature of a POET which is less developed in more traditional teaching and learning approaches is that it engages students in the process of constructing learning in terms of artefacts such as posters (Koshy, this volume), and more creative use of presentations, flipcharts and boards. In workshops this is often integrated with the soliciting and recording of students' views, which provides a sense of contribution and ownership:

> *"I like how we're never told what or how to think about any subject... we're always asked to write down or draw a diagram or represent in some way how we understand something first. Quite often we will then work in our project groups to produce a diagram or poster that represents the group's understanding... Makes you see other perspectives and as a group decide which is most relevant – this is not always easy though"* (Leisure 4)

Whilst to some extent group work can provide a focus, traditionally the tutor chooses the task. Instead, the use of project groups can focus on themes chosen by students (supported by tutors). In turn, these are used to integrate learning into a more coherent framework, which is then shared with the larger plenary group through presentations, posters and panel discussions; a process akin to that inherent in problem-based learning.

Continuity/Progression

The sense of intellectual continuity of learning is often difficult to generate in traditional courses, particularly those trying to acquaint students with a wide range of issues. Often we do not make clear to students the areas of the curriculum that they need to concentrate on and which will enable them to access higher level learning later. Topics that are personally meaningful enable learners to access a different level of thinking about a subject and their ability to grasp these concepts enables them to understand them more deeply and access the next level of learning (Meyer & Land, 2003). Failure to grasp the concept impedes the ability to progress; such gaps in core understanding inhibit both the willingness to engage and further development. A learning environment is most likely to promote deep engagement in students when it can hold its shape and structure to allow for skill mastery, while also being open to change to allow for skill development. It is important that learning activities allow individuals a degree of choice and freedom in order to facilitate change while also maintaining a clear structure that provides discipline in practice wherein students spend time going over topics and concepts and revisiting it from different perspectives in order to promote familiarity, trust and subsequent continuity of experience and the opportunity for personal growth. Extending the amount of time spent on a particular topic appears to have been well received by students on both units, with the comments of one Tourism student typifying the student view:

> *"I have got more from [this] 5 week block than I have from whole modules before. The difference is we build an understanding visiting and revisiting topics on a regular basis but each time in a slightly different way"* (Tourism 8)

When appropriately conceived, learning environments can present the opportunity for deep engagement which is genuinely experiential. This is because students necessarily refer to the stock of past experiences which have been integrated into understanding and to new experiences which spring from interactions with a learning setting. This is not always immediately positive:

> *"It's difficult at first because it's a different way of thinking and working which takes time to get your head around... well it did me?! The expectation of bringing something to contribute every week was very tough for me to start with because I hadn't done anything like it before. I now see why we're doing it – I think it's an attitude thing?"* (Sport 11)

Early experiences of an activity may often be unrewarding because of resistance and unfamiliarity with the task and the mode of delivery. Action at this stage is directed primarily towards overcoming these barriers, requiring continuous personal commitment and perseverance. A Tourism student:

> *"You develop a sort of routine in your work. At first our tutor would provide guidance with readings... what to look for, or ask questions that we should answer using the reading like "what are the key messages?"... I do this automatically now whenever I get anything new to read and actually enjoy doing it!"* (Tourism 1)

Through continued involvement, learned patterns of behaviour are carved out, creating mental and physical habits that can be enacted consistently and smoothly at deeper levels of learning. The ingrained intensity and quality of experience that accompanies effective negotiation of this process denotes the difference between early and later experiences of students on the units.

When considered together, the over-arching principles discussed above can be seen as integrating three interrelated levels of meaning: those of the individual, significant others, and the place of learning or setting. At the individual level are found the subjective interpretations of individual student learning in relation to his/her skills and competencies as they attempt to connect some degree of significance and meaning to their actions. The second level concerns social interaction as students begin to construct a fuller understanding of the nature and quality of their learning experiences which is consolidated in their interaction with significant others (i.e., peers and tutors). The final level includes the relations between the first two levels and the place or setting in which learning occurs. People tend to relate to specific places as contributing to types of "preferred" learning experiences. It is in the information gathered in this interaction between individual, significant others and the learning setting that defines the true meaning of learning and is the material out of which students appear to form conceptions of themselves and others.

Based on this emerging understanding of student engagement, it is clear that effective transition pedagogy must be sensitive to the nature and quality of student learning and its micro-transitions. For those with the requisite experiences, skill and intentions student engagement needs to be functionally bound in a manner that supports specific opportunities for action. It must also provide the opportunity for choice and for challenging independent work, wherein students are supported and guided in managing their own development to identify and negotiate gaps in knowledge, skills and understanding. This takes in both the vertical (involvement on a variety of levels requiring various skills) and horizontal (progression from novice to expert) dimensions of learning transitions, experienced in the present as well as over time. In short, an ecological view of learning is required. Using a POET to articulate an ecological perspective of student learning represents the most nuanced portrayal yet of what is referred to as "optimal engagement". The term optimal is not used here to imply some utopian state, nor the presence of a true or pure form of engagement. Rather it denotes purposeful action and personal commitment of self that brings about an intensity and meaningful resonance between an individual, a learning activity and its setting that is deeply enjoyable.

The Ecology of Optimal Engagement

Implementing a POET promotes an ecological view of learning that permits content to live, and be lived, in its conceptual and contextual richness with a focus on guiding learners to be attentive to those underlying structures that are personally meaningful. The learning environment and its associated learning activities is an enabler for optimal student engagement, wherein clear goals, immediate feedback and manageable levels of challenge orient the individual in a unified and patterned way. The result is that attention becomes completely focused on the present, allowing the individual to become completely involved in the learning act with confidence and self-belief. This resultant sense of competence functions to reinforce the intrinsic motivation and related behaviours that brought it about in the first place, thus holding engagement. Sustaining experiences of deep involvement, and returning again and again to them, sets up an upward spiral of personal growth, cultivating positive learning repertoires to be repeated and honed during subsequent participation.

Such an approach has had a positive impact on student learning outcomes in each of the case units. A POET moves beyond the traditional instrumental gaze of student learning and a view of knowledge (facts, concepts) as acquired for the purposes of assessment, to one of "coming to know" as participation in rich contexts where one gains an appreciation for both context and the situations in which such knowledge has value. From this perspective, knowing is always an activity and not a thing to be transmitted from tutor to learner, it is always contextually bound and not abstracted, and is representative of an individual's relational-functional stance toward a learning interaction that is rarely static. For this reason knowing requires continuous maintenance and evaluation.

When educators fail to engage learners in meaningful relations to knowledge, and instead impart core ideas as isolated facts or abstract concepts, these facts and concepts are no longer connected to the situations and activities that allow them to have any use-value. Treated in this way, such knowledge runs the likely risk of becoming disembodied and effectively disconnected from any meaningful use in the world. It is one thing to "know of" something in order to satisfy some assessment task; it is quite another to function in those situations in which knowledge has value, and yet another to choose to engage in such situations. It is only in the latter that authentic, self-regulated, engagement can be claimed. Self-regulation is required from students at the higher levels of study and is an expectation of professional practice and for anyone functioning in the complex and continually changing environment of modern society.

Conclusion

Conventional expressions of student engagement rely on concepts and methods depicting engagement as something educators can easily frame, that endures through time, and whose essential qualities can be captured in a single image or set of behaviours. The pedagogy of optimal engagement and transformation (POET) introduced in this chapter challenges some of these traditional thoughts and re-addresses deep or optimal engagement as dynamic, emergent, and embedded in personal learning journeys. Such engagement pertains to who teachers and learners are and what they do as they interact with one another for the purposes of learning. A POET reveals to us that the places to search for such meaningful content are not in the still important conventional physical descriptors for individual practice (learning outcomes, assessment criteria etc) but, instead, in the flow of student learning itself and its constitutive micro-transitions. This chapter represents a deliberate attempt to move beyond extant and separated institutional policy and discrete initiatives for student engagement. It has articulated a guiding framework for holistic curriculum design such that educators might realise the significance of embracing situated learning, as well as the longer-term layering of learning experiences. Such an approach has been shown to bring student learning journeys to life moment-by-moment in what is an ecological view of engagement and truly transformational learning. From this perspective, transformational learning is not an add-on; it is the essence of a higher education.

About the Author

Sam Elkington is a Senior Lecturer in Sport Management and a Teaching Fellow at the University of Bedfordshire, UK. He can be contacted at this email: samuel.elkington@beds.ac.uk

Chapter Seven

Learning through Innovation

Paul Bartholomew and Nicola Bartholomew

Introduction

This chapter deals with the implementation, at a university level, of approaches to teaching that are "beyond transmission". When accounts of innovations in learning and teaching are shared in literature, they often focus exclusively on innovation as a product. That is to say: using a case study approach an identified problem is highlighted, an account of the design and deployment of innovative intervention is shared and some results relating to the impact of the intervention are offered for review. Such accounts of academic practice are clearly valuable; indeed we offer a form of case study as part of this chapter; but what of the *process* of innovation? Can innovation as a practice be taught to academic colleagues and if so what would such a course look like and how might it influence the practice of its participants?

The first part of this chapter sets the Higher Education context for and describes a Master's level course Learning Through Innovation – offered at Birmingham City University. This professional development course for academics has been specifically designed to encourage innovative practice in individual practitioners and to catalyse institutional change through their agency. The underpinning philosophy of the course, which is now in its seventh year, is shared with reference to the theoretical frameworks of innovation. Survey data relating to the impact of the course on the academic practice of 24 participants is presented and discussed.

Later in the chapter one of the authors offers a detailed narrative account from the point of view of a participant from the 2005 cohort; her experiences of the process of innovation as facilitated by the course is offered with reference the specific innovative teaching practices that emerged as a result. Additionally, she reflects on where her ongoing innovative practice has taken her since 2005 and the implications her professional development has had on her academic identity.

National Context: Innovation and Higher Education

In the United Kingdom (UK), universities are governed through the Department for Business, Innovation and Skills. As Dobbins (2009) notes, the UK Government's position is that supporting innovation is a fundamental pre-requisite for economic growth and that universities have a key role to play in creating an environment that embraces and nurtures innovation. Although this position is taken in relation to an expectation that universities support outward-facing innovation through their relationships with industry, what can we say of the internal environment within the universities themselves?

Certainly the UK Government, through the Higher Education Funding Council for England (HEFCE), has held a longstanding expectation that universities will support the development of an internal environment that embraces innovation. In its 2001 review of the Teaching Quality Enhancement Fund (TQEF), HEFCE stated that in order to use the funding effectively to catalyse change, universities would need (amongst other things) to develop mechanisms to support projects and innovation.

Although internal frameworks are clearly fundamental for fostering innovative practice, UK universities have not been abandoned to take these steps in isolation. Institutions operate in a nationally supported context, able to draw support and guidance from such agencies as the JISC (Joint Information Systems Committee) and the HEA (Higher Education Academy).

The JISC has a particular role in the support of the innovative use of digital technologies to support education and research. There have been great strides in the development of information and communication technologies (ICT) over recent years and students entering higher education have an expectation that effective use of ICT is a fundamental component of their learning experience at university. It is therefore not surprising that around 50% of all of the innovations developed by participants on our course involve the use of ICT. Nor is it surprising that the JISC has supported innovation in this area. The JISC's Learning and Teaching Innovation grants scheme has been running since May 2008 and has funded 19 projects so far, each with a grant of £50,000. It is easily observed that such funds are more likely to be attracted by institutions able to catalyse and sustain innovative approaches to learning and teaching than those who have a less well-developed culture of innovation in this area.

It is from this national context that a need for the Learning Through Innovation course emerged and has continued to develop. Details of the course, first offered in 2003 are given below.

"Learning Through Innovation": Philosophy and Aims

The Learning Through Innovation course at Birmingham City University is structured as a 30-credit module within the MA Education programme. It is normally studied by participants who have already gained a Postgraduate Certificate in Learning and Teaching in Higher Education. The module has been delivered every academic year since 2003 and attracts between 12 and 30 participants.

The title of the course has an intentional double meaning. The participants (Higher Education teachers) learn from the process of innovation and the students they teach have *their* learning enhanced (hopefully) as a result of the innovations developed and deployed by the participants on the course. By way of seeking verification that this dual intent is reflected in the experiences of those who have undertaken the course we included a question relating to the perceived focus of the course on a survey conducted with current and past participants (see the "Surveying current and past participants" section below for details):

Perceived focus of the course:	Innovation as a "process" it's about me and my organisational context	It is about innovation as a "product" i.e. mainly about developing a real innovation that impacts on my academic practice	It's about innovation as a process and as a product in equal measure
Responses:	12.5%	25%	62.5%

Table 1: Perceived Focus of the Course

As can be seen in Table 1, a majority of the respondents did feel that the module had a dual focus and was "*...about innovation as a process and as a product in equal measure*".

The course has been designed by and is delivered from our University's Centre for the Enhancement of Learning and Teaching (CELT) and as such there are two overarching aims for the course; firstly, to support the personal and professional development of the members of our academic community and secondly to contribute to the institutional capacity to provide the highest quality learning experience for our students.

Central to the underpinning motivations for running the course is the assumption that Higher Education provision is dynamic and requires continuous institutional innovation to remain optimally effective. Through teaching course participants to become confident and competent innovators we hope to create cohorts of change agents on behalf of the institution.

Just as the course supports participants in their development of innovations that ensure their teaching goes "beyond transmission", so this course meets the same challenge. Transmission of information is minimal; the course revolves around peer-supported approaches, including peer-reviewed iteration of projects, with reflection on the outputs of the peer review process a mandatory part of the assessment task. The course's primary aim, to transform academic identities, cannot easily be achieved through participant acquisition of declarative knowledge alone; activities that stimulate multidisciplinary discourse and develop confidence in innovation as an academic practice are fundamental to the course's delivery model.

Course Structure

The course runs over six full days delivered over five months – the cohort meets approximately once a month for five months – with the final piece of assessment due approximately eight months after participants start the course. Participants spend the three months between the last taught session and the submission of their final piece of work deploying and evaluating their chosen innovation in the context of their own academic practice. Although there is online support for the course it has been purposefully designed to run in a face-to-face mode, like many of the courses delivered by CELT. This course design choice is made in order to encourage and foster a strong sense of community and to take maximal advantage of the multidisciplinary nature of each cohort.

The course has two items of assessment. The first is a reflective account of the participants' propensity to innovate (the Self Appraisal) and the second is an evaluative report on the innovative intervention as deployed within the participants' academic practice (the Report).

Course Content

Through undertaking the Self Appraisal assessment, the participants explore their own motivations to innovate and the context in which they work. This exploration leads to the development of a personal development action plan that forms part of this first assessment.

A number of theoretical models are used to help participants make sense of their personal and organisational context. Firstly, participants consider their academic identities in the context of their orientation to educational development (Land, 2000). Land identifies twelve orientations that do not necessarily reflect personal idiosyncrasies but rather describe the *"attitudes, knowledge, aims and action tendencies of educational developers"* in relation to their personal ways of working within organisational contexts.

They then undertake two self-diagnostic questionnaires: one relating to the learning they gain from reflection and another relating to the organisation they work in. The Learning Organisation questionnaire generates three scores relating to whether participants are "allowed", "willing" and "able" to innovate. The "allowed" scores within a cohort will often align very strongly with the area of the university in which the participants work i.e. all participants from a particular department tend to have similar scores to each other but different scores from participants from other departments. This finding shouldn't surprise us since the "allowed" score is directly attributable to the local working environment; managers with particular attitudes towards supporting, or not supporting, their staff in developing innovations will have a similar overarching influence for all of those under their management.

The notion that the organisational culture exerts a strong influence on people's propensity to innovate is well recognised. In his 2006 book *The Enquiring University,* Stephen Rowland explores the tension between compliance and contestation in academic practice and notes that academic development is "*intertwined with the micro politics of the institution as well as the wider politics of higher education*". Our experience is that not only is the development of academic staff intertwined with the micro politics of the institution but that this micro-political landscape has a variable topography across an institution.

As well as sharing tools that help to support reflection, the course also covers innovation theory. Central to the course is the assumption that participants will develop a properly planned, deployed and evaluated innovation with demonstrable effectiveness in the support of student learning. As such, participants are encouraged to develop an understanding of strategies that will aid them in migrating their innovation from their specific context to more mainstream utilisation.

The diffusion of innovation model as developed by Rogers (1962; 1983; 1995; 2003) has been very useful as a basis for exploring the pattern of uptake of innovations within a university context. The model is utilised to elicit appreciation of adoption typologies and what these mean for innovators in Higher Education. These typologies are introduced and explored with the intention of equipping participants with some awareness of the need to be adaptable when trying to gain "buy-in" from peers, managers and students.

Although a description and critique of this model is offered below, a detailed inclusion in this chapter would go beyond our wish to offer a sample of indicative course content. Rather, we contend that understanding the model is central to understanding the way in which the course reaches and influences beyond the enhancement of the learning of the participants and the students they teach. It explains how the course represents an institutional response to supporting a widespread culture that delivers enhanced learning outcomes for students across the university.

For those unfamiliar with the model, a graphical representation is offered below as Figure 1 and summarises the following concepts:

- The uptake of an innovation within a population follows a predictable pattern of adoption;
- The population comprises individuals who can be grouped according to their propensity for uptake of the innovation;
- There are five groupings: Innovators, Early Adopters, Early Majority, Late Majority and Laggards;
- Uptake of an innovation begins with Innovators, with the other groups coming on board in the order given above and as shown in Figure 1;
- Laggards may never adopt at all;
- The most significant differences in propensity to adopt innovations occur between the Early Adopters and the Early Majority. Moore (1991) referred to this phenomenon as the "chasm" (as marked on the graphical representation of the model);
- Those differences emerge from the social and psychological characteristics of the participants of the groupings.

Within our course the concept of the "chasm" is critiqued. Classically, it is described that the Early Majority "cross the chasm" as they come to adopt an innovation. We find this metaphor to be problematical since members of the Early Majority group do not spontaneously change their social and psychological profile to become Early Adopters. On our course we suggest that no one needs to "cross" the chasm, rather it is incumbent upon the Innovators and Early Adopters to take action to "close" the chasm, thus making the innovation readily accessible to the Early (and Late) Majority.

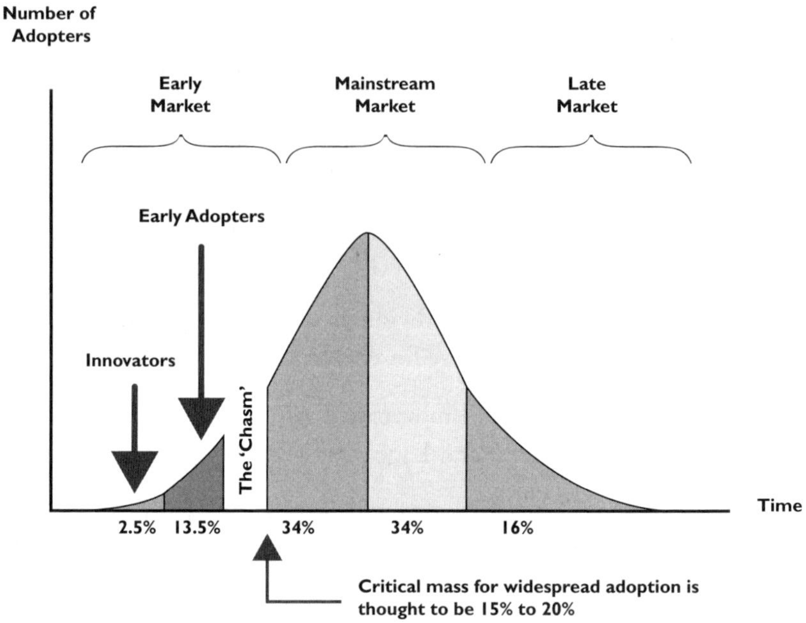

Figure 1: Adapted from Rogers (1983), Moore (1991), Geoghegan (1994)

Geoghegan (1994) refers to the Early Majority as:

> *"...pragmatists... ...who adopt a wait-and-see attitude toward new applications of technology, and want solid references and examples of close-to-home successes before adopting. They are not interested in abrupt, discontinuous change, but are more attuned to evolutionary modification of existing processes and methods. They want to see compelling value in an innovation before adopting it."*

We believe that to meet the needs of the Early Majority, Innovators and Early Adopters need to generate persuasive evaluation data, as it is this evidence of effectiveness that closes the chasm and catalyses uptake of an innovation within the (large) population of the Early Majority. For that reason, a significant part of our course is given over to developing participant competence and confidence in undertaking robust evaluations of innovation and to the ways in which such evaluation data might be communicated to others. Through focusing on evaluation techniques on our course, we offer an opportunity for participants to develop not an "innovator" identity, equipped to deliver enhancements in learning opportunities for their own students, but an "institutional change agent" identity, someone who is able (and willing) to effect positive change much more broadly.

Participants are encouraged to consider the purposes of their evaluations in terms of "evaluation for accountability", "evaluation for development" and "evaluation for knowledge". Frameworks for evaluation shared with participants include the RUFDATA model (Saunders 2000) and Kirkpatrick's Four Levels of Evaluation reaction, learning, behaviour, results (Kirkpatrick 1975). In the context of our course, central to any choice for evaluation is the notion of "audience", so participants are asked to consider (and indeed are assessed on) who is the audience for their innovation, who are *their* Early Majority and what sort of evaluation data would be most persuasive to that audience?

Of course before participants can evaluate their innovation and disseminate their findings they must first create an innovation! Participants on the course are therefore offered tutor and peer support to choose and develop a suitable innovation and are made aware of sources of support for innovative practice. This includes signposting to sources of support both intellectual and financial in nature, both within the institution and more widely through such organisations as (in our British context) the JISC, the Higher Education Academy and the Staff and Educational Development Association (SEDA).

Overall, the course is designed to support the development of academic staff so as to increase their propensity to innovate and crucially to develop their capacity to catalyse innovation beyond their immediate teaching responsibilities.

The course has been running for seven years. To what extent do current and prior participants feel the course has had an impact on their propensity to innovate as a teacher in Higher Education?

Surveying Past and Current Participants

In February 2011 we invited all current and past participants for whom we had email contact details to take part in an online survey relating to the Learning Through Innovation course. Eighty-seven individuals were contacted and twenty-four responded; a 28% response rate. Although this response seems fairly low, twelve of the respondents studied the course within the last two years (from twenty-four participants) and these represented a 50% response rate from those for whom the course was fresh in their minds. Results of the survey can be seen throughout this chapter. In the survey, participants were asked to share their perceptions on the degree to which the course impacted upon their willingness to innovate, their personal capacity to innovate, their ability to make sense of the institutional culture as it relates to innovation and their ability to navigate the institutional culture as it relates to innovation. Their responses to these questions are shown in Table 2 below:

N=24 What impact has undertaking the Learning Through Innovation module had on	**No positive impact**	**Modest positive impact**	**Considerable positive impact**	
your *willingness to innovate* as a teacher in higher education?	0%	54.2%	45.8%	**Personal**
your *personal capability to innovate* as a teacher in higher education?	0%	58.3%	41.7%	
your *ability to make sense of the institutional culture* as it relates to innovative teaching practice in higher education?	8.3%	62.5%	29.2%	**Institutional**
your *ability to navigate the institutional culture* in a way that enhances your ability to innovate as a teacher in higher education?	20.8%	58.4%	20.8%	

Table 2: Impact Analysis of the Learning Through Innovation Course (n=24).

As can be seen, for the most part prior participants report that undertaking the course has had some impact on their willingness and ability to innovate within a Higher Education context. In relation to the data given above, it should be noted that, in the optional free-text sections of the survey, two respondents noted that they embarked upon the course as active innovators (in their eyes) and as such, the impact of the course in terms of their willingness and ability to innovate was necessarily limited they felt there was little room for augmentation. This may beg the question: "What motivates these participants to enrol on the course?" When asked, these participants reveal themselves to be strategic in their behaviour; they refer to the academic credit that accrues towards the award of a Master's degree and they speak of the opportunity the course gives them to secure time and, to an extent, permission to engage in such innovation activity.

In relation to the questions relating to making sense of and navigating the institutional cultural landscape, the results were less positive. Nonetheless, 29.2% of participants report that they feel the course had considerable positive impact on their ability to make sense of the institutional culture and a further 62.5% report modest impact. In terms of actually navigating the institutional culture, 20.8% feel the course had a considerable impact on their ability to do so and another 58.3% report modest impact. Some participants felt that there was a good deal of intransigence and bureaucracy within the organisation and that this was too well entrenched for them to make significant headway. As a consequence, we see generally that participants find it harder to effect change at an institutional level than they do at a personal level. However, we must not forget that each of the participants who completed the course *did* undertake an innovative project related to their academic practice with the intention of improving the learning opportunities they themselves offered to their students. As a consequence of the course, around 150 innovations/projects have been developed, deployed and evaluated by course participants since 2003.

Although the table of survey data offers some insight into the institutional impact of the course, what does the lived experience of having participated in the course "feel like" to one of our participants? One such account, describing experiences of the course and subsequent post-course practice, is offered below:

A Personal Account of Participation and Subsequent Practice

As a participant of the Learning Through Innovation course, I felt empowered and motivated to pursue new methods of learning and teaching that would ultimately encourage student engagement and collaboration.

I coordinated a 2nd year module (course) on the undergraduate Diagnostic Radiography programme in the Faculty of Health. This is a three-year BSc (Hons) programme that requires graduates to be autonomous, self directed professionals who are able to question anachronistic policy and work collaboratively within a multidisciplinary team.

As an educator, developing trust and a degree of partnership with my students is something that I feel is a dominant factor in my teaching philosophy. Encouraging learner engagement is often challenging within the classroom environment due to a range of inhibitors including those that are socially constructed and those emerging from academic-structural deficiencies. Making the transparent links between learning outcomes, module content and assessment and clearly applying them to practice ensures that students will be more likely to understand learning design intent and will engage more fully in class. Of course, I also want to make learning enjoyable for students, our key stakeholders, as this important but sometimes elusive element can also help to break down the barriers that might otherwise preclude learner engagement.

This underpinning motivation for me *wanting* to innovate is aligned with what Land (2000) refers to as the Romantic (Ecological Humanist) orientation, I'll expand on this below but I have found this modelwhich was introduced during the Learning Through Innovation courseto be quite useful from a career planning point of view.

I embarked on the *Learning Through Innovation* course in 2005 as part of an MA in Education and through this study I was afforded the opportunity to reflect on my identity as an educator, my own needs and abilities and the needs of my students. The first assessment, the Self Appraisal, instigated a degree of introspection in relation to personal motivators for change and although the Land paper (*ibid*) is interesting for how it helps you learn who you *are*, it is even more useful in learning who you *aren't*!

Reading the other orientations, it was easy to appreciate how some of them might be useful in making things happenfor instance, I was particularly struck with the Political-strategic (Investor) and the Vigilant Opportunist orientations. Awareness of these approaches was the first stage in me aspiring to develop some of the traits associated with those orientations. As a consequence, since 2005 I have found myself better able to steer myself in ways which have allowed me to manage my orientation and adopt some of the traits to which I aspired.

The second assessment undertaken as part of the course asked participants to design and deploy an innovation within their own teaching practice. As a Learning Technology Champion within my department, I have an ongoing, inherent interest in using and promoting technologies that encourage a student-centred approach that may be used to enhance and encourage learner engagement.

My innovation was based upon generating narrated video demonstrations that depict a series of radiographic techniques to include appropriate patient positioning, manipulation of equipment, and communication. The aim was to provide students with an online, simulated, visual representation of techniques to review in their own time rather than listening to a verbal description of techniques within the classroom. The visual cues provide an additional element of clarity for students as they can see firsthand how a verbal description can match the actual manipulation of the patient or equipment and this in turn can build student confidence in their own abilities before physically attempting these techniques themselves.

Each video lecture can depict a radiographic technique quickly and effectively in a way that can be reproduced by the student in practice. A series of such videos were integrated into first and second year modules and these generated some extremely positive feedback.

In my context, "beyond transmission" does not mean the abandonment of transmission but rather a reference to how we can use efficiencies afforded by technology to transmit information at a time and space to suit the learner thus allowing classroom contact time to be liberated for collaborative group-work and problem-based activities. The additional affordances of repeatability and learner-paced study are a useful by-product of such a methodology.

In 2009 Birmingham City University began to offer a scheme that pairs academics with student partners to develop learning and teaching projects of mutual interest. My experience of the Learning Through

Innovation course and my acquired Vigilant Opportunist habits prompted me to apply to this scheme and I have subsequently been able to employ six student partners to help me with scripting and videoing of new productions. The student partners are clearly passionate about the project because they can see the relevance to clinical practice and the benefits of the products as learning tools. They have also discussed potential content with their peers and have therefore acted as effective conduits for communicating the learning needs of the student group.

I have adopted and developed new methods of teaching locally within my own department, but am I a true innovator? If I refer to the Diffusion of Innovation Model, I would actually align myself with the Early Adopters group rather than the Innovator group because I view myself as a role model to inspire others to take steps towards change. Indeed, my role as a Learning Technology Champion has precisely this intention. Adopting innovations and sharing my experiences with colleagues can help to ensure that the mainstream majority sees the tangible benefits of innovative practice and in this way I can help to close chasms.

Working closely with students also provides an opportunity for me to influence innovative thinking within the student group. When I initially broached the concept of video methods with my current students, one member of the group suggested that we might also build a library of podcasts relating to the module content in order to ultimately enhance flexible learning methods. A simple concept which may not necessarily be at the leading edge of pedagogical design but one that is still somewhat under-utilised within the programme. What excites me more than the innovation itself is that the concept originated with a student for the benefit of peers and that students are now effectively helping to shape the curriculum. I believe that this process of innovation and engagement has influenced my student colleagues and may encourage them to innovate in their future careers.

Chickering and Gamson (1987) identified seven principles of good practice for ensuring student engagement that include student-staff contact, respect for diverse learning styles and co-operation among students. In 2010, on behalf of the HEA, Trowler and Trowler reviewed a large body of literature to find evidence for assertions that student engagement leads to positive educational outcomes; the seven principles of engagement emerge once again. However, this HEA report suggests that students in general are only tenuously linked to curriculum design, as their engagement is too often limited to providing feedback through surveys. The Student Academic Partner project detailed above offers an example of how it is possible to engage students beyond the remit of just providing module feedback.

My innovative practice, with its roots in the staff development activity which I have described, has continued to develop and evolve since 2005. I truly believe that the early support I received has been influential in getting me to think strategically about innovation and about how to gain support for the curriculum developments I continue to champion. By way of sharing future plans for my work, it is my intention that the student partners will ultimately work together to generate formative online assessments through our virtual learning environment in a way that specifically links them to the content covered within the technique videos. Working together in this way will provide students with some insight into my role as an educator, thus enhancing their opportunities for learning. As Dobozy (this volume) states *"As student producers progress in their learning, their understanding of the interplay between learning goals, learning design and learning output grows."* It hasn't escaped my notice that this engagement, even empowerment, of students through partnership, reflects my natural Romantic (Ecological Humanist) orientation.

Innovations/Projects Undertaken by Other Participants

In the above personal account the innovative project section is quite typical of the type and scale of innovation/project our participants undertake. Around 50% (more in the last two years) of the participants choose an innovation that relates to new (to them) use of some form of technology-supported learning. Another 25% or so of the innovations/projects relate to the development of new assessment methods and although these are infrequently fully rolled out within the timeframe of the course, the participants do undertake some pilot work. The final 25% of projects relate to a wide range of activities including, to name but a few, the use of story-telling in teaching, peer feedback techniques, the use of Action Learning Sets, and new ways of working with colleagues.

Specific examples of innovations undertaken by the 2010/2011 cohort include:

- The use of video methods to involve healthcare service users with learning disabilities in the selection of prospective students for a nursing programme;
- The production of a set of podcasts to support the teaching of enterprise level computer networking skills;
- The use of movie clips to assist the education of learners about bio-psycho-social-spiritual facets of healthcare;
- The development of a portfolio based assessment for Media Studies students;
- Video based evaluation of computer-based simulation activity in a healthcare context.

Reflections of a Member of the Teaching Team

It is worth pointing out at this stage in the chapter that neither of the current course teachers is the originator of the course, recognition for that goes to our colleague Alan Mortiboys, now retired. However, it is worth noting that both members of the current teaching team are previous participants of the course and I (Paul) was a participant in the first cohort in 2003 and my co-tutor undertook the course in 2007. For both of us, the course had such an impact on our practice and thinking that we wanted to become involved in its ongoing iteration and delivery.

Although it is now in its seventh year we contend that the need for such a course could not be more relevant than it is today. The recent global financial crisis and the consequent changes in the funding arrangements for universities in the UK, and more widely, means that one thing is certain: simple maintenance of the *status quo* is not a viable option. This realisation has created an environment in which institutional capacity for innovation has become a highly valuable commodity. We contend that the figures we have presented, relating to the impact the course has on the participants' propensity to innovate, demonstrate significant success in bolstering individual innovative activity. Furthermore, we believe that this has led to significant bolstering of institutional capacity for innovative academic practice.

However, our findings also suggest that we have more work to do; the lower numbers of participants reporting considerable positive impact in relation to making sense of, and being able to navigate, the institutional context could be seen as a bottleneck to catalysing innovation and change across the institution. In response to these findings, and through the consultations we have had more widely, the course is about to be redesigned as part of wider redesign work to move our academic staff development provision from an MA Education framework to an MEd framework. Through this work the Learning Through Innovation course will be shifting its emphasis a little, so as to offer more support in relation to helping participants to make sense of, and to successfully navigate, the institutional, micro-political, cultural landscape. In order to reflect this change in emphasis, the new course will be called "Innovation, Identity and Culture in Higher Education".

Conclusion

An enhanced capacity to innovate in learning and teaching *can* be taught. Adopting institutional approaches to delivering such a course to members of academic staff can make a real and positive difference to a university's capacity to innovate. As the Higher Education sector is forced to make changes to the way it delivers its programmes, new ways of working and new ways of delivering courses need to be developed. Innovation thrives in climates of profound change and thus institutional commitment to courses such as Learning Through Innovation could be seen to represent a very good investment.

As our survey data have shown, this approach to enhancing institutional capacity by equipping individuals with the skills and attitude they need to innovate has real potential to transform approaches to teaching. However, and perhaps more importantly, the narrative account offered by a former participant demonstrates the potential for a propensity for innovation to be sustained well after participants have finished the course.

About the Authors

Paul Bartholomew is the Head of Curriculum Design and Academic Staff Development at Birmingham City University working within the Centre for Enhancement of Learning and Teaching. He can be contacted at this email: paul.bartholomew@bcu.ac.uk

Nicola Bartholomew is a Senior Academic within the Faculty of Health at Birmingham City University. She can be contacted at this email: nicola.bartholomew@bcu.ac.uk

Chapter Eight

Contextualised Iterations of Innovative Teaching Practices

Anne Herbert and Elyssebeth Leigh

Introduction

In traditional approaches to higher education teaching the emphasis often falls on transmission of existing knowledge (Phillips, 2005), locating education as a transactional exchange of knowledge which Freire (1970) likened to "banking".

In this chapter, we use the term "innovative teaching practices" to refer to those approaches to teaching and learning which aim for more than transmission in higher education. But innovative practices are not simply transmitted from one context to another without negotiations and adaptations because any specific context always inhibits and enables practices in particular ways (McKenzie *et al*, 2005). The purpose of this chapter, therefore, is to illustrate iterations of a teacher's adjustments in this context in order to go beyond transmission in her teaching practice.

The teacher wants to enact a dialogic and experiential process of teaching and learning (Flecha, 2000) that was "*not a simple transmission, wrought by and large through description of the concept of the object, to be memorized by students mechanically*" (Freire, 1994:67). Her professional values drive her desires to increase the productive interactions between the students in the classes, use formative assessments to emphasise learning, and provide feedback to students transparently. She is an academic faculty member responsible, like most of her academic colleagues, for both teaching and research. Her work context, described more fully in the second section of this chapter, is transmission-centred. Lecturing to impart information and examinations to test memory are the norm. How does the academic innovate and go beyond transmission in her teaching when many unsupportive contextual factors operate in her context?

After illuminating the transmission-centred context, the theoretical basis of the innovative practices is provided. This is followed by the teacher's voice describing three iterations of innovative practices. The discussion section emphasises the negotiated aspect of these multiple iterations.

The Transmission-centred Context

First we describe this context from the viewpoint of a particular teacher. This teacher was recruited to an academic post to research and teach management. Here we focus on this academic's teaching role, understanding that she also enacts the researcher who is not visible in this chapter. Although not immediately evident, lecturing to impart information and examinations to test memory have been the norms in this context. These norms are consistent with the reward system that values research outputs more highly than teaching efforts or outputs, indicating that the "theories in use" (Argyris & Schön, 1974) at the university primarily enact education as transmission.

Recruitment and Induction

The teacher was employed in an established, well-regarded and internationally accredited university to teach management. One argument in the written recommendation for the appointment was that she would introduce, and could help implement, new ideas especially in relation to the practices of teaching and learning. However, the emphasis on the value and validity of new approaches did not extend beyond the recruitment process.

Induction about teaching and learning for incoming academics was informal, like in many other universities. For external appointees, inevitably lacking prior experience of studying at this university, the only formal induction offered is a half-day program offered once a year to deal with employment conditions.

Existing Norms of Teaching and Assessment

In practice, making improvements to teaching and learning practices were peripheral to most academics' regular activity. Under pressure to increase competitive research outputs and complete reports for accreditations and rankings purposes, the emphasis was on producing research to increase the university's international visibility. Resources for teaching shrank and class sizes grew, leaving little time or energy for collegial discussion about teaching and learning. This was, perhaps, not so surprising given the absence of explicit policy about teaching, learning and assessment. Individual faculty members could decide their own teaching, learning and assessment practices according to their course content, abilities and interests. There was a prevailing attitude frequently encountered in corridor conversations (but not explicit in university documentation) that any specific policy on such matters would be undesirable and risked constraining or undermining individual academic freedom and responsibility.

Like many other European universities (ACO, 2005), this one has been primarily staffed by its own graduates who, during their studies, are passively socialised into the values and common practices of the faculty. Experienced professors model for potential new faculty ways to cope with the competing demands of research output and teaching load, which were

- Identifying the latest and best bank of knowledge to deliver;
- Ensuring teaching content is linked to personal research interests so the bank is efficiently maintained;
- Limiting support for students' exploration, identification and pursuit of their own personal interests. (Räsänen, 2009).

Further, since the transmission style of teaching is individually oriented, cooperative construction of knowledge is devalued or ignored. While teamwork may be used as a means to share the workload, little heed is paid to learning how teams work in practice. This approach results in lectures driven by projected slides, with occasional exercises to emphasise key concepts in preparation for a final exam. The primary task is to describe and explain particular banks of knowledge chosen by the teacher as important for students to know. New academics adopt this as the simplest way to manage the dual load of teaching hours and research outputs.

Assessment tasks sustain this view of teaching. Traditional written exams in an enclosed space with limited time frames and without access to information sources other than the student's individual memory are the most used and heavily weighted form of assessment of student learning. One rumour purported a rule that every course was required to have an exam. There are a number of factors contributing to the ongoing status of such traditional examinations:

- The conditions of the examinations can be controlled, so the results are believed to provide reliable measures of learning;
- Their relative ease to administer; and
- They fulfil expectations that the main feedback required is a numeric grade (Lindblom-Ylänne *et al*, 2003).

Another is the ability and willingness to outsource the grading, which some use as an argument that the assessment is independent. Typically, peer and institutional pressures are to conform.

Enacted Values Evidenced in Student Feedback Forms

When a course ends, the feedback system affirms the assumption that students will accept knowledge deposits as sufficient. Students are invited, after each and every course, to rate anonymously their agreement or disagreement on a 1-5 scale in relation to such items as: the teacher motivated me to learn, the teacher explained matters clearly, the teacher was expert, and the course content was factual. The collated results are sent to relevant academics – but such student input is widely disregarded because there is a low response rate. Not many students complete the feedback since there is no evidence it is used. This leads to a pair of dead ends rather than a usable feedback cycle (Ramsden, 2003; Watson, 2003).

This description of the context sets the scene for the challenges encountered by a teacher committed to enacting learning-centred theories when she was given to teach a compulsory first year course for all students studying business disciplines.

Theoretical Underpinnings of the Innovative Approaches

This university context, with many strong institutional elements supporting transmission-centred education, did not fully acknowledge the existence of alternate practices. The theories underpinning the three inter-related components of this teacher's initiatives in the context – an increased level of classroom interaction; a continuing developmental focus on formative assessment; and emerging attention to open, shared assessment processes – were all extant in academic literature. These are outlined below followed in the next by the academic's personal account of the *in situ* iterative implementation.

Dialogic Deep Learning

The underlying operational principle, consistent with dialogic learning (Flecha, 2000) can be expressed as "we know through interaction". This requires interactions between teacher and learner roles to be aligned with the belief that everyone can teach, and everyone wants to learn as much as possible. Deep learning (Ball, 1995) requires appropriating existing knowledge for oneself by personalising understanding through active discussion and reflection on experience. Students who do this "*learn to learn*" (Freire, 1994:68), and are more likely to be actors in the world, not merely the objects of others' actions. Similarly, interactions with concepts and theories relevant to the course require active engagement rather than passive reception. Moreover, interactions with one's own and each other's experiences are considered to have merit and value of their own (see also Dobozy, this volume; Almeida & Teixeira-Dias, this volume).

The Teaching Role

With these values about learning, the teacher's role is non-authoritarian, facilitating learning (Rogers, 1969), formalising learning in a way that makes the process and its outcomes more conscious and enhances its positive outcomes (see also Ramsden, 2003). Negative learning outcomes are possible but beyond the scope of this discussion. Positive learning outcomes are identifiable by observing increases in effectiveness in practices (eg Revans, 1983; Senge, 1990). Harvey (1999:73) calls this *"not*teaching"*, and others have called it *"learning-centred teaching"* (eg Nygaard & Holtham, 2008).

Collective Critical Assessment of Knowledge

A key aim is to engage learners in collectively assess the justification of their claims to knowledge by actively linking their existing foundational knowledge in a subject to the way they interpret their own and others' experiences.

> *"The focus is on discovering the context of ideas and the belief systems that shape the way we think about their sources, nature, and consequences, and imagining alternative perspectives"* (Mezirow, 1997:7).

Ideally the learner will

> *"become (1) more aware and critical in assessing assumptions—both those of others and those governing one's own beliefs, values, judgments, and feelings; (2) more aware of and better able to recognize frames of reference and paradigms (collective frames of reference) and to imagine alternatives; and (3) more responsible and effective at working with others to collectively assess reasons, pose and solve problems, and arrive at a tentative best judgment regarding contested beliefs"* (Mezirow 1997:8).

Thus, learning-centred teaching is not primarily concerned with transmitting foundational disciplinary knowledge, although that is a part of the responsibility. Equally important is to foster identifying, framing and solving skills, critically reflective thought, and discourse awareness. This emphasis on processes as well as outcomes distinguishes a dialogic, experiential learning-centred approach. It is participatory and interactive, involving group deliberation.

Building on personal experience and understanding

Materials to support these kinds of learning include the living experiences of the learners and using those to examine and assess reasons, identify and consider evidence, and arrive at reflective judgments (Bruner, 1960; Mezirow, 1997). The learners' articulation of these experiences and understandings helps the teacher see the learners' current level of knowledge and then the teacher can pitch lessons at the learners' current levels of understanding, working as the "more knowledgeable other" with the learners at their "zone of proximal development" (Vygotsky, 1978). Since it is difficult for the teacher to be the more knowledgeable other for each individual learner at the most pressing or motivating zone of proximal development, constructive working relations between learners in the class are fostered so that they can be more knowledgeable others for each other.

Building on the learners' own experiences and connection with other learners can increase the perceived relevance of the concepts to be understood and examined, which in turn can increase the motivation to engage in the learning process, arousing curiosity and increasing initiative (Dewey, 1952). This can be done using a variety of group and individual methods such as group projects, role play, simulations, life histories, case studies, critical incidents, metaphor analysis, and collective concept mapping, all of which provide opportunities to rehearse existing knowledge experience or practice discourses and also encourage critical reflection.

Making the Learning and Assessment Cycles Visible

The articulation of expected outcomes from learning and teaching helps guide attention and efforts, and guides assessment of the effectiveness of the efforts. Assessment can be a valuable tool to motivate and guide ongoing learning. The processes of assessment and their connection to the learning goals and activities can be made explicit from the very outset of a course. Rubrics are one tool to provide the students with information about how their work to demonstrate learning is assessed. Ideally, a rubric offers students clear signals about what the teacher seeks, and what constitutes acceptable work for various grade levels (Huba & Freed, 2000; Sadler, 2005). The learning progress can become more visible when feedback on assessable tasks is given with reference to the rubric, with time and space for students to understand the feedback, adjust their performance and be assessed again (Yorke, 2003; McMillan, 2007).

Iterations of Innovations

This section provides a first-person account of the negotiations and iterative fine-tuning in one teacher's efforts to implement these practices in the transmission centred context from 2008 to 2010.

In 2008, when I took over the "Introduction to Management" course – delivered in the first semester of each year – the published learning goals course were i) learn basic concepts and models in management theory; and ii) explore uses and criticisms of those concepts and models. Only very general information about assessment procedures was available. The 330 students divided into two groups for the course. I taught one group and an experienced professor taught the other. Generously, he gave me all his detailed lecture slides and those of my predecessor. While briefing me about course objectives, practices and assessment, the professor emphasised the importance of providing a positive learning experience. I questioned the heavy reliance on end-of course exam questions – 75% of the course grade – but initially it seemed that no change was possible.

First: Increasing Interaction between Students

While I wanted to fulfil the public objectives of the course, I needed to maintain my own values about teaching and learning. Playing it safe as a new faculty member, I thought it was best to deliver the same content that was being given to other students in the same course and to make the assessment process as similar as possible. In addition to the final exam, for another 25% towards their grade, students could choose one task: a book review, a case analysis, an interview with a practicing manager, or a position paper on an aspect of management. This work was due and assessed at the end of the course, so provided little opportunity for student action based on teacher feedback. Listening well, rote learning, managing workloads and time and writing exams under pressure were the identifiable means of passing this initial compulsory course. But I knew these would not be sufficient for success in their future studies, and definitely inadequate for working life.

I wished to provide students with opportunities consciously to practice academic crafts, such as identifying different theoretical perspectives in the literature, through such activities as reading, discussing and reporting different viewpoints. Providing this involves assisting students to examine and extend their own learning preferences, and providing them with sustained support to be active learners. The wide variety of student backgrounds (in transition from high school or gap year; locals and foreign students; international exchange and open university students) provided a potentially rich forum where these differences can be effectively mobilised for exchange and for sharing the collective experience in our group.

Thus my first new move was to add the additional learning objective of "practise some key academic crafts like identifying different points of view in reading, discussion and writing". To achieve this I had to reduce the amount of lecturing and substitute some in-class activities. Students were regularly reminded to review lesson content and invited to ask about anything that was unclear. These questions helped to identify ways to improve the mini-lectures, and provided cues for greater discussions during the second iteration. The students were required to do the end-of-course, optional task in pairs but the 25% weighting remained unvaried, with 75% for the final exam.

A rubric describing what I was looking for in this optional task, and what was required for various levels of marks, was given to the students along with the task description. Rubrics for guiding assessment of student work were a virtually unknown tool and certainly unused at this university, but the students could see the point. I gave extensive feedback on the student work but, as it was delivered at the end of the course, I had no opportunity to observe how students used it. There was no rubric for the exam. This was a test of memory of concepts and models requiring short answers, marked right or wrong. At the end of the course, 90% of the class passed the exam, indicating effective acquisition of course concepts, although without much evidence relating to the depth or permanence of their learning, nor how I might improve my contribution.

All my attempts to discuss student learning and my own teaching experience with colleagues were unsuccessful. It was clear that the course coordinator and other academics were too busy and/or were uninterested. However the results and student feedback encouraged continuation of a learning-centred approach in the second cycle.

Second: Formative Assessment to Encourage Learning

For the next iteration, I further reduced the number of sub-topics covered to a) allow more time for discussion and group work, and b) provide more structured support for discussion to generate different perceptions of the topics. I chose not to amend the learning objectives further since my aim was to improve my facilitation of the learning process.

The big change came in the organisation of ways to encourage students to engage with concepts and to criticise them. Students were assigned to teams of three rather than pairs in order to increase the diversity of perspectives and opinions in doing a newly introduced task series. Since most tasks in life are accomplished in coordination with others, and often with their conscious help, assessment tasks were designed to reflect this. In life, we also usually have more than one chance to succeed. The practice of management is learned through cycles of action and reflection (Marquardt *et al*, 2009), so groups undertook cycling through one task three times to demonstrate their understanding of a concept or model (and its limits), examining how it fits with their own experience.

Trios were required to reflect on each other's personal experiences of management and write a joint paper comparing the experiences and linking them to course concepts. The structure of the task allowed members to take turns to build perspectives about their chosen examples, making it evident to the students that theory could illuminate experience in particular ways, and *vice versa*. Another assessment rubric was provided to show the students the levels of performance expected and how they would be judged and awarded marks.

Timely detailed feedback on this task helped students reflect on the state of their learning and how we might better extend and support the learning process for each other during the course – and in the future. Feedback affirmed the strengths of the performance and described where improvement could be made. Since trio members were required to complete the exercise three times, there was scope to improve their work based on feedback given in each cycle. This time my own values about learning were more explicitly enacted than in the first iteration because I was giving students concrete suggestions on how to improve their work and observing their responses during the course.

It was especially encouraging to see students learning to value their own and others' perspectives on their personal management experiences and relate these to the course material. This gave students explicit practice at managing teams while completing tasks related to course topics; an important inclusion since one course topic was team performance. Everyone could reflect on their team's performance in the context of this structured classroom activity, and some students consequently wrote about team performance in their exercises.

After this second iteration, students gave feedback for a second time that the exam was too focused on memory-testing. And they commented that the exercises required a disproportionate amount of work for their grade value. Although I felt conflicted about varying my version of the course too much from its counterpart, nobody questioned when, for the third iteration of the course, I changed the weighting of the exam marks to 50% and increased the weighting of the exercises accordingly.

During both the first and second iterations I had encouraged students to search online for company examples and other related resources and to share any useful additional resources that they found. The students would tell me what they had found and I posted the information on the course website. Being mostly members of the "post-internet" generation the students were often more net-savvy than I, even if not yet as skilled at judging the academic worth of information. Their comfort with internet technology gave rise to the idea of creating a collaborative wiki to enable students to:

- Share company examples and other resources they found useful;
- Discuss topics with everyone online, answering each other's questions, not merely depending on me for answers;
- Use the content contributed to the wiki as their work (i.e. Demonstration of learning) for assessment;
- Read all the students' work and all the feedback I offered.

Third: Sharing the Assessable Work and Feedback

For the third iteration I had searched for peers with the experience of using a wiki to advise me on the feasibility of the wiki concept. One colleague encouraged me and gave good advice on how to manage my own workload with regard to using wiki tools with the students. But, after several false starts, it turned out that the university intranet would not support student use of wikis connected to course websites. Meanwhile, I used a university sponsored web-based learning environment which provided both group folders and a course forum where students could write.

A logical extension to dialogic learning and providing formative assessment opportunities was to open up the assessment processes so they would be available as material for collective learning. Thus all student work for assessments was publicly posted to the online learning environment alongside all the other course material. Each group had its own folder to share resources and work-in-progress and were also required to submit their work for assessment through the website. This student trio work was available for all to read, as was the teacher's feedback and grade – aligned with the assessment rubric for each piece of work. I published the assessment feedback so that I was also accountable for consistency with course principles, namely; to provide feedback in a clear relevant and immediate manner.

The software tracking system indicated that most students read each other's work as well as the teacher feedback within 24 hours of posting At first, when I had informed everyone that this was how this course and its website operated, one student immediately asked *"What if others copy our ideas?"* I was delighted to be able to reply *"Wouldn't that be a compliment?!"* adding that where somebody did use another group's ideas it would be observable for all the learners how those ideas were used and developed. This exchange offered a perfect cue to discuss plagiarism and the academic ethic of avoiding it, stressing the importance of giving credit to others when you use their ideas. In this context it was straightforward to emphasise my expectation that students use their own ideas and experience, as well as those of others. The intention was that students would learn not only from reading feedback to their own group but also from the feedback given to other groups.

The online learning environment provided for an asynchronous conversation, called a forum, structured only by topics the students raised (including the many internet links referred to), responses from among the class, and the linear way the software formatted the discussion. Ideas were mushrooming and it was professionally challenging to provide sufficient scaffolding to ensure students could structure the information and ideas they were gathering. Students openly discussed tactics for getting the assessment tasks done and shared resources and drafts. Even learners with a perceived preference for logical, linear presentation of information were finding this exploratory approach exciting and engaging.

These discussions were only visible to those enrolled in the current course year. Notably, there was no public discussion among students of the feedback given on the work. The next step in this innovative process would be to encourage students to offer feedback to each other in addition to that from the teacher and to discuss the feedback.

This third year of the course coincided with a merger and claims being made by the merged university to be greater than any of its component institutions. Such claims rang hollow when students faced the many practical problems, such as registering for courses, getting passwords and student cards. However these problems themselves provided shared experiences for class discussion about applications of management concepts and models. For example, during the opening class I emphasised management as the practice and theory dealing with many paradoxes. The students' experience of the claims about greatness being accompanied by dysfunctional services became living examples of this paradox.

Discussion and Conclusion

In our opinion an innovation in teaching and learning practice depends on what is considered normal in a particular context. Like many, the vision of the university we have described is to be innovative and to provide an environment that encourages and inspires the active development of new ways of learning and building expertise. Its strategy includes commitment to lifelong learning and developing skills to enter professional life. A continuing paradox permeating the context concerns the fact that those who called themselves "innovative" were often not prepared to practice their espoused theory and were ready to limit the visibility of innovations in teaching. Vision and reality are currently far apart but, as the experiences of the teacher featured in this chapter demonstrate, change is possible.

In any context, an innovation takes time to develop and adjust itself to and with the context until it becomes normalised. The iterations of innovative practices introduced in the particular context described in this chapter are summarised in Table 1.

	Vision	Opportunities in context	Challenges in context	Practices implemented
1.	Increased interaction & dialogic learning	Wide diversity of student background; first year students are unconditioned to traditional norms	Absence of role models or collegial support or openness to dialogue	Reduced content given as input, increased student interaction and responsibility for finding examples
2.	Formative assessment & student learning from assessment	Academics are very free to do what they wish as teachers	Exams prevail as the dominant institutional practice	Cumulative assessment based on a number of team tasks in addition to exam
3.	Openly shared work and feedback	University sponsored web-based learning environment	False starts re support for student wikis	All assessment work and feedback posted into the web-based learning environment

Table 1: Summary of Iterations of Innovative Teaching Practices

The iterative process of innovation has been emphasised here, underpinned by a concept of learning being a process of *becoming* more effective in practice. Both the academic and her students are learning through practice. Thus, opportunities for the students to practice with support and have time to share how experiences were understood were essential new elements incorporated into the curriculum of the compulsory first year course. The academic sorely missed this sort of support from peers for her teaching, but persisted. Motivation and resilience were drawn from energies gained with earlier experiences and the positive feedback of current students.

Recruited partly for her demonstrated commitment to learning-centred curricula, the academic was able to use her preferred approach – albeit in relative isolation. She took advantage of the freedom her isolation allowed, and of the web-based learning environment supported by the university. In the particular context, the freedom to choose to do whatever she wished in the classroom lacked any collegial challenge and support or accountability. Although prior experience created personal confidence in being learning-centred in any context, no doubt this is not always an easy task.

Contextual Constraints on Collaboratively Learning about Innovative Teaching

In a context structurally resistant to change, because of the emphasis on publication outcomes rather than teaching and learning outcomes, faculty members interested in teaching and learning practices feel isolated and sometimes experience outright hostility from peers (Mäntylä, 2007). Peers, already feeling pressured, resist suggestions that they find time to develop their teaching practice even when they are conscious that there may be other ways to facilitate learning. The pressures of work, and suggestions that one may not be an ideal teacher, are difficult and lead to avoidance of discussions about teaching and learning. Research-focused academics may experience feelings of inadequacy, often unexpressed. The teaching innovators are also prone to withdraw behind the thick skin they need to wear to keep their sense of well-being and purpose about teaching and learning. This compounds alienation of each group from one another and individual privacy about their practice. Such conditions are not conducive to flourishing growth of creative innovations in teaching and learning.

Attempting unsupported modes of innovation is challenging for oneself and others. Having the vision, energy and flexibility to work around obstacles to implement innovation requires a great deal of determination. When it causes the innovator to question habits and routines of others, defensiveness and a sense of discomfort may be created which cause the others to remove themselves from the discussion – thus enlarging the circle of disaffection and isolation.

Furthermore, learning-centred education can aim to facilitate but cannot control or guarantee all outcomes. This realisation can be very uncomfortable in a transmission-centred environment where tests of memory are the most common test of learning, and controlled (and controlling) outcomes are explicitly preferred to fit the hierarchy of learning objectives, course goals, program goals and university strategy.

Sustaining and Expanding Innovative Teaching Practices

While it is currently fashionable for universities as corporate entities to aspire to be innovative, it is clear that there are still many institutional and individual barriers to be overcome to sustain widespread innovative activity in teaching and learning. Some individuals, such as the teacher featured in this chapter, try some innovations in the privacy of their classrooms, but for practical adoption of innovations in wider fields, an academic's own learning about teaching and deep learning in their disciplines needs much more public recognition and discussion.

Based on this experience of sustaining innovative teaching practices at least for the life to this academic's tenure at the university described, the need for determination and persistence is obvious. However, it is also apparent that other elements are essential if universities hope that teaching and innovations will be more effectively disseminated among faculties and affect individual academic's practices. At least four of these can be extrapolated from the experiences described in this chapter:

1) Officially counted time to prepare, give feedback, and reflect collaboratively with peers. If the time it takes for these learning-centred processes is not counted or discounted, many academics are understandably unwilling to devote their private or discretionary time.

2) Classroom management skills. If academics do not feel confident about their skills managing classrooms, group work and discussions they will not even try a small step in learning-centred teaching.

3) Valuing students' experience, opinions and interactivity in the classroom. If academics do not value these it is difficult for them to promote them during coursework and allow students to identify difficult questions and problems with course content. This is closely linked to the fourth, most fundamental element in higher education.

iv) Giving learners responsibility for their own learning and knowledge.

Giving learners responsibility for their learning is familiar rhetoric in higher education nowadays. But in practice it goes hand in hand with the need for academics to take responsibility for their own learning about teaching practice. If academics can model collaborative, deep learning in their area of expertise they are likely to be able, with encouragement, to collaborate in learning about teaching in their disciplinary area. In turn they may take more interest in what are innovative and effective means of teaching and learning.

About the Authors

Anne Herbert currently works on enhancing the graduate learning experience for students at the University of Melbourne. She can be contacted at this email: trebrehenna@gmail.com

Elyssebeth Leigh is a freelance educational consultant, and sessional lecturer at the University of Technology Sydney. She can be contacted at this email: Elyssebeth.Leigh@uts.edu.au

Chapter Nine

Implementing a Constructivist Learning Environment: Students' Perceptions and Approaches to Learning

Patrícia Albergaria Almeida and José Teixeira-Dias

Introduction

This chapter is based upon a growing body of work shaped by a research project aiming to promote the advancement of the scholarship of teaching and learning (Almeida, 2010), through the implementation of classroom research at the University of Aveiro in Portugal. In recent decades, the scholarship of teaching and learning has emerged as a fundamental concept underpinning the development of good teaching practices in higher education and, consequently, the enhancement of the quality of student learning. Several studies (e.g., Abraham *et al.*, 2007) have revealed that the quality of student learning is dependent on students' approaches to learning. The approaches adopted by students to their learning have been shown to be related to their perceptions of the learning environment (Case & Marshall, 2009), their conceptions of learning (Minasian-Batmanian *et al.*, 2006), and their performance on assessment tasks (Baeten *et al.*, 2008).

Contemporary society is characterised by fast and complex change processes (Barnett, 2000) covering all spheres of life. Consequently, learning should also be seen as a process of change. However, in a society that is rapidly changing and requiring informed citizens, the educational system has changed very little. We concur with Johnston (2010) in arguing that first-year university students should become engaged in learning activities which encourage the development of higher-order skills. These skills can be achieved through the design and implementation of learning environments that go beyond transmission, aimed at stimulating students' active (Meltzer & Manivannan, 2002) and deep learning (Entwistle *et al.*, 2001).

According to Case and Marshall (2009), the way students perceive the learning context significantly influences their use of a specific approach. Therefore, in a chemistry course intentionally conceived and designed to promote higher-order competences, such as questioning, argumentation, creativity, and critical thinking, do students with better grades adopt a deep learning approach? Or is it possible to obtain high grades using a strategic or a surface learning approach? And what is the predominant learning approach adopted by students with the lowest grades? Do students with the lowest grades have a surface approach to learning?

In this chapter we will describe the constructivist learning environment (Gijbels *et al.*, 2008) designed and implemented in the General Chemistry course for 1st year students at the University of Aveiro in order to stimulate deep approaches to learning. We will then discuss how the students with the highest and the lowest grades perceived these strategies, and how students' perceptions of the learning environment influenced their approaches to learning.

The sections that follow present a brief literature review on approaches to learning. Later, the study context and the methodology are described in detail. Finally, findings and conclusions are discussed.

Approaches to Learning

The higher education literature suggests that approaches to learning might be a useful mode of conceptualising different ways in which students experience a learning context (Tennant *et al.*, 2010). Identifying a student's approach to learning has been considered as a means of:

(i) Increasing students' metacognition (Papinczac *et al.*, 2008);

(ii) Identifying students at risk because of ineffective approaches (Tait & Entwistle, 1996);

(iii) Assisting teachers who are concerned with monitoring and improving the effectiveness of their practices (Pedrosa de Jesus *et al.*, 2005);

(iv) Designing and implementing teaching, learning and assessment strategies to enhance learning (Struyven *et al.*, 2006).

In 1976, Marton and Säljo identified deep and surface approaches. In the deep approach, the intention to find meaning generates active learning processes that involve looking for patterns and relating information on the one hand, and using evidence and examining the logic of the argument on the other. This approach also involves examining the progress of one's own understanding. In contrast, the intention of the surface approach is just to deal with the task. A surface learner sees the course content as unrelated fragments of information which directs to much more confined learning processes, particularly to memorisation (Entwistle *et al.*, 2001).

In 1978, Biggs identified a third learning mode: the strategic approach, which is predominantly influenced by assessment. Learners adopting this approach are motivated by a desire to succeed and will use processes that they believe will most likely to achieve high grades. Here the emphasis is on organising learning specifically to obtain a high examination grade. Later, Entwistle and colleagues (2001) concluded that the strategic approach can be associated with the deep or the superficial approach. For instance, a student that usually adopts a deep approach may use some strategies typical of the surface approach to meet the requirements of a specific activity such as a test. Case and Marshall (2009) underline that the way students perceive the learning context significantly influences their use of a specific approach.

Setting the Scene: the First-year General Chemistry Course at the University of Aveiro

Having in mind the promotion of students' higher order skills, the construction of the General Chemistry course curriculum at the University of Aveiro aims at meeting the learners' and societal demands. Our major concern is to develop a curriculum which has a sound basis in the nature and methods of chemistry as a discipline, with its important place in a modern society. We also aim to equip students with transferable skills and competences which will enable them to make a contribution to society within and beyond chemistry. These skills should be seen in generic terms (like verbal and written communication of chemical ideas, team working) as well as in cognitive terms (such as objectivity, creativity, conceptual understanding, reflective, critical and logical thought).

The fundamental idea is that by adopting student-focused teaching strategies, active and deep learning in chemistry can be accomplished. With this in mind an action research (Henning *et al.*, 2009; Watts, 1985) project was developed involving 150 1st year chemistry students and aiming to promote student-centred teaching approaches. Following the suggestions of Mbajiorgu and Reid (2006) and Johnston (2010), the following three strategies were implemented.

Lectures, Laboratory Classes and Tutorials

The general chemistry course comprises three kinds of classes: lectures, laboratory classes and tutorials.

Lectures (not compulsory) should provide the students with an understanding of the content being covered. Lectures should be seen as hours of active study. Before each class, students are expected (i) to read the material provided by the teacher; (ii) to identify topics that could represent obstacles to learning; and (iii) to identify topics that could raise doubts or questions. During lectures students are stimulated to ask questions orally or in a written format.

Laboratory classes. The main aim of these is to initiate the student in the research process in chemistry. During laboratory classes the teacher acts as a facilitator, assisting the students to overcome their difficulties. These classes are compulsory, as students are assessed in each class and their attendance is monitored.

Tutorials provide the student with pedagogical guidance about learning methods. Students should use these classes to clarify their doubts and ask questions about the content taught in lectures and also about the practical tasks. These are not compulsory classes.

Innovative Teaching and Learning Strategies

Besides the formal classes described earlier, the following strategies were also implemented:

(1) *Small "pauses for thought"* during lectures to encourage students' oral questions. In the middle of the lesson, the teacher stopped lecturing for two or three minutes and invited the students to think about or to discuss the class topics with their colleagues. At the end of the break, students had the opportunity to raise oral questions;

(2) *Teacher's written questions* during lectures to facilitate the organisation of teaching and learning and to serve as a role model to students. These had diverse degrees of difficulty and served different functions;

(3) *The "Questions and answers in Chemistry" online forum* to encourage and facilitate students' questioning. Students could use this tool to ask written questions related to the topics taught during lectures and/or practical laboratory sessions. Questions related to everyday phenomena with a chemical background were also welcome;

(4) *"Problem-based cases" online forum* to encourage students to ask questions and suggest possible explanations for the phenomena proposed by the teacher. This kind of activity also aimed to enhance the discussion between students. Students were invited to analyse these situations through the eyes of a scientifically informed citizen;

(5) *Chemistry mini-projects* where the students are given the opportunity to creatively develop a small group project on a chemistry topic, display their research in a poster format and present it to the whole class at the end of the semester. Examples of these topics would include "Melting below zero" and "The ice of life".

Assessment Strategies

In order to promote the alignment between teaching, learning and assessment (Biggs & Tang, 2007), the following assessment strategies were considered:

(1) *A multiple-choice test* due to the large number of students in the chemistry course. This test also included two open questions: a question-posing case (students should raise questions) and a problem-based case (students should propose explanations).

(2) *Participation in the two online forums* considering both the number and the quality of the participation;

(3) *Performance in laboratory work* considering both students' performance in practical classes and the content of the lab book;

(4) *Participation in the mini-projects* considering the development of the project, the quality of the poster, the quality of the poster presentation, the questions students asked of other presenters and their answers to questions asked of them during the mini-projects presentation session. Koshy (this volume) has also used poster presentation as an effective assessment strategy.

Methodology

Participants

The main sample was composed of 150 undergraduate students (78 female, 72 male; mean age 19 years) who were tackling foundation chemistry, although following different degree programs such as physics, environmental engineering and materials engineering. This class did not include students enrolled in a chemistry degree program. For this particular research, the 10 students with the highest grades (all over 75% in the final test of the course) and the 10 students with the lowest grades (all under 40%) were selected for interview. These 20 students were contacted by email at the end of the semester and invited to participate in interviews. All the students agreed to being interviewed.

Data Gathering

Throughout one semester, from February to June 2010, data were gathered by means of students' semi-structured interviews, non-participant observation of chemistry classes (mini-research projects sessions, lectures, tutorials), documentary analysis (posters produced for the mini-research projects, participation in online forums, assessment instruments) and the administration of the Portuguese version of the Approaches and Study Skills Inventory for Students (ASSIST; Valadas *et al.*, 2009).

Findings and Discussion

The results of the ASSIST, including conceptions of learning, learning approaches and preferences for different types of courses and teaching, are presented in Table 1.

The ten students with the highest grades conceived of learning as understanding. During interviews, all the students remarked that it was important to memorise and apply knowledge, but all agreed that learning could not be, and should not be, solely memorising and applying. For instance, João said that:

> *"Learning... is not only memorising, because when we try to memorise we don't learn anything... eventually we forget what we memorise (...) learning is to understand the meaning of things... I think this is the most important feature of learning... the most important is to understand. If we comprehend we can connect ideas and even if we forget something, we can relate what we know and move ahead..."* (João, a deep learner)

All students emphasised the role of understanding in the learning process. Bruno and Carlos went beyond this and also stressed the importance of questioning and critical thinking in the learning process. For instance, Bruno, a strategic-deep learner, said that:

> *"Learning is to gather information and knowledge in a way that allow us to reflect about it and reach new conclusions or ask new questions, in order to gather more information... it is a cycle because it is always repeating itself: the more information and knowledge we have, the more knowledge we need to have to answer our own questions about the knowledge we have acquired before... it is like a spiral... it has no end."*

	Student	Conception of learning	Learning approach	Different types of courses and teaching
Students with the highest grades	Carlos	seeking meaning	strategic-deep	supporting understanding
	Ricardo	seeking meaning	deep	supporting understanding
	Liliana	seeking meaning	deep	transmitting information
	André	seeking meaning	deep	transmitting information
	Fábio	seeking meaning	surface	transmitting information
	Bruno	seeking meaning	strategic-deep	supporting understanding
	João	seeking meaning	deep	transmitting information
	Pedro	seeking meaning	deep	supporting understanding
	Ana	seeking meaning	deep	transmitting information
	Luís	seeking meaning	deep	supporting understanding
Students with the lowest grades	Rita	reproducing knowledge	surface	transmitting information
	António	reproducing knowledge	surface	transmitting information
	Fernando	reproducing knowledge	surface	transmitting information
	Maria	reproducing knowledge	strategic--surface	transmitting information
	Afonso	reproducing knowledge	strategic--surface	transmitting information
	Joana	reproducing knowledge	surface	transmitting information
	Francisca	reproducing knowledge	surface	transmitting information
	André	reproducing knowledge	surface	transmitting information
	Mara	reproducing knowledge	surface	transmitting information
	Álvaro	reproducing knowledge	surface	transmitting information

Table 1: Students' Conceptions of Learning, Learning Approaches and Preferred Types of Teaching (ASSIST results)

In contrast, the ten students with the lowest grades presented a conception of learning associated with rote learning. In the course of interviews, all these students underlined the importance of memorising and reproducing information. When asked about her notion of learning, Maria said that:

> *"I had never thought about this (...) but I think learning is remembering what we listen to in classes and remembering the information we have in our notes and on the slides"* (Maria, strategic-surface learner)

António went a bit further and referred to the importance of applying chemical knowledge:

> *"Learning is having the ability to apply the theoretical knowledge gained in lectures. OK, so now we know what is a redox reaction, but what does this mean if we can't apply this knowledge in a practical sense? Yes, I think learning is applying what we know"* (António, surface learner)

However none of the students with the lowest grades went beyond the three conceptions of learning at the bottom of the hierarchy proposed by Van Rossum and Schenk (1984), namely; increasing one's knowledge, memorising and reproducing, and applying knowledge.

We agree with Trigwell and Ashwin (2006:244) when stating that students' conceptions of learning will *"to a large extent, define the nature of the task, and the way they approach that task."*

All the students that possess a conception of learning associated with memorising and reproducing did adopt a surface approach to learning, or a combination of a surface and a strategic approach. On the other hand, nine of the 10 students that have a conception of learning related to seeking meaning did approach learning in a deeper way, or through a combination of deep and strategic modes. These results confirm the assertions made by Marton and Säljo (1997) that students using a more sophisticated conception of learning are more likely to adopt a deep approach than students who regard learning in a limited way. However, our results contrast with those obtained by Minasian-Batmanian *et al.* (2006), who found no significant differences between the students' final grades and their conceptions or approaches to learning.

The results of the ASSIST show that seven of the students with the higher grades predominantly adopted a deep learning approach, two used a strategic approach (Carlos and Bruno) and only one was identified as a surface learner (Fábio). In fact, during interviews, the students that were identified as deep learners through the ASSIST also said that they used a surface approach at specific moments or for specific tasks. Deep learners revealed a capacity to use both learning modes (deep and surface) according to the learning phase. Initially they felt the need to memorise some facts. Later, they used these facts to understand other topics. This kind of performance was identified by Entwistle (2009) as typical of students who have sophisticated conceptions of learning.

On the other hand, it was noted that surface learners lacked the ability to switch learning approaches according to the learning phase or according to the task. These students used a surface approach systematically throughout the semester. The constant use of a surface approach within a learning environment designed to promote understanding leads to low achievement and, consequently, to poor final marks. In his quantitative study, Diseth (2003) also found a clear relationship between surface approach and low achievement.

Students Carlos and Bruno were identified as strategic learners through the ASSIST; the interviews showed that these students associated the strategic approach with a deep approach. Deep-strategic students tried to obtain higher grades through reflective organisation. For instance, these students put consistent effort into studying and were alert to assessment requirements. This emerged as the most successful way to cope with the learning and assessment tasks in this course, since these learners were the ones with the highest grades.

The two students with the lowest grades (Maria and Afonso), identified through the ASSIST as strategic, were characterised as strategic-surface learners after analysis of their interviews. These students associated the strategic approach with a surface approach. This combination of approaches led to weak results in the final marks of the chemistry course. Papinczac *et al.* (2008) characterise these as a dissonant combination of approaches to learning.

According to Case and Marshall (2009) the strategic approach can be combined with a deep or a surface approach, as supported by our findings. However, as stated by Entwistle (2009), when understanding becomes a fundamental criterion in assessment only deep approaches to learning combined with a systematic organisation will be rewarded.

As suggested by Biggs (1994) the assessment of the chemistry course was aligned with teaching and learning. Assessment tasks were designed in order to assess students' understanding and not students' rote learning. This may be the reason why students adopting a combination of surface and strategic approaches did not obtain good marks. Even if all students were exposed to the same assessment strategies these were perceived in distinct ways. For instance, deep and surface learners disagreed in their opinion about the multiple choice test:

> *"It seems easy at first sight, because it's a multiple choice test, but it is not easy. It's not about memorisation, it's about applying our knowledge... We really must understand the topics; otherwise we will not be able to choose the right answer (...) I like this kind of test."* (Ana, deep learner)

> *"I feel that I do not need to study so much... I do not need to know everything in a deep way because I do not need to explain why I am choosing that option, I just choose it and that is all"* (Fernando, surface learner)

All the students with the worst grades agreed that the multiple choice test was a "good" assessment method, because it enabled them to have a good grade with a limited effort to study. The deep learners realised that this multiple choice test was designed to assess understanding and not merely memorisation. However, they agreed that it made it easier for students who had not prepared properly for the examination to achieve acceptable grades:

> *"I think this kind of test is good for those students that do not study a lot... if they are in a lucky day, they can pass the exam... but I think it is not so good for me... because I want to have higher grades and I feel that I would perform better if it was an exam with more open questions"* (Carlos, strategic-deep learner)

These findings are in line with those reported by Baeten *et al.* (2008). This study demonstrated that deep learners prefer assessment procedures which support understanding. When referring to the two open questions on the final test, the opinions of the surface learners were quite different from those about the multiple choice questions:

> *"The two last questions [the open questions] were very difficult... The teacher asked us to ask questions about an experiment and I really did not know what I should ask... I thought it would be better to try to answer the other questions [multiple choice questions] and not spend time with the two last questions"* (Maria, surface learner)

When approaching the questions requiring deep reasoning, most of surface learners did not try to answer them. Those who tried to answer to these questions did not approach them in the correct way: these students perceived a demanding task as if it was simple. For instance, when invited to ask meaningful questions about an experiment these students raised basic or acquisition questions, as characterised elsewhere (Pedrosa de Jesus *et al.*, 2006).

Besides the multiple choice test, the assessment also included two voluntary assessment tasks during the semester (participation in online forums, and participation in the mini-research projects) and one mandatory task (performance in practical laboratory work). Participation in the voluntary activities enabled the students to enhance their grades by a small margin where they felt this additional work might benefit their overall assessment. The deep learners participated in the voluntary assessment tasks, while the surface learners did not.

When asked about his participation on the online forums, Carlos emphasised the challenge of discussing daily life situations from a chemical point of view. All the students who participated in these discussions said that the bonus in their final marks was an interesting stimulus, but also mentioned that they would participate anyway, since they were intrinsically motivated.

The students who participated in the online forums were mainly deep learners. These students were motivated to participate because they felt they would learn while discussing and arguing with their peers and with the teacher. Bruno, one of the strategic-deep students, also emphasised the importance of learning by discussing problem-based cases with his peers. This student underlined the importance of assessment in his approach to learning and studying:

> *"Probably I would not participate so much in the forums if my grade could not be enhanced. In this case I guess I would read my peers' messages,*

> *but I would not post so much... I had a lot of work searching information to support my arguments in the discussions...*" (Bruno, strategic-deep learner)

The two strategic-deep learners also participated in the mini projects. Both students emphasised the challenge of conducting a mini-research project but also underlined the importance of improving the chances of increasing their final grade.

Deep learners participated in all the activities proposed by the teacher. This revealed that they had the ability to manage their time positively, as described by Case and Marshall (2009). Furthermore, deep students demonstrated an intrinsic interest in these activities. On the other hand, surface learners adopted a minimalist approach to learning, performing only the mandatory tasks. None of the students with the lowest grades participated in the online forums or in the mini-projects. The reasons pointed out by these students are diverse:

> "*we have so many classes, and we spend so much time at the university... so, I did not want to spend more time here... and this is my first year, I have a lot of time to perform a mini-project.*" (Rita, surface learner)

> "*I went to the online forum one or two times... I did not think it was very interesting (...). If I would participate in the forums I know I could increase my grade, but in that case I had to find information and read it... It is not as easy as it could seem to be.*" (Álvaro, surface learner)

Other major differences were also found between the study habits of the students with the highest grades and those of the students with the lowest grades. The latter stated that they usually only studied a couple of days before the exam, and that they frequently tried to memorise the concepts and rather than try to understand them:

> "*I read my class notes and also read the teacher's slides and I try to memorise the information... since I only study a couple of days before the test I do not have time to do more than this.*" (Mara, surface learner)

All the students with the lowest grades revealed a preference for a type of teaching that emphasises the traditional transmission of knowledge.

This incongruence between their preferred teaching approach and the type of teaching used in this chemistry course can be one of the reasons for their weak grades. During the interviews these students said they were not familiar with this kind of learning environment. On several occasions during the semester these students did not understand the aim of some teaching strategies, such as the "pauses for thought" in lectures. Even if the teacher explained at specific points the intention of the innovative strategies most of the surface students did not understand their purpose.

According to Biggs (1994), students' perceptions of the context are a function of both the context and of students' prior experiences. He found that the majority of students had prior learning experiences that focus on reproduction rather than on seeking meaning and understanding. Probably because this was the first time that these students were exposed to a constructivist environment and they needed additional support to face the demands of this kind of learning. We believe that introducing a new course design requires detailed and systematic explanations by the teacher. Furthermore, continuous feedback should be provided to students to guide their learning. It seems that deep learners have the ability to understand easily the teacher's aims and engage straightforwardly in the learning tasks in the intended way. On the other hand, surface learners seem to need more guidance in order to connect with the real purpose of the learning tasks.

Of particular interest is the variation in the teaching preferences of the students with the highest grades. This was an unexpected finding. Even though these students adopted a deep approach to learning, four students show a preference for types of teaching that emphasise the transmission of information, while the other four prefer teaching strategies that enhance understanding (Table 1). It was the first time these students were exposed to this kind of learning environment and, even if performing well, some of them felt that it was easier to study in a traditional learning environment.

Concluding Remarks

This chapter has investigated students' approaches to learning and students' conceptions of learning in a course intentionally conceived to promote understanding.

From this study it is clear that it is possible to create a constructivist learning environment focused on the promotion of deep approaches to learning. Elkington (this volume) also implemented a learning environment aiming to foster deep learning; this was based on the pedagogy of optimal engagement and transformation. The research reported in this chapter shows that, with appropriate and diversified strategies, stimulus and motivation, students can enhance their interest and engagement with learning chemistry and, consequently, adopt a deep learning and obtain high grades. This concurs with what was reported by Entwistle and Peterson (2004:422):

> *"University teachers using approaches indicating a student-oriented approach to teaching and a focus on student learning (as opposed to a transmission approach) are more likely to have, in their classes, students who describe themselves as adopting a deep approach in their studying".*

Herbert and Leigh (this volume) argue that methods to foster deep learning are not easily transmitted from one context to another. Furthermore, the findings of our study confirm prior research postulating that even in the same learning environment different approaches to learning can coexist (Abhayawansa & Fonseca 2010; Entwistle 2009; Prosser *et al.*, 2000). Not all the students on this course adopted deep approaches to learning. In our study students with distinct perceptions of the learning environment approached learning in opposite ways. Consequently, these students obtained different final marks.

The results of this study indicate that the students with the lowest grades were all surface or strategic-surface learners. These students seem not to have the ability to adapt their usual learning approaches to a situation that requires the use of a deep strategy. On the other hand, nine of the 10 students with the highest grades adopted a deep approach to learning. These results confirm previous studies which suggest that higher performance is related to deep learning approaches and lower performance with a surface approach to learning (Booth *et al.*, 1999; Davidson, 2002). In addition, we have found that deep learners have the ability to accommodate their learning approach to the task, as noted by Entwistle (2009). When the learning task suggests the use of a surface approach to learning deep learners showed the ability to adopt this kind of approach. However, surface learners were not able to engage in a deep approach when they were required to. Surface learners seem to lack awareness about the real meaning and purpose of the learning tasks.

Students adopting a surface approach seem not to have perceived that this constructive learning environment could be more supportive of their learning. Consequently, these students also approached the assessment tasks using a surface strategy. The results obtained by Gijbels *et al.* (2008) agree with ours, also concluding that implementing assessment methods focused on understanding does not necessarily promote deep approaches to learning.

Perhaps the most significant educational implications of this research are that:

(i) Students learning chemistry gained transferable skills which can be used to gain new knowledge. Enomoto (this volume) also reached this conclusion when implementing a scaffolded curriculum within a language course;

(ii) It reminds teachers about the diversity among students in higher education. Barriers to learning may result from several issues: incorrect perception of the learning environment, lack of awareness about demands of the learning environment, and inadequate approaches to learning.

As stated by Case and Gunstone (2003:67):

> *"What matters is not how a lecturer might define a course context, but rather how it is perceived by students."*

About the Authors

Patrícia Albergaria Almeida is a researcher at the Research Centre for Didactics and Technology in Teacher Education, Department of Education, at the University of Aveiro, Portugal. She can be contacted at this email: patriciaalmeida@ua.pt

José Joaquim Teixeira-Dias is a Full Professor of Chemistry at the Department of Chemistry, University of Aveiro, Portugal. He can be contacted at this email: teixeiradias@ua.pt

Chapter Ten

A Centralised Tutor System to Support the Affective Needs of Online Learners

Aileen McGuigan

Introduction

Web 2.0 social media tools are increasingly being used in online programmes in Higher Education to supplement and complement course materials. In this chapter, I consider how such tools have been utilised innovatively on an online, distance learning programme for college lecturers. The new tutoring system moves beyond transmission on the part of the tutor, towards self-reliance on the part of the learner. The conclusion I reach is that the needs of both cognitive and affective domains of these professional learners may be satisfied without resorting to the time and labour intensive mainstay of online learning programmes: the "Personal Tutor".

If, as this book and the wider literature suggests (see, for example, Phillips, 2005; Laurillard, 2002), university students largely continue to be passive recipients of knowledge, the problem is greatly accentuated when the context is that of distance learning. Here, there is no face-to-face contact: there are no lectures, no tutorials, and no direct oral transmission of course content, except for that mediated through the learning environment. Learners in this context are much more heavily reliant on the written word than their peers in the face-to-face context and the notion of the self-directed learner (Knowles, 1975) becomes even more acutely pertinent.

An online programme offers a lot of flexibility; students can access materials whenever it is convenient for them and can work at their own pace, unaffected by that of others in the cohort. Along with this flexibility comes a weight of responsibility upon the learner for their own learning. There are no class attendance registers and no-one will notice if, in spite of having the opportunity to study at any time, the individual learner chooses instead not to study at all.

Learning does not just happen cognitively, the student being the passive recipient of the teacher's transmissions. There is a significant body of literature stretching back to Krathwohl, Bloom & Masia (1956), and continuing ever since, which points up the importance of the emotional response of the learner. Theorists such as Beale and Creed (2009), writing about the context of the computer user, also pertain here. In the face-to-face teaching context in Higher Education, the lecturer can offer reassurance to a class as a whole. And there are, or should be, various institutional support mechanisms in place for those individuals who need it: the personal tutor, Student Support Services and so on. In the online learning environment – with the largely epistolary nature of communications in this context – this supportive network can be more difficult to put in place.

One of the ways in which online programmes frequently attempt to surmount the problem of the struggling or non-engaging learner is to allocate a personal tutor to each student. The purpose of this tutor is to keep in touch with individual students and motivate them to engage with the learning material and each other if necessary. As well as reinforcing the "transmission" role of the tutor (in the sense of teacher-centredness) this is somewhat labour-intensive for them. For example in this support and guidance role, the onus is on the tutor to establish and maintain contact and, if this breaks down, a lot of time and energy can be expended in attempting to build it up again. Although many learners may enjoy and find helpful this kind of one-to-one support, it can lead to "learned helplessness" (Seligman, 1975) much to the detriment of the learner.

This chapter examines ways in which the online Teaching Qualification (Further Education) (TQ(FE)) programme at the University of Dundee has developed beyond the mere transmission of information, with the teacher at the centre, towards self-reliance amongst the learners supported by a centralised tutor mechanism. Instead of providing a personal tutor to support the affective and cognitive needs of individual learners, an innovative tutoring system supports learner self-direction. This system includes a blog that is the "hub" of this enterprise, enhancing support by tutors and enabling peer support.

Learning and Teaching and the Affective Domain

The affective domain pertains to the learner's attitudes and values; it influences the motivation to learn and is tightly linked with the learner's emotional state. From the writings of earlier theorists such Vygotsky (see Enomoto, this volume) to a host of writings on the first year experience, the importance of educators taking account of the affective needs of learners continues to feature prominently in the educational literature (Yorke & Longden, 2008. See also Harvey *et al.*'s (2006) review of the literature. The centrality of the affective domain to all kinds of learning is succinctly summed up by Miller (2005) citing Smith and Ragan (1999) who suggest that:

> *"any 'cognitive' or 'psychomotor' objective has some affective component to it (if at no deeper level than a willingness to sufficiently interact with learning resources to achieve the learning)."*

Whether educators need their learners to remember, understand, apply, analyse, create or evaluate – to use Anderson *et al*'s (2002) revised taxonomy of the cognitive domain – the affective domain of the learner is paramount. In this study, the author demonstrates how the TQ(FE) programme's new tutoring system challenges the assumption that in an online learning context learners' affective needs necessitate the provision of a personal tutor.

The research conducted for the purposes of this chapter – like the TQ(FE) programme itself – draws on a social constructivist epistemology that views reality as socially constructed and subjective. I adhere to the belief that there are "multiple truths" rather than subscribing to a positive, objective world view. Jennifer Moon (2004:16) conjures up a useful metaphor for the development of learning in a constructivist view, writing that it is:

> *"a vast but flexible network of ideas and feelings with groups of more tightly associated linked ideas/feelings. In the network some groups are far apart and some are near to each other and there are some relatively isolated ideas that have very few links to the network while others are well interconnected".*

The TQ(FE) Programme

The TQ(FE) programme is an online professional education and training programme for lecturers in the Further Education (FE) sector. It has been delivered online since 2006, having been until that time a paper-based distance learning programme. The programme participants (or learners), all of whom are in-service lecturers, are encouraged to construct and co-construct their learning, building upon both their own practical experience and reading as well as their interactions with peers and the teaching team. The tutor is in place to facilitate and support the process, but the onus is upon the learner to make sense of their own new learning, elaborating and adapting previously held knowledge to accommodate the new.

Underpinning the TQ(FE) programme are the Scottish Executive's (2006) Professional Standards for Lecturers in Scotland's Colleges, a number of which are concerned with attitudes and values, rather than the accumulation of knowledge *per se*. In the preamble to the particular standards relating to Professional Practice and Development (2006:28) it is noted that *"Lecturers must be flexible, reflective, innovative and committed to their continuing vocational and professional development".*

Standards that pertain to this area require, *inter alia*, that lecturers should be able to:

- *"Critically reflect on own values and deal with issues in accordance with the values and ethics that underpin professional practice"*
- *"Manage self, relationships and work demands to promote personal, emotional and physical well-being."*

Of course, these standards cannot be met by the straightforward transmission of knowledge. They require the learner to adopt a particular set of values and affective rather than cognitive objectives.

The Innovative TQFE-Tutor Communications System

Rationale

Until the 2010/11 cohort, participants on the TQ(FE) programme were each allocated a personal tutor who oversaw their progress through the course of study and kept in touch via email. As email traffic soared and tutor numbers decreased (an effect of recent staffing efficiencies at the University) the team was forced to consider ways in which to cut down on email correspondence without negatively impacting upon the programme participant learning experience. In addition to email, a the teaching team used a course blog and an announcements page (both tools being on the TQ(FE) Virtual Learning Environment (VLE) on the Blackboard platform) to communicate with programme participants.

Possible solutions were discussed with stakeholders including not just the teaching team, but also programme participants and their employers, whose sponsorship usually meets the programme fees. As a result it was decided that a fully integrated, centralised communication system – which the team named "TQFE-Tutor" – could offer a solution that would work for all.

After a successful small-scale pilot early in 2010, involving just 15 programme participants, a new blog was created using Wordpress, an installation of which was set up on a University of Dundee server. The new blog took account of feedback from the participants on the pilot programme and particular attention was paid to the aesthetic features as well as the blog's accessibility and utility.

Participants on the 2010/11 intake (numbering 200) were given access to the TQFE-Tutor blog and email and a bespoke Twitter account, all three of which were integrated throughout the programme content on the TQ(FE) Blackboard VLE. Participants encountered the TQFE-Tutor communication system from the earliest point in the programme. This was a mandatory induction exercise at which they were introduced to a navigational pathway, comprising a number of activities which involved interaction on the blog and communication via the central TQFE-Tutor email. Participants were also alerted to the programme's Twitter account and invited to sign up for text messages from the microblogging site.

The potential of the proposal is summarised in Table 1.

Previous communication on the VLE	TQFE-Tutor communication
One-to-one with tutor via tutor's email	One-to-one with tutor via TQFE-Tutor email
Telephone tutorial by arrangement	Telephone tutorial by arrangement
One participant benefits from tutor advice	TQFE-Tutor's advice available to all participants
Personal feedback from named tutor	Personal feedback from named marker
Tutor availability varies	TQFE-Tutor availability known
Participant uncertainty regarding time of response	Guaranteed response time from TQFE-Tutor
Potential mismatch of tutor/ participant	All participants have access to the full teaching team
Cumbersome "clickery" on VLE to move between content and announcements/ blog	News available by RSS feed direct from TQFE-Tutor blog
No knowledge database	Dynamic knowledge database
No search facility on Blackboard VLE	New blog facility fully searchable, with categories and tags in use

Table 1: Comparison between TQFE-Tutor and the Previous Communications Set-Up

The idea of the central TQFE-Tutor system was primarily driven by the need to make staffing efficiencies on the programme due to a 20% budget cut in relation to the previous year. However, members of the team share a wholehearted commitment to the programme participants and they resolved that there should be no detriment to the learners. The TQFE-Tutor system gave the team confidence that appropriate support would be in place for the programme participants. Indeed, in various ways the new system would improve the support available.

After the introduction of the TQFE-Tutor communication system participant-generated communications were submitted either to the central TQFE-Tutor email address or to the TQFE-Tutor blog, each of which was staffed by members of the tutor team on a rota basis.

Advantages of TQFE-Tutor

The TQFE-Tutor system ensures appropriate support for learners by allowing the TQ(FE) tutor team to:

- Guarantee participants a response to any enquiry to TQFE-Tutor email enquiry or blog posting within two working days.
- Provide high quality individualised support by email or telephone tutorial.
- Promote independent, self-directed learners, through tailored responses to enquiries which are subsequently made available to all via the TQFE-Tutor blog – all learners potentially benefit from advice sought by just one.
- Quality assure the teaching online – all tutors, regardless of their FTE on the TQ(FE) programme have access to all the teaching (by the full tutor group) via TQFE-Tutor, leading to tutoring that maintains a high standard and does not vary in quality or content.
- Gradually build a fully tagged and categorised knowledge data-bank for programme participants on the customised blog, allowing participants to access accurate information both easily and quickly, thereby quelling future learner anxiety without reference to a tutor.
- Tweet snippets of news and programme information via Twitter, for example drawing attention to current developments in the FE sector and alerting programme participants to forthcoming online tutorials on the programme as well as looming deadlines.

It was posited at the design stage and, once the system was launched, fully realised that TQFE-Tutor further afforded the programme participants a range of benefits. These included:

- A forum in which to raise issues and consider postings from their peers, as well as the tutor team.
- Opportunities to interact and collaborate with each other as well the tutor team, thereby enhancing the potential for authentic social constructivist learning.

- An introduction to innovative use of Web 2.0 social media tools, which they can in turn incorporate into their own teaching. This is in keeping with the Scottish Government's (Scottish Executive, 2006) recommendations in the *Professional Standards for Scotland's College Lecturers* as well as wider European ambitions. In the latter regard, TQFE-Tutor pertains to two of the Lifelong Learning Programme's Key Competences for lifelong learning (European Communities, 2007): digital competence and learning to learn.

In short, TQFE-Tutor was intended to give programme participants much more than they might expect from a personal tutor without, however, experiencing the problems associated with that kind of provision. The former personal tutor who would have transmitted information in response to participant enquiries would be replaced by an integrated support network to which the participant would have full access, thereby meeting affective needs and promoting learner autonomy.

In addition to these many benefits for TQ(FE) participants, TQFE-Tutor provides a range of benefits to the tutor team. In this regard, TQFE-Tutor:

- Enables team members to learn from each other and thereby improve practice.
- Allows each member of the team an easily accessible oversight of all contact with all of the programme participants.
- Negates the need for one tutor to deal alone with a participant who requires a disproportionate amount of support – responsibility for this is shared.
- Avoids the necessity of repeat effort: once one tutor has dealt with a question or appeal for advice, all tutors have access to that information (as of course do all the participants).
- Provides a convenient central repository of all programme tutoring, with associated advantages, such as affording a swift overview of the "state of play" during staff absences as well as an ideal resource for the induction and training of new tutors on the programme.

Methodology

Here I write from an "insider/outsider" perspective – as Director of the programme upon which the research is based. I am "inside" in respect of my post but, because I am not one of the learners, I am simultaneously "outside" the community I am studying. Naturally, as Director of the TQ(FE) programme I have a bias – it is very much in my interests for the programme to be successful. As well as wanting the participants to benefit from their learning experiences on the programme I have a staff team to motivate, institutional targets to meet, stakeholders to satisfy. I am aware of my somewhat precarious stance as insider/outsider and have tried not to make assumptions based upon my knowledge of the programme and its participants. As far as possible, I have followed advice offered by Asselin (2003:100):

> *"It is best for the* [insider] *researcher to assume he or she knows nothing about the phenomenon under study and start gathering data from a fresh perspective with his or her 'eyes open.'"*

The discussion below, about the participant experience, is based upon a triangulation: (1) examples of communication via the TQFE-Tutor system (2) data gathered via end of module online questionnaires (the programme comprises two separate modules), utilising the Bristol Online Survey (BOS) tool and (3) quantitative comparison of the numbers who successfully completed the first module (of two) in the current and previous years.

In regard to the tutors' experiences, data was also drawn from semi-structured interviews with the teaching team at the end of the first semester of the academic session.

The Participant Experience of the TQFE-Tutor System

Participants on the TQ(FE) programme tend to be "strategic" learners; by necessity "*strategic learners are ... characterised as: looking for the most expedient way to complete coursework*" (Naughton *et al.*, 2010:673). TQ(FE) participants are all busy professional lecturers, usually in full-time employment in the FE sector. Furthermore, many are not on the programme by choice but rather due to a Scottish Government directive which requires colleges to ensure their lecturing staff are appropriately qualified. This strategic inclination towards their learning was reflected in some of the comments made in response to module evaluation questionnaires in previous iterations of the programme (in which an earlier blog was sited, but rarely utilised by participants). Participants' written comments included: *"Didn't really have time to blog"* and, in agreement with the view that strategic learning was the reason for inactivity on the blog: *"Very few students interact through the blog, choosing to use the available time for individual research (essential) rather than sharing/discussing on the blog (optional)".*

There were, however, sufficient positive written comments to suggest to the team that a blog was viewed by participants as potentially useful:

- *"Did not use Blog; possibly could have benefited from this site".*
- *"I enjoyed reading it more than putting comments on it ... Some people probably enjoyed putting comments on it, we are all different; to me it served a purpose".*
- *"The university may need to do something to encourage participants to take part in it".*
- "[the blog] *has been used infrequently and I am disappointed about how little it is used".*

These kinds of statements chimed with the team's conviction that the potential affective learning benefits to be had from the use of such a tool outweighed the somewhat negative response towards it from some of the programme participants.

For the 2010/11 cohort, the new TQFE-Tutor blog was put into operation and programme participants were encouraged to take part in a variety of activities there from the very start of the programme. Previously it had been left to participants not only to find the blog but also to decide whether or not to participate in activity there. Activities in the new blog began with a straightforward "Introduce yourself" task, for which a specific area had been set aside on the site. This served to separate purely social postings from the more scholarly activity expected elsewhere within the TQFE-Tutor blog environment.

Earlier feedback to the teaching team had indicated that many programme participants had no previous experience of blogs so this social task gave participants an opportunity not only to greet each other but also to familiarise themselves with the blog environment. Prior feedback had also shown that some participants felt anxious about posting on the programme blog; for instance, for fear of exposing gaps in their knowledge. The "Introduce yourself" task, being social and requiring no prior knowledge of the programme content, was designed to alleviate such concerns. Of the 200 participants on the 2010/11 intake of the programme, some 170 posted on the optional "Introduce yourself" page and many of these participants also responded to others' postings there. This was just the first of a number of introductory blog tasks set; others included participants being invited to blog on their response to particular resources on the VLE and to post reflections having first undertaken tasks set within the VLE. Responding to each others' postings, comments were often affective: for instance offering reassurance to each other when anxiety was indicated, as in the following example:

> *"I agree about the mass of literature, and also the contradictory nature of some of it. I'm hoping to apply relevant literature to my own teaching but it is a time consuming process sifting through the various theories. However, I am enjoying the process – it broadens the possibilities of self evaluation and critical analysis."*

Here there is peer reassurance in response to an issue together with implied advice about how to respond positively to the challenges of the programme. The new set-up allowed learners to not only take responsibility for their own learning but also to support each other, actively constructing networks that promoted each other's self-direction, circumventing "learned helplessness" and enhancing personal motivation.

As the participants progressed through the programme materials on the VLE, they were prompted to take part in blog activity that requires increasingly complex cognitive effort. For instance, in relation to the concept of "professionalism", discussed in the programme materials on the VLE, participants are directed to interact with each other on the blog, and thereby to collaboratively reach a consensus on "professionalism" in the context of an FE lecturer. Tasks such as this are constructively aligned (Biggs & Tang, 2007) with the programme outcomes although none are summatively assessed. In previous iterations of the programme, participants tended to omit these optional elements of the course. However, since TQFE-Tutor has been operational there has been a significant increase in blog activity pertaining to such tasks.

Table 2 shows how blog traffic has soared since the advent of the TQFE-Tutor site, especially when compared with the same period in the previous year.

	Number of active participations	**Number of new "prompt" blog postings by tutors**	**Total number of responses to postings**	**Number of responses by participants**	**Number of responses by tutors**
Sept – Dec 2010	658	19	639	585	54
Sept – Dec 2009	260	10	250	237	13

Table 2: Comparison between Participations on the TQFE-Tutor blog and the Previous Blog

In 2009/10 more than 50% of respondents to the evaluation questionnaire at the end of their first module disagreed with the statement: *"I have found the blog a useful way of taking part in an online community"*. In contrast, in 2010/11 when the TQFE-Tutor blog was launched, some 70% of respondents agreed with the statement. in spite of Although 85% of respondents disagreed or strongly disagreed with the statement *"I frequently visit other blogs for educational purposes"*, the team was heartened to see that more than 70% agreed or strongly agreed with the statement, *"I would like to introduce a blog to my own teaching"*. In the same vein, 76% of respondents agreed/strongly agreed with *"I found tutor postings on the blog useful"* and 62% were in agreement with *"I found it useful to read postings by other participants on the blog"*.

The TQFE-Tutor blog has introduced programme participants to the intrinsic potential of a blog environment to enhance learning-by-peer as well as tutor support. The potential positive affect of the blog has been realised. Attitudinally, participants are increasingly falling into line with the standards of their profession by becoming:

> "... *flexible, reflective, innovative and committed to their continuing vocational and professional development*" and by "*Manag[ing] self, relationships and work demands to promote personal [and] emotional ... well-being*" (Scottish Executive, 2006).

Analysis of the figures showing successful completion of the first module in the TQ(FE) programme reinforces the teaching team's confidence in the efficacy of the TQFE-Tutor model: progress through the programme has remained high and stable – some 95% of the learners successfully completed their first module. The remaining 5% have yet to complete for a variety of reasons: e.g. extensions granted due to illness/ personal issues. This is marginally better than the previous year's results, although this could be influenced by other factors such as a higher incidence of illness amongst participants at that time.

It is not my contention that a blog can alone fulfil all the affective needs of the in-service lecturer in training. TQFE-Tutor is, of course, much more than just a blog. In addition, participants have access to the central TQFE-Tutor email account and those who prefer can correspond one-to-one, privately, with a member of the tutor team. However the blog plays a role here too; issues raised within email correspondence which are judged by the tutors to be of use to the whole of the cohort are posted on the blog anonymously, in the form of a tutor-composed blog posting. This allows the response to an issue raised by just one participant to be of benefit to the whole cohort. Occasional "tweets" from the TQFE-Tutor microblogging tool have also been used by the tutor team for brief alerts to the participants, though the full potential of this tool to enhance affective learning remains to be explored.

The Tutor Experience of the TQFE-Tutor System

Whilst the social constructivist tenets upon which the TQ(FE) programme is built puts the learner firmly in the centre, the needs of the teaching team, particularly the affective needs, must be addressed as well. Tuition on the programme is necessarily underpinned by the Professional Standards for Lecturers in Scotland's Colleges (Scottish Executive, 2006) and these imply an expectation that the professional values tutors wish to enable in the programme participants must equally be held by the tutors themselves. In this regard, work on the TQFE-Tutor system by the team members, collectively and individually, has brought about substantial changes in the online TQ(FE) programme. TQ(FE) has been transformed from a somewhat static programme which transmitted information into a flexible, networked learning environment where new possibilities are constantly occurring (Moon, 2004).

TQFE-Tutor has resolved numerous issues experienced by the personal tutor system that it replaced. These include:

- Variation in tutor availability: there is only one full-time tutor on the TQ(FE) programme. The other eight tutors vary in FTE from 0.1–0.7, thus a participant whose tutor was part-time could have a long wait – up to and sometimes even more than a week – for an email response to an enquiry made to their own personal tutor.
- Personal differences: sometimes there is an unavoidable "personality clash" between a personal tutor and a programme participant and by "sharing" all the participants, TQFE-Tutor allows the team to neutralise that problem.
- Range in quality of response: the central TQFE-Tutor system means the team is able to quality assure and members may moderate each other's tutoring as a matter of course.

The TQ(FE) team's response to the TQFE-Tutor innovation is perhaps best illustrated in their own words:

- *"Since joining the team at the beginning of this academic session, I've learned so much from TQFE-Tutor. I can easily browse around other tutors' assessment feedback to participants and responses to questions raised by the learners. This has been great for inducting me into the role of the tutor and to consolidate my learning. TQFE-Tutor has made me feel confident about giving advice to participants on a complex programme that is all new to me."*
- *"TQFE-Tutor saves lots of time – I can quickly get an overview of any participant's progress without having to refer to lots of different sources of information."*
- *"TQFE-Tutor has meant that there's much less repetition of effort on the part of tutors."*
- *"Working together on TQFE-Tutor has helped to strengthen the team."*

Team morale has been very positively affected by the TQFE-Tutor system. Gone is the rather solitary work of the personal tutor, "alone" with their learners on a one-to-one basis. Instead, the team members are reaping the many benefits of what is, in essence, a thoroughly innovative kind of team-teaching that minimises the transmission mode whilst simultaneously promoting learner support.

Future Plans

Building upon participant feedback from the 2010/11 intake, the TQ(FE) teaching team plans to refine the TQFE-Tutor system further for the 2011/12 intake and future deliveries. The microblogging site has been somewhat underutilised by the programme team thus far. However, Twitter's enablement of "short, timely messages" has lots of potential for tweeting snippets of news (e.g. reminders of assignment deadlines and requirements) and plans are in train to make more use of this facility in future.

The team has yet to fully realise the knowledge databank that was envisaged in the plans for the TQFE-Tutor system. The Wordpress TQFE-Tutor blog has a great deal more functionality than the Blackboard one that it replaced and work on setting up reliable and helpful tags and categories/sub-categories is continuing. This will allow future participants to straightforwardly find any programme-related information they require, whenever a posting on the topic has already been generated. The knowledge databank is a cumulative project which will be built up gradually over time.

My own plans include further research into the online learner and the affective domain, for instance; into the demographic factors that affect participant activity on the programme blog, and into differences in blog usage between academic disciplines. A study is also planned that will follow up on comments from participants who have indicated an intention to introduce Web 2.0 social media tools into their own teaching.

Conclusion

Use of the TQFE-Tutor utilities has brought together the TQ(FE) tutor team into a collective "team-tutor". This ensures that programme participants have access to the same high quality level of support throughout their studies and that their affective needs, as well as cognitive needs, are taken into account as they make their way through this professional development programme.

The TQFE-Tutor case study shows that it is not necessarily the "personal tutor" that is needed in order to affectively support the online distance learner. Web 2.0 social media tools, such as the blog used in the TQ(FE) programme, can be highly effective in this pursuit – for instance, in their potential for enabling peer support. Similarly, tutor support can be just as effective when provided centrally, one-to-all, utilising a blog rather than one-to-one via email correspondence. However, the system also accommodates one-to-one tutor support for individual participants where this is needed.

Lecturers should exemplify in their own values and practice the life-long learner they aspire to ignite in their own learners. By designing the TQFE-Tutor's integrated utilities with the learners' affective, attitudinal domain always in mind, the tutor team believe they significantly enhance the TQ(FE) programme participants' learning. The personal tutor, once a given in distance education, is no longer a *de facto* necessity – at least in the context of the TQ(FE) programme.

About the Author

Aileen McGuigan is Programme Director, Teaching in the College Sector, at the University of Dundee, Scotland. She can be contacted at this email: a.mcguigan@dundee.ac.uk

Chapter Eleven

Fostering High-quality Learning through a Scaffolded Curriculum

Kayoko Enomoto

Introduction

The meaning of high quality learning (HQL) in higher education (HE) is a topic of significant debate. A growing body of literature argues that HQL can no longer be measured solely by students' grades or readiness to work in a specific discipline area (Anderson & Hounsell, 2007; Barnett, 2007; Entwistle, 2008). Rather, it should also measure student attitudes, knowledge, conceptual understanding, and ability to practise more general ways of thinking, with a shelf life beyond both discipline and university. Indeed, these latter measures are clearly reflected in current graduate attributes statements in Australian universities, as core to learning-centred university education. Any curriculum innovations focusing on improving the "transmission" of subject knowledge alone can no longer be considered appropriate or adequate for promoting current graduate attributes in Australian HE.

This chapter, therefore, explores a way to provide a learning environment where HQL could be brought about and experienced by students. The chapter disseminates a learning-based innovative curriculum encompassing the integration of subject-specific skills development with the broader intellectual development of the individual student. Such a student can analyse and evaluate a range of ideas, perspectives and viewpoints to generate their own effective and creative solutions to current and future problems. For such curriculum innovations, thinking-skills development is crucial; thinking-skills activities and content need to be well-structured and "scaffolded" to effectively assist students to consciously engage in deep thinking.

In contemporary HE, such thinking-skills development has become more important than ever – we face a generation of university students accustomed to daily engagement in non-reflective and non-attentive thinking via instant communication media such as Twitter and Facebook. Therefore, the curriculum innovation I will describe actively integrates thinking-skills development to help equip this student generation with the skills and attributes necessary to successfully cope with complex demands of the real world and the workplace in the 21st century.

Background for the Scaffolded Innovation

Learning cannot be achieved in a single bound, rather it is the result of multiple learning experiences (Vygotsky, 1978). Learning is achieved through accretion, with courses offering scaffolded incremental stages to guide students through tasks, challenging enough to stimulate self-regulated learning, but without becoming overwhelming. This allows students to experience a series of successes, build the skills and confidence necessary to progress through the stages, and remain resilient when learning becomes more difficult. Therefore, to facilitate self-regulated learning, associated learning environments need to provide carefully staged, scaffolded tasks (Verenikina, 2004). The mapping of such tasks must also allow for explicit acknowledgement of the incremental skills developed (Jacobson *et al.*,1996). However, this can be particularly difficult in foreign language programs in Australian universities given the variety of disciplinary backgrounds of language students and the diverse academic experiences they bring to the language classroom.

Advanced Japanese is a third-year advanced language course for non-native speakers of Japanese; it is the highest level of Japanese course offered at the University of Adelaide. The enrolled students are from a wide variety of degree programs across the university, including Engineering,

Computer Science, Science, Health Sciences, Psychology, International Studies, Media, Business, Economics & Finance, Education, and Law. Such a diverse student cohort inevitably has profound implications for language teaching. To facilitate HQL, it is imperative to create and deliver learning environments where all students can equally achieve quality learning outcomes. In this instance, there was also a general perception in the cohort that studying Advanced Japanese was mostly about developing their advanced language skills, with learning Japanese language-specific skills as their learning goal. Therefore, it was vital to help students see the knowledge of a foreign language as a learning tool for gaining new knowledge, not just as a learning goal in its own right.

Thus, there was the need for innovative teaching practices to enhance learning for all students beyond the transmission of linguistic knowledge, through language curriculum revisions to establish the level of scaffolding provided. It was so framed that, in this language learning context, skills developed from experiencing scaffolded tasks could in turn become available and relevant to other learning scenarios in the students' own disciplines: i.e., transferable generic skills.

As a result, a curriculum innovation – a scaffolded curriculum (SC) – was piloted and evaluated as a key component of the Advanced Japanese courses. This chapter examines the effectiveness and benefits of an SC model to improve student learning and develop discipline-specific and generic skills, using Student Experience of Learning and Teaching (SELT) surveys and post-course personal reflections.

Evaluating Scaffolding Theory for Pedagogy

The metaphor of scaffolding has been increasingly applied to Australian educational contexts, incorporating Vygotskian socio-cultural theory; in particular the notion of the zone of proximal development (ZPD) (Vygotsky, 1978). ZPD is defined as the difference between what children can do with assistance and without assistance (Vygotsky, 1978). Vygotsky believes teaching should provide children with learning experiences within their ZPD. Thereby teachers assist children as necessary by supporting their "active" position in their learning and then removing such scaffolding as it becomes unnecessary. This enables the nurturing of self-regulated learning in such processes (Verenikina, 2004).

This conceptual framework, derived from socio-cultural psychology primarily based on childhood learning, provides a powerful theoretical platform for teaching in HE. Yet, as Verenikina (2004:5) points out, *"there is no consensus of opinion among educators on the specific characteristics that constitute successful scaffolding"*. Furthermore, applying a learning theory in an actual non-experimental educational context requires educational researchers to examine and determine its validity, applicability, practicality and limitations.

> *"It is not sufficient for a pedagogical theory simply to explain how people learn; it has also to provide clear indications about how to improve the quality and efficiency of learning"*. (Entwistle, 2008:2)

Therefore, in light of this apparent gap in scholarly understanding, this chapter addresses what types of scaffolds and their characteristics could constitute successful scaffolding within a foreign language teaching context. Following Vygotskian teaching philosophy, I will argue that co-construction of knowledge within student-centred learning activities, along with transfer of responsibility from teacher to student, could contribute significantly to the provision of successful scaffolding.

Requisites for Student-Centred Learning Activities

An increasing body of literature suggests that student-centred learning enhances the development of higher-order skills such as problem-solving and critical-thinking skills (Brush & Saye, 2002). In a student-centred curriculum, activities are embedded, giving students opportunities to become active learners by shifting responsibilities from teacher to student (Cadman & Grey, 2000). Unlike traditional teacher-centred activities where goals are predetermined by the teacher, in student-centred activities students set their own goals for completing a certain activity and assume more responsibility for meeting these goals (Brush & Saye, 2001). Therefore, in such classrooms, teacher-directed imposition of a structure on the student is minimised.

Furthermore, past studies have found that student-centred activities require a different set of skills – metacognitive thinking skills – from those required to succeed in more traditional classroom activities (Brush & Saye, 2001). With such metacognitive skills, students can not only monitor, regulate and evaluate a plan of action but also their behaviour and motivation. In other words, student-centred activities assume that students would practice and exercise their self-regulation in learning; the primary aspiration of teaching and learning in the ZPD.

However, in practice we see some disorientated students frustrated or overwhelmed during activities when they cannot solve a problem or complete an activity. There are two chief reasons for such situations. The first is when content and activities are ill-structured due to the teacher's limited experience in student-centred teaching, resulting in unclear structure and inadequate support to guide students towards successful completion. The second reason, which may accompany the first, occurs when students do not yet possess sufficient metacognitive thinking skills to be able to locate, analyse and evaluate information to generate their own solutions to problems (Brush & Saye, 2001). It is therefore crucial that student-centred activities are sufficiently well-structured and supported to guide students towards completion while facilitating their metacognitive thinking-skills development. To address this the scaffolded curriculum I will describe maps out well-structured student-centred activities with the gradual transfer of responsibility from teacher to student, together with active integration of thinking-skills development.

The Scaffolded Curriculum Innovation

A crucial role for HE teachers is the provision of the scaffolding necessary for students to become self-regulated learners (Verenikina, 2004; Enomoto, 2010). Such scaffolding is not limited to any particular discipline area. Ideally it involves a student-centred, gradual shift of control from teacher to student as a course develops (Cadman & Grey, 2000). One way in which this control shift can be achieved is by designing a course which utilises and builds upon students' existing skills. In the case of Advanced Japanese, this common skill base was identified as IT skills.

In order to meet the academic needs and interests of this diverse cohort, scaffolded tasks embedded within the curriculum were presented as immediately relevant to students' own realities, to maintain student motivation and course engagement. Previous research indicates that

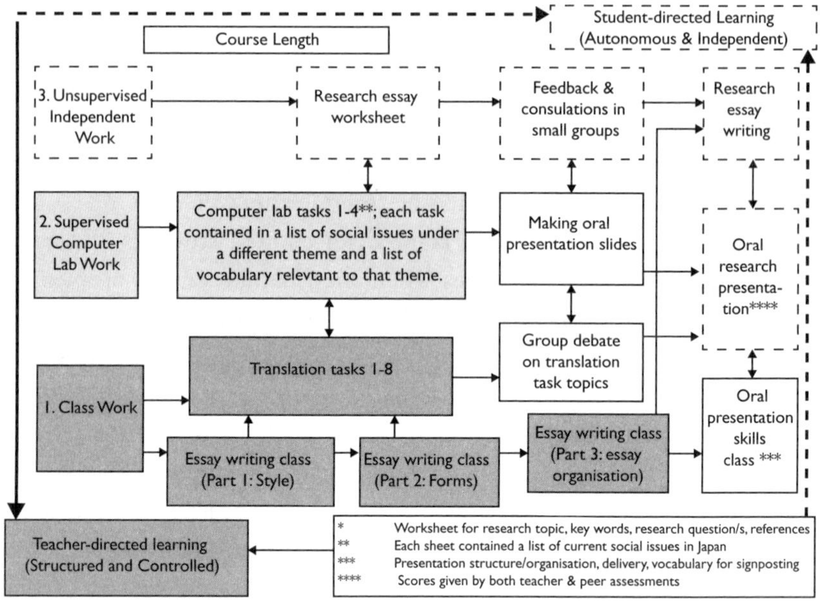

Figure 1: Control-Wedge-based Scaffolded Curriculum in an Advanced Japanese Course

authentic activities provide students with a meaningful purpose for exploration of complex multimedia resources (Herrington & Oliver, 2000). Thus, authentic student-centred activities with students using their existing Internet skills as a tool for learning Japanese would engage them in challenging, real-life tasks. These activities would then provide students with opportunities to view problems from a variety of perspectives and to generate their own views of and solutions to problems.

Using and building upon their existing Internet literacy in English, their first language, students conducted a research project in order to write a research essay and give an oral research presentation, both in Japanese, at the end of the course (Figure 1). They investigated self-determined social issues to develop both their research and Japanese language-specific skills, utilising Japanese search engines to locate and read authentic online materials in Japanese. It was intended that this "double tasking" would help students develop their research skills, particularly thinking skills, for later utilisation in their own disciplines and beyond.

The students were provided with four computer laboratory tasks (Figure 1); each task contained a different themed list of social issues and also a list of vocabulary relevant to that theme (Table 1). The selection and planning of the topics (in this case, social issues) in each laboratory task was crucial for stimulating the students' individual interests, curiosity and desire to learn, helping them see Japanese as a learning tool to gain new knowledge. Each task was given to the students over the first six weeks of the course during the laboratory sessions where teacher assistance was available on demand. To develop their research skills, they investigated every topic listed in each task, utilising Japanese search engines and a variety of online tools to locate and read authentic online materials in Japanese.

Task 1. Society – Japan's reclusive shut-ins, NEET (Not in Employment, Education or Training) phenomenon in Japan, parasite single, working poor, aging population & old age care, homelessness in Japan
Task 2. Education – school refusal, bullying & suicide, childhood depression, classroom collapse
Task 3. Women – abortion, baby post in Japan, Japanese single mothers, parenting leave, working women & child care
Task 4. Other social issues – child abuse, Internet dependency, working to death, death penalty, whaling, recycling, etc.

Table 1: Social Issues Contained in Four Computer Laboratory Tasks

To research each social issue, students engaged in free voluntary reading, using the Internet as a medium of exploration, guided by their own opinions, interests and curiosity to learn more about that topic. To put forward their own views of and solutions to each topic, they had to locate, analyse and evaluate information. To do so, they engaged in deep thinking, making their own judgements as to which pieces of information were relevant and useful to their arguments amongst virtually inexhaustible Japanese language resources. Thus, such laboratory task exercises naturally encouraged students to adopt a deep rather than a surface approach to learning (Enomoto, 2010; Almeida & Teixeira-Dias, this volume). Furthermore, research in second language pedagogy has shown that such free voluntary reading activities can effectively increase second language competence (Krashen, 2003). It was intended that such information-retrieval activities would develop their research and critical-thinking skills and further extend their knowledge of advanced vocabulary, reading comprehension, skimming and scanning skills in Japanese.

Concurrent to these laboratory tasks and in order to develop language-specific skills, students were given in class eight translation tasks (2 topics x 4 themes) closely related to the laboratory task topics (Figure 1). The students, as a group, chose from each theme two topics to translate. This scaffolded link between the laboratory and translation tasks enabled the students to be familiarised with the vocabulary, grammar, etc. relevant to a particular topic or theme, before independently reading about that topic online during the laboratory sessions and outside class., Because the authenticity of relating translation materials was equally important, such translation tasks for each topic were created by exploiting up to the minute Japanese texts from online Japanese newspaper sites. This showed students real examples of the language use (vocabulary, kanji characters, grammar, register/style) on that topic.

These laboratory and translation tasks served to help students decide which Table 1 social issue to pursue further in order to write independently their research essay and give an oral presentation in Japanese, while developing in class the essay writing and oral presentation skills depicted in Figure 1. To help them formulate any feasible research question(s) for their own research project, the students completed a research essay worksheet by filling in their self-selected research topic, research question(s), key words, and useful references that they found online. This worksheet was followed up by feedback & consultations in small groups where every student could receive feedback on their research questions from the teacher and peers.

Figure 1 summarises the above process and shows how a variety of staged learning tasks were scaffolded so that each task component in each of the three streams – Class Work, Supervised Computer Laboratory Work, Unsupervised Independent Work – was interlinked across the curriculum in a developmental grid pattern. Such "thematic criss-crossings" (Jacobson, *et al.*, 1996) provide students with important conceptual links – i.e. scaffolding within embedded activities across the SC – to guide them to complete a given task.

By supporting students in this way to pursue their own research topic independently, this SC innovation enabled students both to determine and to follow through with different types of individual learning goals at each stage. As the course developed they gradually received a lessening amount of teacher direction, support and guidance. Such guidance can take on various different forms, termed as soft and hard scaffolds (Brush & Saye, 2002). Soft scaffolds are situation-specific assistance, provided by a teacher or peer to help with the learning process. In contrast, hard scaffolds are static assistance or support structures planned and embedded in advance by a teacher, based on typical student difficulties with a certain task (Brush & Saye, 2002).

In this Advanced Japanese SC, both soft and hard scaffolds were mapped. In the first case the teacher provided soft scaffolds to those students asking for assistance or those students whom the teacher deemed to require assistance. Support from both teacher and peers took place during in-class activities, supervised computer laboratory activities, and during feedback and small-group consultations (Figure 1).

In the second case hard scaffolds were built between, for example:

- Translation and computer laboratory tasks – learning necessary vocabulary and grammar before researching each topic in the laboratory;
- Laboratory and group debate sessions – forming their own opinions on a topic based on their laboratory research before debating on that topic;
- Essay writing classes and independent essay writing – learning academic writing/referencing conventions in Japanese before writing the essay;
- Laboratory ppt-slide making sessions and oral presentation -creating ppt slides in Japanese with teacher/peer feedback, before presenting;
- Oral presentation skills class and oral presentation – learning set-phrases, manners of presentation, and common oral presentation structures in Japanese, before presenting their own research.

This SC innovation is based on the Control Wedge model of curriculum design (Cadman & Grey, 2000) with a gradual shift of control from teacher to student (from left to right and from bottom to top in Figure 1) resulting in maximum student autonomy in the top right corner.

Such a continuing increase in the amount of student independence in learning directly mirrors a continuing decrease in the amount of teacher control, as the course develops. This is depicted by the two incorporated wedge shapes in Figure 1; the top wedge focuses more on student-directed learning and the bottom more on teacher-directed learning. These core principles of a gradual control shift have been adopted and successfully implemented not only in various projects within English for Academic Purposes (EAP) contexts (Cadman & Grey, 2000), but also in other non-EAP contexts, such as the Introductory Academic Program (Warner, 2010) and Integrated Bridging Program (Picard, Warner & Velautham, 2011), both offered at the University of Adelaide. The study I report in this chapter extends the application of this model to the Japanese teaching context.

Methods of Exploring the SC Effects on Learning

Participants

The effects of using an SC on development of language-specific and generic and thinking skills was explored using students' responses and feedback obtained from standard SELT course surveys. The surveys were conducted in Advanced Japanese courses in 2005 (n=15), 2006 (n=15) and 2007 (n=15) and the results were then compared.

An SC was not used in 2005 so this student cohort served as a control group. However, this control group was not experimentally designed as a "control" for the SC implementation; it was chosen for the purpose of comparisons with the other two groups to explore the effects of SC here. Indeed, it was not practical or ethical to intentionally create an experimental control by implementing the SC teaching with some students but not with others within the actual teaching context of Advanced Japanese. On this point, Entwistle (2008:3) tellingly critiques the predominance of experimental approaches in psychology applied directly to educational research contexts.

> *"Controlled experiments allow greater precision in investigating learning, but are almost impossible to carry out in everyday contexts of teaching*

> *and learning, particularly in PSE [post-secondary education] where introducing specific experimental interventions, or allocating students randomly to differing educational treatments, is generally unacceptable".*

A partial SC had been implemented with the 2006 group. Whilst the mapping of horizontal links and the incremental skills developed along each stream were explicitly acknowledged (Figure 1), the mapping of vertical links between task components across each stream and the whole curriculum were not made as explicit as the full SC to the students. This was largely because the horizontal streams were taught by different lecturers in 2006.

The 2007 group experienced a full SC, with each task component linked both horizontally and vertically in Figure 1; all streams were taught by one coordinating lecturer. Hereafter, the 2005 group is abbreviated as NS (No Scaffolding), the 2006 as PS (Partial Scaffolding) and the 2007 as FS (Full Scaffolding).

Quantitative Data Collection and Analysis

In this study, the use of formal SELT surveys was considered appropriate to the measurement of evidence for the SC effects on student learning. Such surveys provided students with a point of comparison for rating. Advanced Japanese students are third-year students familiar with both the rating format and questions in the standard course SELT, and have already experienced identical SELTs every semester for every course since their first year (4 courses x 5 semesters = 20 SELTs). Therefore, when these students are completing the Advanced Japanese SELT, it is likely that they rate their experience of learning and teaching in Advanced Japanese relative to how they rated their previous experience in other courses. Thus, such familiar SELT results are less likely to represent potentially misleading over- or under-rated scores, which could result in questionable generalisability.

The surveys were administered by an independent survey administrator in class during the 11th week (out of 12 weeks) of Semester 2 in each year. This survey included a total of 15 statement questions (Q1–Q15) and two open-ended questions (Q16 & Q17) as shown in Table 2. Students indicated the extent of their agreement/disagreement with each statement question (except Q1, Q16 & Q17) on a 7-point-Likert scale (from 7 ="strongly agree", to 1 ="strongly disagree"). All questions also offered a "not applicable" option. Broad Agreement (BA) percentages were calculated on the basis of responses where students indicated their agreement as between 5 and 7, and then compared between the groups.

To further examine whether obtained ratings differed significantly among the three groups, a Kruskal-Wallis H test was used to compare the three sets of rating for each question; this non-parametric test, unlike its parametric counterpart (one-way ANOVA), does not assume normal distribution of data. Because small sample sizes tend to fail to present normal distribution (Mori & Yoshida, 1990), the non-parametric test was more appropriate in this study because of the small sample sizes (n=15/group). In this study, the distributions of the obtained data, tended to be truncated at the high end of the scale. Significant H test results were further analysed by post-hoc multiple comparisons using Mann-Whitney U tests with Bonferroni correction, to pinpoint exactly which two groups differed significantly. Finally, the students' qualitative comments from the open-ended SELT questions were used to further support the interpretations of the above quantitative responses.

Qualitative Data Collection and Analysis

In order to explore possible long-term Scaffolded curriculum benefits in the "Full scaffolding" group, qualitative data were sought by contacting all 15 students in this group 12 months after they completed the Advanced Japanese course. They were invited by email to participate in a research project by writing their personal reflections on their course learning experience in relation to Advanced Japanese. Five students responded; three did not respond and seven email invitations were undeliverable because these students had already graduated and left the university. The element of self-selection in response to the invitation may have weighted the sample in favour of students who tended to be enthusiastic about their university experiences. The five respondent graduates of Advanced Japanese were advised that such personal reflections on their course experience may include what and how they learned in this language subject and how specific aspects of teaching affected that learning. No page limit was set and the amount of their commentary varied between 2–4 pages.

The analyses first entailed the author's reading and re-reading the returned reflective commentary, searching for key themes and issues which "emerged" from the written data to explore the range of experiences within a group, rather than to capture any particular individual's experience within that group (Åkerlind, 2005).

Findings and Discussions

As Table 2 shows, the Broad Agreement percentage (BA%) results clearly demonstrate the benefits of using a full scaffolding for student learning, showing overall improvement in ratings in all questions between No Scaffolding (NS) and Full Scaffolding (FS); most markedly "thinking skills" (Q9) (BA: 80% to 100%, Median: 5 to 7). The non-parametric test results revealed significant differences among the three groups for Questions 3 and 6–11. The multiple comparisons tests were then conducted for these seven questions and the results shown in Table 2, with *1 indicating a significant difference ($p<0.05$) between NS & Partial Scaffolding (PS), *2 between NS & FS, and *3 between PS & FS groups.

Key Findings

1) For the students' perceptions of "workload" (Question 1), no significant differences were found among the three groups. The implementation of an SC did not affect students' perceptions of workload.

2) The students' "enthusiasm for further learning" (Q3) differed significantly between NS and PS, and also between NS and FS. This means that not only the FS but the PS contributed to developing student motivation to continue learning in the future.

3) In contrast, "motivation to learn in this course" (Q7) was significantly different only between the NS and the FS groups, but not so between the NS and PS. This suggests that "full" scaffolding of each task both horizontally and vertically, is required for enhancing student course engagement and motivation to learn.

4) For developing "thinking skills" (Q9), it was found that the difference between NS and FS was significant, indicating that FS contributed significantly to developing their thinking skills.

GP	Question	Min	Med	Max	BA %	Question	Min	Med	Max	BA %
N	Q1. Overall, how would you rate the workload in this course?	4	5	6	60	Q9. This course helps me develop my thinking skills (e.g. problem solving, analysis)	2	5	6	80
P		4	6	7	87		4	5	7	73
F	(Very Heavy - Very Light)	4	6	7	73	(*2, *3)	5	7	7	100
N	Q2. Overall I am satisfied with the quality of this course.	4	6	7	93	G10. The learning resources are valuable for my understanding of the course.	5	6	7	100
P		4	7	7	93		5	6	7	100
F		5	6	7	100	(*2)	5	7	7	100
N	Q3. This course stimulates my enthusiasm for learning.	3	6	7	93	Q11. I am satisfied with the course information provided.	5	6	7	100
P		4	7	7	87		6	7	7	100
F	(*1, *2)	6	7	7	100	(*1, *2)	6	7	7	100
N	Q4. I feel part of a group committed to learning.	4	6	7	93	Q12. The learning environment is free from discrimination.	5	7	7	100
P		5	6	7	100		NA	7	7	93**
F		6	7	7	100		6	7	7	87**
N	Q5. It is made clear what is expected of me.	3	6	7	93	Q13. The learning environment takes into account the diversity of students' backgrounds.	5	6	7	100
P		5	7	7	100		4	7	7	80**
F		6	7	7	100		6	7	7	87**
N	Q6. I receive adequate feedback on my work.	3	6	7	80	Q14. My ability to work independently is being increased.	5	6	7	100
P		4	6	7	93		6	7	7	93**
F	(*2)	6	6	7	100		6	7	7	100
N	Q7. I am motivated to learn in this course.	5	6	7	100	Q15. I understand the concepts presented in this course.	5	6	7	100
P		4	6	7	93		4	6	7	87
F	(*2)	5	7	7	100		5	7	7	100
N	Q8. The assessment allows me to demonstrate what I understand.	2	6	7	87	Q16. What are the best aspects of this course and why?	Qualitative comments			
P		3	5	7	73	Q17. This course could be changed in the following ways to improve my learning.	Qualitative comments			
F	(*2,*3)	5	6	7	100					

N=No scaffolding group, P = Partial scaffolding group, F = Full scaffolding group
*1 = Significant Difference between N & P, *2 = Between N & F, *3 = between P & F
**Two students responded "not applicable"

Table 2: The SELT Survey Questions & Statistical Results

The student feedback comments from Q16 further support these quantitative responses, as well as the use of SC and authentic tasks, and research and thinking skills development in this course. Students commented on how they enjoyed and benefited from a wide range of tasks and topics embedded in the SC, perceiving such tasks as immediately relevant to their own realities. Many students commented on how involved they became in the topic they had chosen; they took on the responsibilities of their roles as *"producers of knowledge"* (Dobozy, this volume), engaging in *"knowledge production"* (Piihl & Philipsen, this volume) with enthusiasm. Furthermore, they also commented that they gained general knowledge as well as Japanese words through that knowledge, noting that researching current issues in Japanese was challenging but rewarding. Students also commented that they learned significant vocabulary for each topic in a unique way through Internet research.

These comments suggest that students saw the staged series of tasks principally as a means of acquiring information to inform their opinions on their topics, rather than as a language learning exercise, leading them towards personal understandings of Japanese social issues. That is, they were using their existing IT skills to develop both their research skills and knowledge base, but through a foreign language: Japanese. Additionally, students noted that their independent work and better understanding of the language were encouraged through a research project and gaining these new skills, particularly research skills, was deemed to be the best aspect of this Japanese language course.

Qualitative analyses of all five reflective commentaries revealed two common key issues, as represented by the following comments by the graduates of Advanced Japanese. Firstly, authentic tasks and the way they were scaffolded were effective for improving their learning (n=5), and, secondly, this SC developed transferable generic and thinking skills (n=5). These comments also clearly indicate the positive long-term effects of scaffolds provided in the course beyond university.

> *"[The course] taught us techniques for understanding pieces of text... in advance. These skills along with the confidence gained from reading the news articles...gave us the ability and self-belief that we needed to successfully complete the research projects".* (Graduate A, who is now teaching English in Japan)

> *"Advanced Japanese course has given me the skills necessary to be an independent learner...Furthermore, I now have much more confidence in public speaking, whether it be in English or Japanese...the skills I developed in delivering presentations will be beneficial in the future".* (Graduate B, who has just completed her second degree)

> *"Reading "real" Japanese was very interesting, and I often found myself continuing reading of such issues independently".* (Graduate C, who is now an engineer)

> *"...the strategies for developing effective presentations covered in the class have been invaluable to me following university".* (Graduate D, who is now a practising teacher of Japanese)

> *"Since studying Advanced Japanese in 2007, I have been able to maintain self-directed study".* (Graduate E, who is now working in a government office)

One reflective commentary that typifies the responses from this group clearly indicates that research skills developed from experiencing scaffolded tasks became available and relevant to other learning scenarios, so students can continue learning independently with the confidence gained though experiencing scaffolded tasks.

> *"I have used ... the fundamentals of the research skills I learned in my Japanese course on numerous occasions during my Engineering studies ... The most important thing to come from my [Advanced Japanese] study... is the confidence and enthusiasm that I have gained".* (Graduate C, who is now an engineer)

Overall, the personal reflections of these five students strongly support the pragmatic value of this scaffolded curriculum for improving student learning and developing both subject-specific and generic and thinking skills. This learning-centred scaffolded approach, involving authentic utilisation of existing IT skill bases and interests, successfully developed self-regulated learners, thus paving the way for independent lifelong learning.

Implications, Limitations and Future Directions

There are major challenges in fostering High Quality Learning (HQL) in today's more diverse teaching and learning environments in Australian HE, especially in the teaching of foreign, Asian languages. To tackle such challenges and to contribute new understanding to the field of HE research, this study examined the effectiveness and benefits of implementing an SC for improving student learning and for enhancing thinking skills.

This study found that scaffolded authentic tasks embedded in the curriculum effectively developed both Japanese language-specific skills and transferable generic and thinking skills without increasing student perception of workload in a third-year Japanese language course. Through double-tasking language-specific and research skills development in a research project, students engaged in deep thinking stimulated by both their personal interests and a desire to learn more. They actively practised generating their own opinions and perspectives of and solutions to problems, which is core to HQL. Simultaneously, this curriculum innovation successfully enabled students to see and use Japanese as a learning tool for gaining new knowledge.

Furthermore, the results show that the SC significantly increased motivation and course engagement with students from diverse academic backgrounds. This is because they saw scaffolded tasks as immediately relevant to their own realities, other learning scenarios and the world beyond. In other words, this study strongly points to the importance of enabling students to identify lasting values from completing given tasks. Thus, this study sheds light on the question of what specific characteristics constitute successful scaffolding.

The implications of these findings are that an SC should:

1. Allow the gradual transfer of responsibility from teacher to student as the course develops, to facilitate students' self-regulation in learning.

2. Map out well-structured student-centred tasks, characterised by explicit acknowledgement of the incremental skills developed.

3. Integrate metacognitive thinking skills development actively into student-centred tasks.

4. Make embedded tasks authentic in a way that interacts with life beyond university, to provide students with a meaningful purpose for such tasks.
5. Provide a sufficient amount of appropriate soft and hard scaffolds to guide students towards successful completion of each task.
6. Allow students to experience a series of staged successes in order to build the skills and confidence necessary to continue from one stage to next.

However, these findings and implications are limited here to a Japanese learning context, for those undergraduate students completing a wide variety of non-Arts degrees. Therefore, future research projects could explore possible applications and impacts of an SC on student learning in other learning contexts in HE. Since 2008, we have continued to apply and implement the six required characteristics of scaffolding in a first-year Japanese course curriculum (n=250) to successfully promote students' self-regulated learning and their deeper approaches to learning (Enomoto, 2010).

While this Control-Wedge-based, scaffolded curriculum is by no means "the one and only" way to encourage high quality learning, my experience of its effectiveness convinces me that its application in other discipline areas could be equally beneficial.

About the Author

Kayoko Enomoto is a Lecturer at the Centre for Asian Studies at the University of Adelaide, Australia. She can be contacted at this email: kayoko.enomoto@adelaide.edu.au

Chapter Twelve

The Use of RISK® for Introducing Marketing Strategy

John Branch, Lewis Hershey and David Vannette

Introduction

In 2001, I (John) was charged with the task of teaching an undergraduate, final semester course in marketing strategy. The course was the capstone for those students who were concentrating in marketing and, as underlined by the Director of Undergraduate Studies, ought to finalise their undergraduate marketing education by integrating all previous core and elective marketing courses within a strategic framework.

Adopting an experiential learning perspective (like other authors in this volume), I decided to use one of the many computer-based marketing strategy simulations which were available, in order to provide students with a hands-on opportunity to "do" marketing strategy. With one practice year, an eight year simulation, and one debriefing session – a total of ten classroom sessions – the simulation would consume almost the entire second half of the course.

I also wanted to use an experiential activity at the beginning of the course which, like the simulation, would move beyond transmission and introduce marketing strategy in a more hands-on way. Its main objective would be to highlight some different concepts of marketing strategy: mission statements, strategic postures, and sustainable competitive advantage, for example. Additionally, I hoped that the activity would expose students to the dynamics of competitive markets, and emphasise the importance of a strategic approach to marketing.

While thumbing through my office library in search of a "good idea", one single text jumped out at me – *Even More Offensive Marketing: An Exhilarating Guide to Winning in Business* (Davidson, 1997). In it, the author suggested that there are eight archetypal marketing strategies for exploiting competitive advantage: 1. head on, 2. flanking, 3. encirclement, 4. diplomacy, 5. guerrilla, 6. regional concentration, 7. product range, and 8. niche. It is obvious from these titles that, with the exception of product range and niche, Davidson viewed marketing strategies as analogous to military strategies... and it could even be argued that product range is like bombardment and that niche is a sort of isolationist strategy. Coincidentally, one of my MBA students dropped by shortly thereafter in order to chat about marketing, wondering if I had ever read *Marketing Warfare*, the international best-seller which claims that "*marketing is war*" (Ries & Trout, 1986:1). These two books prompted me to consider developing an activity with a military theme.

A quick Internet search uncovered several board and computer-based military strategy games on the market. One of the most popular of these games was RISK®. Created and marketed by Parker Brothers, a division of Hasbro Games, RISK® is touted as The Game of Global Domination™. It requires that players manipulate their armies on a map of the world which is divided into geographic regions. Battles between players are won and lost by the throwing of dice, and armies are accumulated by conquering geographic territories. In order to win, according to the RISK® rulebook, "*[y]ou must launch daring attacks, defend yourself on all fronts, and sweep across vast continents with boldness and cunning*".

Although not all companies have aspirations to dominate the market (Indeed, according to Davidson's eight marketing strategies, some are better off isolating themselves.), I was convinced that RISK® highlights many of the different concepts of strategy. Being a game, it is certainly competitive in nature. And, as I remembered from my childhood, it emphasises a strategic approach. Consequently, I developed an instructional and assessment activity using RISK®, calling it *Family Game Day* which alludes to an amusing series of advertisements at the time which attempted to convince families to set aside an hour or two per week for a night of board games. Since then, I have adopted *Family Game Day* in all my marketing strategy and marketing management courses, following a "pharmaceutical logic" that if the new pill is working, why return to the old one.

The purpose of this chapter, therefore, is to document the use of RISK® for introducing marketing strategy. More specifically, it aims to detail the *Family Game Day* instructional and assessment activity, situating it within the context of games and simulations. My co-authors and I begin by reviewing this literature on games and simulations. We then describe *Family Game Day*. Finally, we discuss *Family Game Day* in the context of the literature on games and simulations.

The Literature on Games and Simulations

Games have existed for millennia. The ancient Egyptians, for example, were avid gamers, and their games can be seen painted on the walls of ancient tombs and temples (Costello, 1991). The natives of North America loved games of chance and dexterity (Culin, 1975). And the board which is used in today's version of chess is a direct descendant of a game which originated in India more than 5,000 years ago (Kaye, 1973).

However, it is claimed that the first organised use of simulations, dates to only the nineteenth century, when the Prussian army used tabletop battles as a device for recruiting suitable officers (El-Shamy, 2001). So effective was this recruitment device that the practice of using simulations was adopted thereafter by both the British and American armies. Soon afterwards simulations found their way into such professions as law, medicine, and engineering (Adams, 1973).

As pedagogical tools, both games and simulations gained widespread appeal in the 20th century in a variety of disciplines including mathematics, science, communications, urban studies, political science, and international studies (Dukes & Seidner, 1978; Ellington, Addinall & Percival, 1981; Horn & Cleaves, 1977). History teachers, for example, suspicious of the efficacy of traditional lecture and reading approaches to the subject, turned to mock-ups of medieval towns and to replays of the Russian Revolution, in order to bring historical events to life for students (Birt & Nichol, 1975). Games and simulations also became the focus of scientific research, with a Sage Publications journal – *Simulation and Games: An International Journal of Theory, Design and Research* – dedicated to their study.

Business Games and Simulations

Games and simulations have been especially popular in the discipline of business, *"where the complexities of the business world, and the decision-making focus of management, make a wonderful combination"* (Carlson & Misshauk, 1972:3). Indeed, business schools and companies across the United States and around the world have adopted games and simulations extensively in their teaching and training (Faria, 1987; Keys & Wolfe, 1990).

The first business board games debuted in the late 1950s and early 1960s: *The Management Game* at UCLA in 1957 (McFarlane, McKenney & Seiler, 1970); *Top Management Decision Game* at the University of Washington, also in 1957 (Barbian, 2001); and *The Carnegie Tech Management Game* in 1963 (Cohen, 1964). These were meant to offer insights into the "nuts and bolts" of running a company. They were adopted quickly into the curricula of American business schools (Dale & Kalsson, 1964; Editor, 1972) and, by 1961, more than 30,000 executives in American companies had played them (Keys & Wolfe, 1990).

The late 1960s and early 1970s witnessed greater classroom and boardroom interest in games, with a 50% increase in the number of commercially-available products from 1970 to 1972 alone (Horn & Cleaves, 1977). The advent of the computer also made simulations more complex and interactive, and therefore more attractive to professors and human resources professionals alike. *The Harvard Business School Management Simulation* (McKenney, 1967), for example, used early computer technology – an IBM 7094 mainframe – in order to produce accounting reports from decision data which were entered by students with the aid of punch-cards.

The popularity of business games and simulations seemed to drop in the 1980s, but interest resurged in the 1990s, especially in the decision sciences (Lane, 1990). As suggested by Bolt (1990), this resurgence was due, in part, to the growth of executive education which welcomed experiential learning methods – outward bounding, case studies, role-playing, games, and simulations (Broscow & Kleiner, 1991) – and which shirked the 1980s glitz of high-priced lecture circuit speakers for the guts of solid management training.

Today, business games and simulations are more common than ever.

Business schools around the world, and companies from Johnson & Johnson to British Airways, are using them as fundamental components of their teaching and training. At the Boeing Leadership Center in St. Louis, for example, company executives develop strategic objectives in the classroom using customised management games.

Computer-based business games and simulations, however, are usurping the tried-and-true board games and paper-and-pencil simulations (Barbian, 2001). By 2001, they accounted for about 2% of the entire e-learning industry (Hoban, 2001). Computer-based games and simulations can be calibrated to individual companies more readily. But more obviously, they fulfill students' entertainment needs which are so much more a part of education in the 21st century. Monte Cristo Multimedia in Paris, for example, use engrossing video-style graphics of cartoon-like characters which react to students in realistic office environments (Fister, 1999). *Strategy CoPilot*, another commercial product, places real actors, whose images have been filmed against a blue-screen backdrop, into virtual worlds.

Business games and simulations (computer-based or otherwise) are also moving increasingly beyond the strategic level to the integration of strategy and operations (Hapgood, 2001). They allow for front-end experimentation, using extant concepts and skills (Broscow & Kleiner, 1991), and offer both students and managers a way in which to gain the experience which they require, long before they must take the "test". In new product development, for example, games and simulations can play a significant role in a company's success; it *"may only have one shot at launching a new product or making another competitive move"* (Reibstein & Chussil, 1999:35). Similarly, Schrage (2000) suggested that games and simulations provide the vehicles for "serious play". As such, they are the core media for managing risk and creating value, and have become a key to innovation in some of the world's best companies.

Learning from Games and Simulations

These concrete examples, however, only hint at the many reasons why games and simulations have become so popular in business schools and companies. Larreché argued that *"the traditional educational approach exclusively using readings and lectures provides an incomplete coverage of the learning process of action-oriented disciplines*" (1987:561). But from a broader pedagogical perspective, it is believed that games and simulations are simply a more effective mode of learning.

As summarised by Bowen (1987), learning has greater impact when it is accompanied by an optimal amount of emotional arousal. Games and simulations provide it. They are inherently experiential – they begin and end with student action, rather than with the transmission of information (Dukes & Seidner, 1978). As such, they are affectively-charged. Participants become emotionally-engaged in the experience by focusing on the competition and the goals (Barbarian, 2001). Similarly, games and simulations are more memorable experiences. And when an experience is more memorable, skills and concepts are more likely to be retained (Fister, 1999).

Most games and simulations present learning as fun. The drudgery which too often accompanies teaching and training is removed and a kind of playfulness is injected (Barbian, 2001). According to Huizinga (1950), play is considered a universal human phenomenon and is central to the development of the self (Mead, 1934) and of cognitive abilities (Piaget, 1962). In the early twentieth century, the great American educationalist and philosopher John Dewey (1928) even advocated games as an integral part of the curriculum.

Games and simulations couch this play in safety. Their appeal "*as education techniques derives, in part, from the capacity [which they create] for utilizing lifelike situations without the attendant complexity and dangers of the real world*" (McGuire *et al.*, 1976:2). They strip away the extraneous details, hazards, costs, and inconveniences, thereby producing an accelerated course of action so that they can be more efficient than their real-world counterparts (Keys & Wolfe, 1990), and allowing a much broader set of problems than is feasible in a real-life situation (Jones, 1987). Consequently, students become owners of their learning, and are "*afforded full responsibility for their decisions, allowing them to careen down their merry way to disaster without risk to anyone or anything*" (McGuire *et al.*, 1976:2).

According to El-Shamy (2001), games and simulations also meet the criteria for effectiveness of a teaching method as dictated by the key learning theories in the educational literature (See Table 1). For example, adult learning theory which was introduced by Malcolm Knowles in his seminal 1973 text *The Adult Learner* enumerates the distinguishing characteristics of adults which influence their learning. Chief among these are a goal-orientation, a need for relevancy, and practicality. Games and simulations account for these and other adult learner characteristics. Similarly, games and simulations appeal to the learning theories which were proposed by Harvard University psychologist Howard Gardner (1999), including enhancing understanding, learning styles, and multiple intelligences. Games and simulations hit them all.

On a more pragmatic level, games and simulations appear to students as more relevant than textbooks or other conventional methods which rely on transmission (McGuire, Solomon & Bashook, 1976). They often allow for geographically-dispersed participants (Barbian, 2001). They build social and communication skills in their participants (Birt & Nichol, 1975). And they allow participants to self-evaluate their learning (Greenblatt, 1988).

Games and simulations, however, have not escaped criticism. Fister (1999) suggested that some educationalists view them as playing and not learning, with play assuming a negative connotation. It has been argued that they over-emphasise competition and reduce interpersonal and knowledge objectives (Adams, 1973). Lane (1995) contended that the technology of games and simulations often becomes the focus, resulting in a lack of well-defined learning objectives and in a neglect of alternative teaching methods. And according to Reibstein and Chussil (1999), they can be expensive and difficult both to construct and to manage.

Academic research of games and simulations has also been equivocal in its results (Keys & Wolfe, 1990). Early studies which focused on player motivation and involvement (Raia, 1966; McKenney & Dill, 1966; Dill & Doppelt, 1963), team composition effects (McKenney and Dill, 1966; Deep *et al.*, 1967), and the role of chance versus rational decision-making (Wolfe, 1975) offered little evidence – other than anecdotal – that games and simulations are more effective pedagogically than other learning methods.

And finally, outside the discipline of education in which games and simulations have two distinct meanings (Jones, 1985), the literature on games and simulations has lacked definitional rigor. Indeed, the two terms are often used interchangeably. For clarity, therefore, a game is "*a contest (play) among adversaries (players) operating under constraints (rules) for an objective (winning, victory or pay-off)*" (Abt, 1968:73). In a game there is overt, rule-bound competition and participants in the game agree upon both the rules and the game's objective (Suits, 1967).

According to the learning theories which are listed on the right, for a teaching method to be effective, it ought to meet the criteria which are listed below. A check mark indicates that a specific criterion is supported by a specific learning theory.	Accelerated Learning	Adult Learning Theory	Brain-Based Learning	Classical Learning Theory	Constructivism	Control Theory	Enhancing Understanding	Learning Styles	Multiple Intelligences	Neuroscience	Right-Left-Whole Brain	Small Group Dynamics	Social Learning Theory
1. Repeat/reinforce information			✓	✓									
2. Give immediate feedback			✓	✓									
3. Provide safe practice of skills			✓	✓									
4. Develop new concepts					✓								
5. Provide meaningful challenge		✓	✓			✓							
6. Stimulate senses	✓						✓	✓	✓		✓		
7. Promote discussion					✓		✓						
8. Furnish social contact		✓										✓	✓
9. Immerse in realism		✓	✓				✓			✓			
10. Encourage reflection					✓			✓					

Table 1: Effectiveness and Learning Theories (Adapted from: El-Shamy, 2001)

A simulation "*refers to the dynamic execution or manipulation of a model of some object system*" (Barton, 1970:6) of an abstraction of some situation in the real world (Adams, 1973). Often, this abstraction is a simplification of reality which focuses on specific aspects of the situation rather than the situation as a whole (Dukes & Seidner, 1978). Typically, however, it provides sufficient information for participants to adopt a functional role (Jones, 1987) in order to enable execution or manipulation.

Family Game Day

As mentioned previously, *Family Game Day* is an instructional and assessment activity using the board game RISK®. It comprises one classroom session during which students play RISK®, and two corresponding assessment tasks.

Typically, the classroom RISK® session is scheduled as the fourth session of the course. It follows the first session during which both marketing strategy and the course are overviewed; the second session during which a framework for marketing strategy is outlined; and the third session during which mission statements, goals, and objectives are explored. Students come to the session prepared to play; the rulebook is provided in advance to those students who have never played. Tables are organised for groups of six students, with one set of RISK® per table. Students seat themselves, after grabbing some snacks which are provided. For the next 90 minutes, the battles rage.

The first assessment task, a journal, requires students to chronicle their play during the 90 minute session. They are instructed to record not only what they do, but also why they do it, how they feel about it, etc. The journal must be submitted in the session one week after the classroom RISK® session. Assessment of the journal is based on:

- Depth and breadth of journal entries;
- Organisation, structure, and logical flow; and
- Creativity of presentation.

A poor entry, for example, might be simply *"I attacked Germany and rolled a 3"*. A better entry, on the contrary, is deeper and broader in scope. An example might be:

> *"My new strategy is to attack RED in Kamchatka so that I can cross over to North America. If it works, I can dominate the Pacific region, then sweep down across North America, followed by Asia. I am feeling*

> *confident because RED is getting thin in Alberta, but I must be careful because I only have 8 armies and cannot afford to lose, otherwise BLUE might try to attack from Alberta."*

The second assessment task calls on students to reflect on RISK® with respect to marketing strategy. More specifically, it asks students to reflect first on RISK^{Ò} as an abstraction of a competitive market, and then on their play as chronicled in their journals. The reflections must be submitted in the session two weeks after the classroom RISK® session, during which they are also discussed in a debriefing. Assessment of the reflections is based on:

- Depth and breadth of reflections;
- Application of the concepts and theories of marketing strategy;
- Organisation, structure, and logical flow; and
- Creativity of presentation.

A good reflection here might be:

> *"Australia has one entry point: Indonesia. Controlling Indonesia, therefore, makes defending Australia easier. This is analogous to a company which controls a distribution channel to a specific market, thereby making it easier to maintain market dominance."*

Discussion

To begin, the classroom RISK® session is certainly a success with students. Many of them have played RISK® and they welcome the opportunity to play again. One year, a student even showed up to the session in the Russian military overcoat which he bought in Prague while on holiday, and which, he announced, must be sported during a round of RISK®. The activity is wonderful at energising students. It gets them enthused about marketing strategy and can be a fast-acting and long-lasting medicine for "senioritis" – that horrible disease which afflicts final year, final semester undergraduate students. It creates a buzz in the school for several days; students are often overheard talking about the fun which they had in the course. Many students purchase RISK® for themselves after *Family Game Day*... once it was even suggested that RISK® ought to be played during every session of the course.

Perhaps more importantly, *Family Game Day* overall always exceeds expectations with respect to the learning objectives of the activity. First, RISK® exposes students to the dynamics of competitive markets in a very tangible way. Indeed, they begin to appreciate very quickly the evolutionary, dis-equilibrating, resource-intensive nature of competition (Hunt, 2000; 2002). Although it is a relatively simple board game, RISK® also emphasises the importance of a strategic approach – each player's turn encompasses a full cycle of research, analysis, planning, implementation, and evaluation/control.

Most surprising, however, is the extent to which RISK® highlights the different concepts of marketing strategy. Indeed, the links between the board game and marketing strategy are uncanny, and students often raise concepts in the reflections assessment task which could not be envisaged. Ben, for example, wrote that:

> *"While the defender can only roll two dice, any tie is in his favour. The defender is like the market leader, or maybe like the company with first-mover advantage, who can more easily defend market share for a given level of effort."*

Lucy noted that:

> *"I found myself continuing to attack, caught up in the excitement of the game, without thinking consciously about the outcomes. When making a decision, businessmen are just like players in Risk. They are affected by their emotions and personality. People are not necessarily rational when making decisions."*

And for Shivania:

> *"One of the departing lessons taught by the game is that long-term goals are key to success but short-term tactical maneuvers are the vehicle to obtaining them. You can have a strategy, but if you do not execute properly, you won't win."*

A general criticism about the use of RISK® for introducing marketing strategy is that it lacks some of the more consumer- and marketing-specific concepts of marketing strategy – customer lifetime value or the 4 Ps, for example. It could be argued that the rolling of dice is like the fickleness of the consumer. But it appears that the locus of the activity remains at a relatively higher strategic level which is consistent with its learning objectives.

With respect to the literature on games and simulations specifically, it is important to note first that, technically, RISK® is a simulation-game. Considered an educational innovation in the 1960s (Boocock & Schild, 1968), a simulation-game is a game with a simulated environment or, conversely, a simulation which runs like a game. More specifically, a simulation-game, according to both the Society for the Advancement of Games and Simulations in Education and Training (SAGSET) and the International Simulation and Gaming Association (ISAGA), combines the functions of a game (competition, cooperation, rules, players) with those of a simulation (incorporation of critical features of reality). As a game, RISK® has a built-in scoring mechanism which is a consequence of its inherent competition, and has rules which govern play. As a simulation, RISK® reflects a simplified version of real-world military strategy and provides players with the opportunity to adopt the role of military strategist.

Beyond its technical role as a simulation-game, however, RISK® also serves a "meta-level" pedagogical purpose. As mentioned in the introduction, *Family Game Day* was developed in order to address specific learning objectives. In addressing these objectives, therefore, RISK® became that which El-Shamy called a training game:

> *"… a competitive activity played according to rules within a given contest, where players meet a challenge in their attempt to accomplish a goal and win, and in which the* ***skills required and competencies being built in the game are those that are applicable beyond the game itself to the particular subject matter being studied****"* (2001:16, authors' emphasis).

The question which must be asked, however, is whether or not RISK® is effective for addressing these learning objectives.

Effectiveness of RISK® for Introducing Marketing Strategy

At first glance, RISK® seems better than the "tell-and-test" method which transmits information to students and then tests them on their memorisation of it (Hoban, 2001). Indeed, anecdotal results of the classroom RISK® session, plus overall impressions of student performance on the two corresponding assessment tasks, suggest that it is very effective.

First, the use of RISK® for introducing marketing strategy is entirely appropriate. The complexity and dynamics of a competitive market would be difficult, if not impossible, to convey in a non-experiential mode. The decision-making focus of management cannot be appreciated to the same extent outside the iterative process of a simulation, a game, or a simulation-game.

In terms of emotional arousal, RISK® scores higher than other imaginable teaching methods with the exception, perhaps, of internships or consulting projects. It also brings unfamiliar problems to light for students. And it shields them from the dangers of real-life marketing strategy, thereby promoting trial-and-error.

Additionally, all the criteria for effectiveness of a teaching method which were developed by El-Shamy (2001) seem to be met by *Family Game Day*. For example, RISK® utilises the three instructional techniques of brain-based learning (Weiss, 2000): firstly, orchestrated immersion (a learning environment which immerses students in an educational experience), secondly, relaxed alertness (the elimination of fear in the learning environment, but with a challenge), and thirdly. active processing (the internalisation of information through active cognitive processing). Similarly, it provides limitless opportunities for social learning (Bandura, 1971) – learning by observing the behaviour of models, either positive or negative.

On a more pragmatic level, the game appears relevant to students; the familiarity of RISK® makes marketing strategy more approachable, and according to student feedback its use for introducing marketing strategy was germane. The classroom RISK® session provides the vehicle for considerable social interaction, from relatively formal personal introductions to spirited "in-your-face" taunts. And it allows students to self-evaluate, both in terms of on-going strategic decisions, and of extant knowledge.

For some students, however, the classroom RISK® session is seen as playing and not learning; they place too much emphasis on the game, and give little thought to the two corresponding assessment tasks. For others, competition becomes the focus, and their journals are thin on strategic insight. For still others, the two corresponding assessment tasks (especially the reflections task) are too vague – the lack of specific, directed questions leaves them asking "*What am I supposed to do here?*"

Beyond these anecdotal results of the classroom RISK® session, and overall impressions of student performance on the two corresponding assessment tasks, we were able to perform a basic statistical scatter plot (See Figure 1.) using students' evaluations – specifically, the question which measures overall satisfaction with the course. The data is taken from the 15 earlier courses run without *Family Game Day,* along with the 19 courses run after the intervention, in which *Family Game Day* was used. Although the size of the dataset is small, there was a statistically significant improvement in students' evaluations of the courses after the intervention. Indeed, as can be seen from the scatter plot, the slope of the fit line for the total has a significantly steeper slope (R Sq Linear = 0.043) than the line for the data points before the intervention at Time

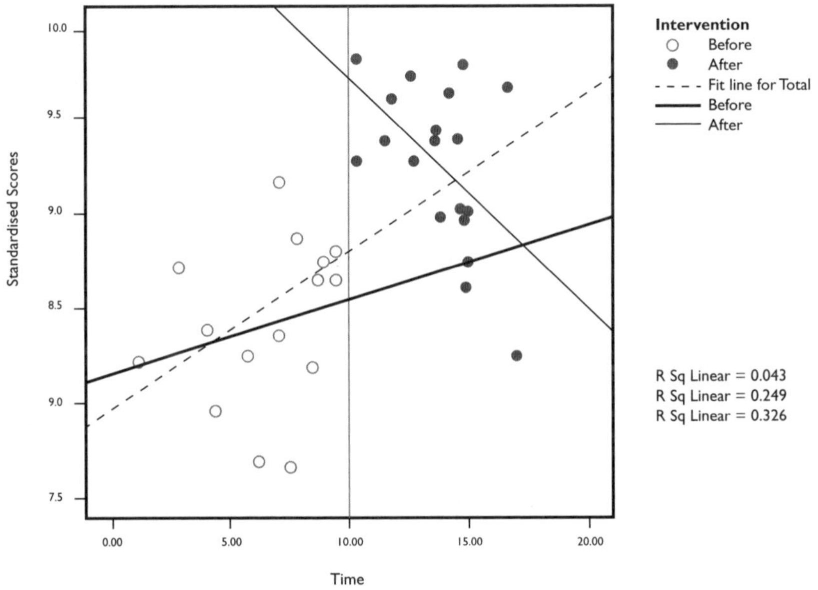

Figure 1: Scatter Plot of Course Evaluations

= 10.00. However, covariates and potentially confounding factors (the courses were not taught at the same institutions, for example.) have not been considered. Nevertheless, the results do lend credence to the anecdotal results and my overall impressions.

In summary, therefore, *Family Game Day* is an inexpensive, easy to manage, and highly engaging activity. It exceeds expectations with respect to the learning objectives for the activity. And anecdotal results of the classroom RISK® session, overall impressions of student performance on the two corresponding assessment tasks, and statistical analysis of overall satisfaction with the course, all suggest that it is an effective pedagogical tool for addressing these learning objectives.

Final Thoughts

I (John) shall definitely continue to use RISK® for introducing marketing strategy. Going forward, however, I plan to schedule the classroom RISK® session immediately following the introduction session, thereby making it even more of an introduction to marketing strategy. In concert with this move, I shall also use the third session to debrief the students as a lead in to a lesson on the dynamics of competitive markets.

I also plan to experiment with an alternative format of playing RISK® which requires that each player draw a MISSION card at the start of the round. A MISSION card (despite its confusing terminology from a marketing strategy perspective) defines a specific objective, the accomplishment of which results in victory for the player. These MISSION card objectives are possibly more realistic than "Global Domination" and, additionally, shorten the length of a typical game considerably. The drawback, however, is that students will not have the opportunity to learn by setting their own strategic objectives.

Recently, while leafing through an in-flight airline magazine, I came across a book by best-selling author and motivational speaker Brian Tracy (2002), which I am now considering as a complement to the eight military-like archetypal marketing strategies of Davidson and to the lessons of Ries and Trout. Entitled *Victory*, it outlines twelve principles which have been key to military successes throughout history and which, Tracy argues, are key to business successes. The principle of "mass", for example, suggests that an organisation must concentrate combat power at the decisive place and time. Similarly, the principle of "concentration" encourages organisations to focus all their energy on specific strategic objectives.

I am also exploring how other military strategy books might provide insight into marketing strategy. *The Art of War* by Sun-Tzu (1983), for example, which is considered the oldest military treatise in the world, is often cited as a key influence in Chinese business practice. Likewise, Japanese business men and women claim that Musashi's 300-year-old Kendo manual, *A Book of Five Rings: The Classic Guide to Strategy* (1974), provides a template for business success.

All these modifications reflect an iterative approach to innovation (Leigh & Herbert, this volume) – the on-going process of simulation-game development. Indeed, Jones (1987) suggested that it is through observation that learning objectives are discovered. In other words, the learning objectives of an activity such as *Family Game Day* become more and more refined through successive iterations. Likewise, evaluating the correspondence between reality and a simulation as an abstraction of reality is a useful exercise (Klein, 1985), helping to clarify its purpose and limitations.

Finally, the use of RISK® for introducing marketing strategy might raise interest in the broader application of play in higher education. Piaget (1976) defined play as "functional pleasure", alluding to both the practical and hedonistic consequences of play. According to Callois (1961:23), however, play is a:

> *"free, make-believe activity that, although it may be governed by rules, is characterised by uncertainty in that neither the course of the activity nor its final end may be ascertained before the fact".*

It is this uncertainty which suggests a significant limitation of play in higher education – indeed, how can play be used as an experiential learning method, when specific learning objectives cannot be assured? But whatever the answer, it continues to motivate us to develop innovations in university teaching which move beyond transmission.

About the Authors

John Branch is a Lecturer of Marketing at the Stephen M. Ross School of Business, and a Faculty Associate at the Center for Russian, East European, & Eurasian Studies, both at the University of Michigan, USA. He can be contacted at this email: jdbranch@umich.edu

Lewis Hershey is a Professor of Marketing at the School of Business and Economics at Fayetteville State University, USA. He can be contacted at this email: lhershey@uncfsu.edu

David Vannette is a PhD. student at the Department of Communication at Stanford University, USA. He can be contacted at this email: vannette@stanford.edu

Chapter Thirteen

Poster Presentation: an Effective Assessment for Large Communication Classes?

Swapna Koshy

Introduction

In the past few decades there has been an unprecedented increase in student numbers in most institutions of higher education (eg: Hoban, 2010). In turn this has led to heterogeneous multi-skilled classes with students from diverse cultural and educational back grounds. From the lecturers' perspective the challenge of assessing large multi-skilled classes with limited tutor support necessitates the use of assessment approaches that are easy to correct and also promote active learning. Educators have had to adopt new practices to facilitate the teaching and learning process without compromising quality.

This chapter evaluates the use of Poster Presentation as an assessment in a large class studying communication in an off shore campus of a Western university. Its Middle East campus hosts students from over a 100 countries. The subject considered here – Business Communication – is a core subject for Bachelor of Business Administration students and an elective for students majoring in other disciplines including accounting, finance and IT. Business Communication is a 100 level subject but many final year students chose it as an elective because of its comprehensive nature and relevance to the work place. Typically the class has a heterogeneous population with mixed skill levels and learning backgrounds.

The current practice is to assess students using group oral presentations. However, I have found that this type of assessment does not stimulate student participation or deep learning. The involvement of the presenters themselves was also minimal. Students are currently being trained in public speaking skills from a very young age because schools have incorporated communication as a key learning outcome in their curricula. Students who are confident do not seem to put enough effort into organising or researching the matter presented. The lack of involvement of both presenting and non-presenting students also called for a change in the assessment used. In an earlier study (Koshy, 2009) students clearly indicated their preference for workshops, case studies and problem solving as compared to oral presentations. I introduced the new form of assessment – despite the risk of it being rejected by students – because I perceived that it would lead to more active learning and better use of class time. It was also in alignment with the learning objectives for the subject. The speaking time for presenters and non presenters would increase through the informal interactions among the students. For the instructor it would mean being able to closely examine students and better assess their learning and also to assess students individually in a large class.

Learning – the Purpose of Higher Education

From the time of its medieval origin the term "university" has been used to refer to an institution that provides teaching and learning at the tertiary level. Effective learning should be the central purpose of every university. Therefore, teaching and associated activities, including assessment and grading, must facilitate effective learning. With the commercialisation of higher education there seems to have been an inevitable dilution of the fundamental purpose of universities. Therefore it is vital constantly to evaluate the quality of learning in universities. This process does not have to be relegated to quality assessors. Academics who develop curricula, course content and assessments and deliver this to the student community must serve as the first evaluators of effective learning. They must continually assess and improve teaching and associated academic activities that aid student learning.

Theories of Learning

Many theories of learning have been developed but a detailed analysis of each is beyond the scope of this chapter, I will summarise some that I feel are most relevant for developing a framework for good teaching and learning.

The constructivist theory refined by Jean Piaget views learning as a subjective process of constructing meaning from experiences (Merriam *et al.*, 2007). Understanding of subject matter is essential and individual students cannot rely on regurgitation or relayed meaning. Assessment has to be a part of the learning process and must allow students to evaluate their learning. It is assumed that the primary responsibility for learning rests with the learner. The teacher should perform the role of facilitator supporting and directing students and not that of a lecturer disseminating information.

The American psychologist Carl Rogers also furthered the view of teacher as facilitator (Rogers, 1969). Rogers' humanistic approach advocated a student centered learning method where students were actively involved in the learning and were not merely passive receptors (Knowles *et al.*, 2005; Merriam *et al.*, 2007). Similar theories were posited by John Dewey (Knowles *et al.*, 2005; Passer & Smith, 2011). Dewey's focus on "experience and education" (1938) was on the connections between life experiences and learning (Merriam *et al.*, 2007). More recently, educators like John Biggs (1999) have effectively assimilated earlier concepts to make seminal contributions to learning theory. Biggs' theory of Constructive Alignment has been well received by new teachers and seasoned teachers who are looking for ways to improve the learning process:

> *"Learning is the result of the constructive activity of the student. Teaching is effective when it supports those activities appropriate to achieving the curriculum objectives, thereby encouraging students to adopt a deep approach to learning. Poor teaching and assessment result in a surface approach, where students use inappropriate and low-order learning activities. A good teaching system aligns teaching method and assessment to the learning activities stated in the objectives, so that all aspects of this system are in accord in supporting appropriate student learning. This system is called constructivism in learning and alignment in teaching."* (Biggs, 1999:11)

Constructive Alignment has been used to align teaching activities, curriculum objectives and assessment tasks to ensure that students learn what educators intend them to learn and they are tested on what they learn. Curriculum developers who practice Constructive Alignment have been able to streamline their courses and to achieve deep learning to a great extent. However, appropriate assessments are crucial for constructive alignment to work.

Measuring Learning through Assessments

Evaluating students' learning is an important step in the learning process; assessment is the time-tested way of performing this. However, because of the many changes in education – including larger class rooms, higher student/teacher ratios and a fall in standards of the "masses" entering the portals of higher education, assessment methods need to be continually reviewed (Biggs,1999:1). Most universities require that assessment tasks and the standards to measure them have to be set before the commencement of the course and clearly communicated to students. Good assessments that are designed to facilitate learning will help not only the learners but all stake holders in the education system. Dunn *et al.* (2004:16) lists the benefits of assessments to the student body:

- Diagnosing students' difficulties;
- Measuring improvements;
- Motivating students to study;
- Judging mastery of essential skills and knowledge;
- Ranking the student's capabilities in relation to the whole class;
- Evaluating the teaching methods;
- Evaluating the effectiveness of the course;
- Encouraging the tacit learning of disciplinary skills and conventions

Assessments are therefore not just an instrument to measure student learning. As this chapter will argue, good assessments are a pedagogical tool that encourages deep learning. They also help to measure the efficacy of teaching methods used, thereby encouraging learning which is beyond mere transmission.

The Need for Innovative Assessments

Academics may decide to develop new assessment formats for various reasons. As curriculum objectives are regularly updated to satisfy the demands of the changing workplace, the need for constructive alignment between teaching activities, curriculum objectives and assessment tasks necessitates new types of assessment. Unfortunately, innovative assessments are not always introduced when traditional assessment methods are found lacking. Repetitive use of assessment formats, such as oral presentations or essay writing, can cause boredom for both teacher and student. Students, depending on their learning style (Honey & Mumford, 1982) may prefer one style of assessment to another and perform better in their preferred style.

Another factor is the teacher's intellectual and emotional involvement in the assessment process. A tutor who assesses oral presentations in every tutorial, semester after semester, – as is the case in many universities – can eventually become a victim of burnout. Psychologists warn that burn out can cause exhaustion, cynicism and inefficacy. Maslach and Jackson (1981) point out that for energy, involvement and efficacy there needs to be engagement. Without engagement it is not possible to assess effectively for prolonged time periods.

Today's classroom, which is a unique mix of skill levels and cultures, also demands innovative assessments (Koshy, 2008). For the teacher, assessment is what happens at the end of the learning process but for students it usually comes right at the beginning; especially when their focus it to only pass the course. As Biggs (1999:160) describes, assessment is for the teacher *"a necessary evil, the bad news of teaching and learning, to be conducted at the end of all the good stuff."* Related to this is the interesting idea of "backwash" that Biggs puts forward. For most students, assessments are at the centre of their learning process; for many it is the only learning they do. Biggs (1999:141) explains *"this is backwash, when the assessment determines student learning, rather than the official curriculum"*. Constructive Alignment ensures that backwash has a positive effect on the learning process. In Biggs' (1999:141) words *"learning for the test is bad only if the test is bad."* Thus, backwash also initiates the need for innovative assignments.

Assessments for Business Communication Courses

The focus of most Business Communication courses is on oral and written communication. For this reason assessments typically used in Business Communication courses are oral presentations, writing business letters and reports. Though not widely used, other assessment types include discussing principles of communication evident in a newspaper article, rewriting sentences using active/passive voice, summarising business articles, revising business documents, interviewing a business contact and writing advertisements. In large classes it is difficult to handle multiple written assessments. Group oral presentations with the aid of PowerPoint™ presentations are therefore the most common assessment type.

Group oral presentations are however not without drawbacks. In my experience the objectives of presentations have been mainly to help students build confidence in public speaking, learn to organise thoughts, conduct research and incorporate support material, respond to questions, and use PowerPoint™ slides. Although oral presentations can achieve these objectives, some students will resort to learning the material by rote and will show little involvement in the learning process. This merely promotes surface learning which is detrimental to effective learning. Prosser and Trigwell (2002:91) remark that in a surface learning approach students complete the assessment with *"the minimum effort"* required and engage in *"reproduction"* and *"rote memorising"*. Moreover, the non-presenting students have minimal involvement in the activity going on except for asking questions during the discussion session – if there is one. So precious class time can be lost without any active learning.

An Innovative Form of Poster Presentation Assignment

The inadequacy of using group oral presentations to assess first year Business Communication students led to the introduction of an innovative assessment – the poster presentation. Around 20% of the student cohort had worked on posters before but for the rest it was a totally new experience. It was therefore important to familiarise students with the format of the assessment. In the first tutorial students were given extensive information about the organisation, content, topics, presentation and other factors related to the assessment. Sample posters in the dimensions and format recommended were made available for review. Information on the poster presentation assessment was provided in the subject outline as well as in handouts. Links to online material on poster development and presentation were also included. The poster presentations were scheduled to start towards the middle of the 13 week course. In each tutorial five to seven students were to present posters on different topics related to the course. The posters were to have a clear title that reflected the content, an introduction, body, conclusion and reference list. Students were instructed to avoid verbosity and to use bullet points wherever possible. This was expected to build their skills in summarising and in critical analysis. This had the benefit of discouraging plagiarism as students could not copy and paste text from outside sources. The use of graphics was encouraged and this ensured that students did not read from the poster while presenting.

Students were to put up the posters anywhere they chose on the classroom wall. They were to stand near their posters for 30 minutes to speak to observers and later they were to view other posters exhibited. Non-presenters could choose to view posters in any sequence. As the poster topics were connected to the course content and covered in the final exam, non-participating students were enthusiastic about reading others' posters. The presenters were encouraged to respond only to questions from the viewers and not to summarise their presentation for every individual or group viewing their poster. This encouraged interaction between students and in-depth discussions of the topics presented. It not only promoted deep understanding of the topics but also helped to practice communication skills.

Most students took pride in their work and were happy to explain the contents of the poster to their peers. However, there was some initial resistance to the assessment, because it was new, and a quarter of the students feared that they were not artistic enough to work on posters effectively. These students were reassured that the criteria did not grade them on artistry. Some students thought it was very childish to work on posters and it was embarrassing to carry the posters around as it attracted a lot of attention. In the event, student attitudes changed to a more positive one as the course progressed.

In the last lecture of the session selected posters based on topics covered and on highest grades attained were presented to the whole cohort and to visitors including students from other courses as well as teaching and administrative staff of the university. Each member of staff was given the opportunity to choose his/her favourite poster and give a best poster certificate. By the end of the 90 minute display, every presenter had received a best poster certificate. This was to reward and encourage the extra efforts that the presenters had put in. Students proudly displayed their certificates next to their posters. Guests were appreciative of the poster display session and said they benefitted from the diverse topics covered. Students enjoyed the experience of presenting their posters to the university community. They were encouraged to present themselves in a professional manner. The dress code was expected to be formal/semi-formal and some students took the effort to co-ordinate their wardrobe with the theme of their poster. Presenting students were also given tips on how to greet and thank strangers and to introduce themselves and their topic succinctly. The students gained much exposure from the whole exercise and it was a simulation of what they would do in their future career.

Poster Presentations – Expectations

When dealing with large communication classes it is necessary to have assessments which will increase the speaking time available for each student and will enable the teacher to evaluate students individually. Posters have been used to assess students in several different disciplines, including marketing and medicine. Almeida (this volume) refers to the use of posters in chemistry. However, in spite of analysing over 30 learned journal articles I could not find evidence of its use in Business Communication courses.

The merits of poster presentation are many. It encourages higher order learning and, as Biggs (1999:200) identifies, the most likely kind of learning assessed by posters is *"concentrating on relevance and application."* The brevity demanded by posters encourages critical analysis, and selection of relevant information. The poster presentation is expected to:

1) Increase quantity and quality of speaking time;
2) Improve class participation;
3) Permit individual assessment in a large class;

4) Encourage deep learning;
5) Offer immediate feedback to students;
6) Involve the whole class and;
7) Cater to visual, auditory and kinesthetic learners.

Practitioners have cited several other advantages which focus on the learning and teaching process with benefits to students as well as teachers. A disadvantage of oral presentations is the tendency for students to read from notes or learn the material by rote and present without any involvement with the material. In poster presentations there is *"little or no reading of notes"* (Firth, 2006). Unlike in oral presentations, the teacher gets the opportunity to discuss work with individual students *"to assess the level of understanding of information presented"* (Mulnix & Penhale, 1995). Crowley-Long *et al.* (1997) point out that students also acquire more favourable attitudes toward research as a result of their active participation in the creation and presentation of a poster. Kemp and Clark (1992:398) who support this view add that this form of assessment improves students' interest and motivation. Co-operative learning is also encouraged. Evaluations can be more accurate because faculty have a chance to interact with students on a one-to-one basis. Students with fear of public speaking find it easier to converse in an informal setting with individuals and small groups. Poster sessions are *"less intimidating... because the audience is one to one and discussion can flow readily"* (Crooks & Kilpatrick, cited in Akister *et al.*, (2000). Akister *et al.* (2000) also point out that the whole class benefits from the *"shared learning environment"* as students see each others' posters and discuss them. There is also the possibility of quick feedback.

Posters can be displayed easily and this can make the practice a community event. Dunstan and Bassinger (1997) observe that poster presentation *"extends activity beyond the classroom walls, involving the college community at large"*. This boosts the confidence of presenters and gives them exposure through presenting to and meeting several guests. Among the benefits to teachers with large classes, poster presentations can help in *"achieving a balance between worthwhile assignments and faculty work load"* and allow instructors to assess multiple students individually in a class (Kemp & Clark, 1992:398). Walker (2005) points out a very important merit of posters:

> *"The prospect of plagiarism is dramatically reduced because while the advent of internet assignment sales has seriously compromised academic credibility, there is also no prospect of copying another student's poster because of their unique characteristics."*

In my experience poster presentations meet and surpass the seven expectations listed above. Bracher *et al.* (1998) observe that poster presentations help to practice the principles of adult learning put forward by Knowles (2005) who emphasised the importance of *"involving them [students]in a hands-on, problem focused activity which encourages relation of knowledge to a specific question of interest and stimulates demonstration and comprehension."*

Methodology

The primary data for this study were collected through a survey and informal interviews with under-graduate students enrolled on the Business Communication course and who had worked on the poster presentation assignment. Participants were assured that their responses would be anonymous and confidential. Their participation was voluntary and no monetary rewards were provided. The sample size was 36, of which 25 were female students. 25 students were in the age range of 17–20; eight were aged between 21–25 and three were aged above 25. The nationality break-down was: 68% Indian sub continent; 15.6% Arab; 9.4% from CIS countries (the Commonwealth of Independent States, being 12 former Soviet Republics) and 6.3 % from the African continent.

Survey

An anonymous survey of students enrolled in the course (N=160) was done to evaluate their responses to the innovative assignment. The questionnaire consisted of 19 ordinal questions on a 4 point Likert scale and one ranking question about the preferred type of assessment. The core areas covered were: working on the poster, viewing others' posters, presenting the posters, and a comparison with other assignments. Frequency and cross tabulation functions in SPSS were used to tabulate the data. All values are expressed as percentages.

	Strongly Agree	Agree	Disagree	Strongly Disagree
Area 1: Working on the poster				
I enjoyed working on the poster	30	50	14	6
I like to work on new types of assignment	44	53	3	0
The tutor gave clear instructions on the assignment	47	42	11	0
I would like to work on posters again	20	58	14	8
Preparing the poster was more time consuming than other assignments	22	19	56	3
The poster presentations should be done in groups	22	28	42	8
Area 2: Viewing others' posters				
I enjoyed reading other posters	22	72	6	0
I learned much from other posters	30	53	17	0
The topics covered in the posters were interesting	25	58	14	3
The topics covered in the posters were useful	28	66	6	0
Area 3: Presenting the posters				
I am afraid of speaking in public	6	30	42	22
One to one speaking gave me confidence	22	70	8	0
The presenters answered the questions about the posters well	22	67	11	0
I was asked stimulating questions about my poster	17	48	29	6
Area 4: Comparison with other assignments				
The weighting of 20% for the poster was too much	14	38	31	17
It was easy to score marks in the poster presentation	11	44	34	11
Posters help to understand difficult topics	14	72	14	0
Poster is preferable to oral presentations	25	55	17	3

Table 1: Summary of Survey Results

In general the response was very positive about poster presentations. In answer to questions about their working on the poster, between 80–90% students strongly agreed/agreed that they had enjoyed the experience, had enjoyed reading others' posters and had learned from others' posters.

A similarly high proportion felt that presenters answered questions well, the topics were useful and interesting, the poster format is helpful to understand difficult topics and the tutor gave clear instructions.

97% students strongly agreed/agreed they would like to work on new types of assessments; 92% strongly agreed/agreed that the one to one speaking format was helpful; 78% strongly agreed/agreed they were willing to work on posters again; 50% of students believed that poster presentations should be done in groups; 54% commented it was easier to score in posters; 43% remarked that it was time consuming and 36% admitted they were afraid to speak in public. Over 50% made posters their first choice for assessments over essays, reports and oral presentations.

The majority of students in each age band said they had enjoyed working on the poster. All students aged above 25 strongly agreed/agreed that they enjoyed the assessment.

A minority of students strongly agreed/agreed that it was easy to score marks in the poster assignment. 83% disagreed and 75% strongly disagreed strongly. Despite this spread of opinion, a majority of respondents in each case said they had enjoyed working on the poster. Among the different nationalities in the sample, all Arabs, Africans and students from CIS countries and 85% of students from the Indian sub-continent strongly agreed/agreed that they enjoyed working on the posters.

Interviews

Twenty students participated voluntarily in an informal interview. There was only one male participant. The informal interviews were conducted to analyse students' motives, beliefs, attitudes and feelings in relation to the assessment. The discussions were recorded and transcribed. The participants did not identify themselves and the following extracts from the interview transcriptions are presented anonymously.

The most popular observation was that it was a fun assignment to do. Some students also said it was easier than other assignments. A few students felt that the individual work required was too great. This view was counter-balanced by a similar minority who felt that working on a poster in a group would be difficult because *"[there would be] too many conflicting ideas."*

A student who won a best poster award for a poster on career choices said he felt as though he had been at an exhibition:

> *"I've been a part of many corporate exhibitions and it feels great when you exhibit your poster and you get views from different professors".*

The need to work on the information was highlighted during the interviews. One student commented:

> *"You cannot put everything on the poster, only the stuff which is appealing to the public and ... you needed to filter a lot of information ... the use of diagrams was really good because it says more than words."*

The same student shared the sentiment that the new assessment seemed childish at first. She said:

> *"It seemed ridiculous in the beginning that we were doing posters as it was something we did in high school."*

Another student who also won a best poster award commented that the reason why she would not want to repeat the assignment was

> *"Once was enough. ... No, because it's kind of embarrassing you know, carrying the posters in the university, it really is."*

Three students expressed their preference for the poster over the oral presentation. Comments included:

- *"I think you learn more than what we learn in presentation because no one is really paying attention [to a presentation] and here everyone is interested, it's visually appealing."*
- *"Somehow – because here I was concentrating on something specific – I actually learned more."*
- *"I actually learned more to answer your [lecturer's] question, I learned more from my posters because in presentations ... I just memorize everything more like not necessarily understand what I am saying, so definitely posters are better."*

Another student shared a similar experience:

> *"Poster presentation is much better because you are talking one to one and you can explain research a lot and you can explain them by putting the pictures and all. But then in presentation it's like you have your part. I mean all the group is presenting together so even if you worked for the entire presentation that doesn't show it. I mean you will be credited only for your part. Poster presentation you can show your individual creativity and you are not limited by, let's say, software. I mean I had much more work rather than just presenting on a power point slide."*

Another comment was:

> *"[Posters are] much better than [oral] presentations ... more interactive, way more interactive. You get to see one thing in many different ways. Many people are doing one topic ... you know different points of view and stuff. You don't have to read from slides or something you just have to talk about. In [an oral] presentation you just go on talking ... you don't care if anyone is listening or not listening".*

Students commented that the poster presentation improved speaking skills. Typically: *"I gained bit of confidence ... what I didn't have, maybe I thought I couldn't present ... now I am fine with it, I can do it maybe in the future as well."*

Many students agreed that presenting one to one was better than whole class presentations. For example:

> *"One to one was much better because you can actually see if a person is interested or not because in an entire class of students some are interested and some are not. When you are presenting to an entire class it's a bit more daunting when you want to answer and everyone is silent. When there is one to one, one person is actually sincere and up close and personal so it is a little less daunting."*

A similar sentiment was shared by another student:

> *"I feel that many of the students ... are very nervous presenting to a whole group of audience. But when it's one to one it's like normal talking to a person and you can actually build an emotional bond and present it."*

Students also felt very involved with the assignment. As one said:

> *"It was a great experience from start to end ... from making your poster till presenting it and explaining it to other people. You yourself get a bit more interested and it's not scripted so it is very simple."*

Commentary

Review of the Survey Findings

It can be concluded from the survey data that the respondents enjoyed many aspects of the poster presentation. They enjoyed working on it as well as reading others' posters. They learned from others' posters and were asked relevant questions about their own. This is evidence of active learning and efficient use of class time. Students got the chance to learn from their peers and there were meaningful interactions between students. Students also commented that the topics covered were useful and interesting. With poster presentations there is flexibility in the way the class is conducted; students move around, choose which ever poster interests them and spend as much time as they need with each poster/presenter. When they engage in discussions they are not observed by the whole class.

Students commented that presenters answered questions well and this could be because presenters were not under pressure to perform before the whole class. The fact that they worked well with the material and not just learned their part by rote may account for their strong belief that posters help to understand difficult topics. Biggs' (1999:107) observation: *"being active while learning is better than being inactive: activity is a good in itself"*, supports the involvement of students in the assignment.

Some believe that students do not like to be exposed to new assessments because it is difficult to learn the format in the restricted time available. However 97% of my students said they like to work on new assessments. Hess and Brooks (1998) observe that *"the sheer novelty of creating a poster can also increase interest and motivation among the students."* This should encourage educators to work on innovative assessments. Comments that the teacher gave clear instructions suggest that this made it easy for students to work on the new assessment and also enjoy it. Clarity of instructions is necessary for students to perform well and without pressure.

The observation by half of the respondents that the poster assessment should be done in groups could be because those students found that they had had to do a lot of work. This view is supported by the 43% who opined that it was time consuming. Though only half the students felt it was easier to score on posters the overall positive learning experience caused them to comment that they would like to work on posters again. And for the same reason half the students commented that posters were their first choice of assessment.

Demographic factors like age and nationality did not show significant differences in students' attitude towards posters – in each case a majority had liked the experience. It is notable that though many initially commented that it was childish to work on posters the students aged above 25 all strongly supported the use of posters.

Though students usually fear the group discussion after a presentation, the students who were asked stimulating questions confirmed that they enjoyed the poster presentation. This could be because of the informal atmosphere which boosted students' confidence. Kemp and Clark (1992:402) also note that the highlight of the poster presentation in their subject was *"meeting people from the class"* and *"interaction with others"*. This view is supported by Akister *et al.* (2000) who point out that the whole class benefits from the *"shared learning environment"*.

Review of the Findings from the Interviews

The comments offered by the interviewed students fully support the findings of the survey. Students saw it as a fun assignment and some felt it was easier than other assessments they do. One of the sentiments repeated was that it was less intimidating to speak one to one. They were also happy that non-presenting students actually listened to them and asked pertinent questions. Students also spoke about increased involvement in the preparation and research process. As Palomba and Banta (1999:71–72) write:

> *"Assessment must be seen as an activity done with and for students, rather than to them. Students need to be active partners in assessment.*

> *... If educators are thoughtful about how they include students in the assessment process, they can help overcome motivation problems that hinder assessment."*

The fact that students enjoyed and learned from the assessment shows that it motivated them. Posters enable students with different learning styles whether visual, auditory or kinesthetic to enjoy and work well on the assessments. This is confirmed by Walker's (2005:287) observation that students, while working on posters, *"seem to invest the work with a large amount of creative energy and individual flair often missing from assignment production"*.

Future Plans

Though the poster session I have reported in this chapter was successful in overcoming some of the drawbacks of oral presentations, there is scope to improve this form of assessment. Many changes can be made to the current format of poster assessment to improve the learning process for students. In future it would be beneficial to follow Farber and Penhale's (1995) idea of asking students to submit a one page summary of another group's poster. Dunstan and Bassinger (1997) gave out one page handouts to attendees which included summaries of the topics presented and a reference list. Poster sessions were also recorded on video for later viewing and for future students. Peer marking was used by practitioners, including Orsmond et al (2002), who also used student generated marking criteria.

Another method to increase student participation and interest would be to apply the demands that Mulnix and Penhale (1997) placed on their students. They asked groups presenting posters to append a question based on the contents; these were later used in the final examination in the course. Moradi and Townsend (2006) had a follow up assignment. This would be appropriate if the weightings for the assessment is high.

Conclusions

Poster presentations offer benefits both for students and teachers. I have found this form of assessment useful for gauging the level of preparation of the presenters and their understanding of the topics. It made it easier to grade students individually and also to give instant feedback; this would not have been possible in most other assessment formats. It took on average 10 minutes to assess a student according to the criteria provided and this suggests that this form of assessment would also be suitable for large classes.

Communication time increased greatly because presenters spoke to multiple visitors. Students who had a fear of facing the whole class had the opportunity to speak to individuals or small groups. As intended, the holistic development of the students was achieved to a large extent as students learned to greet and talk to strangers and to present themselves in a professional manner. Another major merit was that plagiarism could be minimised because students could not copy and paste chunks of digitised text.

In short, the whole class was engaged and class time was used beneficially.

About the Author

Swapna Koshy is an assistant professor at the University of Wollongong in Dubai. She can be contacted at this email: swapnaKoshy@uowdubai.ac.ae

Chapter Fourteen

"Be Original, but not too Original": Academic Voice, Text-matching and Concordancing Software

Michelle Picard and Cally Guerin

Introduction

"This is plagiarised!" That dreaded judgement, tantamount to academic death (Howard, 1995), continues to haunt academics and students despite repeated warnings, threats, explanations and teaching. If it really is so simple – you may not use other authors' work without appropriate citation – why, then, does it remain a problem? Clearly, it is more complex than simple definitions suggest, and we need to move beyond warnings and traditional transmission approaches to a teaching method that involves novice researchers becoming aware of and reflexive (Nygaard *et al.*, 2008:36) in relation to plagiarism. The following chapter provides details of a learning-centred teaching method we have developed with research students to offer a new approach to solving this dilemma and reducing instances of unintentional plagiarism. Like other chapters in this anthology, we offer a detailed description of the process we use in our practice with students.

Avoiding plagiarism and developing appropriate citation and academic voice, like all learning, engages students' identities at the deepest level. Indeed, authorial voice is closely linked to notions of authority.

Developing an academic voice includes a sense of being sufficiently competent in one's field and therefore confidently identifying oneself as a legitimate member of the community of practice who has something original, and thus the authority, to contribute to disciplinary debates. Postgraduate research students, in particular, are expected to develop a high level of autonomy and display originality, challenging norms and being innovative, yet remain obedient to the expectations of their supervisors and academic norms and conventions (Goodman, 2006:203). In short, they are expected to take on disciplinary identities and operate as full members of their various academic tribes and territories (Becher & Trowler, 2001). Not only must they learn the relevant knowledge, theories, models and arguments of their field, but they are also expected to apply them in analysing data and solving problems within the university and, eventually, in their professional lives (Nygaard *et al.*, 2008). While it is assumed these research students will meet the behavioural norms of their discipline, they are also required to develop a separate, distinct, original voice of their own.

Of course, it is reasonable that they are expected to develop high levels of autonomy, but we argue that *"thrusting"* autonomy upon these students can result in *"setbacks and perhaps greater dependence"* (Brown & Krager, 1985:406). Thus, we promulgate the development of competent autonomy (Gurr, 2001) through an explicit pedagogy that involves students in reflection (deep and careful thought about previous action) and reflexive (self-directed) thought and action in relation to academic voice, as well as all other aspects of academic practice. This pedagogy involves a learning-centred approach (Nygaard *et al.*, 2008) where reflective thinking (Chan *et al.*, 2002) and reflexive actions related to academic voice are scaffolded in order to achieve competently autonomous researchers

> *"who, independently of their supervisor, are cognisant of the norms, expectations and standards within their discipline and are able to assess their own plans and actions to ensure compliance with these"* (Gurr, 2001:85).

In this chapter we outline an innovative learning-centred process using text-matching software (or plagiarism-detection software (PDS)) in conjunction with concordancing tools (that is, text-searching software that highlights words in context to indicate the other language elements that surround the chosen word). Trials of this teaching practice with doctoral candidates have resulted in significant improvements in their ability to independently develop appropriate authorial voice in their academic writing.

Responses to the Development of Authorial Voice

In the academic sphere, despite notions of authorship reigning supreme, the line between transgressive and nontransgressive intertextuality (Chandrasoma *et al.*, 2004; Eira, 2005; Share, 2006; Moody, 2007) is often unclear and requires much more detailed unpacking. Academic writing is necessarily intertextual in that authors must situate their research in the context of what other researchers have done before. They must refer to the publications reporting that research and they must use the language of the discipline as it appears in those publications. And authors must do all of this in their own words. Further confusing the issue for today's students, contemporary communication technologies and digital-age attitudes towards information can easily result in uncertainty and indifference regarding the ownership of text (Flowerdew & Li, 2007; Gabriel, 2010).

Traditionally, the academic community has responded by actively detecting plagiarism and punishing those who commit this crime. Many universities still use the legalised language of penalty in their policies on plagiarism. The development and increasing use of different versions of PDS bear witness to the desire on the part of educational institutions to ensure that students do not succeed in what is perceived to be deliberate dishonesty.

However, recent years have witnessed a move towards a formative approach to plagiarism education which recognises that students do not always understand the complexities of how to use others' texts appropriately in their own writing. Transgressive intertextuality, as Chandrasoma *et al.* (2004) label it, is thus seen as a (perhaps necessary) stage in learning about the relationships between one's own text and that of other authors, and how other texts are appropriately used to support one's own writing. Many academics themselves – and academic developers in particular – recognise that the development of appropriate citation and referencing is a complex business; explicit instruction is necessary before most students develop a nuanced understanding of the conventions of citation and voice in academic writing (Howard, 1995; Pennycook, 1996; McGowan, 2008a, 2008b; Gilmore *et al.*, 2010).

Admittedly, there are clear cases of plagiarism, ranging from wholesale copying of another's work to *"patchwriting"* (stitching together various portions of texts, reorganising sentence structures and one-to-one substitution of synonyms) (Pecorari, 2003:317). Students' reasons for presenting such writing are varied and complex, but one significant underlying factor can be an inadequate sense of one's own voice as a legitimate participant in debates within a discipline. Our concern here is with the unintentional plagiarism that results in heartache for those students who are genuinely trying to produce appropriate, acceptable writing that engages in the debates of their discipline.

In order to appreciate just how complicated the rules of plagiarism really are, consider the paradoxical situation of research students who are caught between competing demands as they negotiate this treacherous territory. They are required to demonstrate their synchronicity with the literature of the field and use discipline-specific formats, yet are instructed to *"be original"*; they should use the language structures of their (sub)community, yet do so *"in their own words"* (Eira, 2005).

Stolley and Brizee (2010) outline the contradictory messages students receive:

- They must develop a topic based on what has already been done, yet write something new and original;
- They must rely on opinions of experts and authorities, yet improve upon and/or disagree with those opinions;
- They must give credit to researchers who came before them, yet make their own significant contribution;
- They must improve their english to fit into a discourse community, yet use their own words and their own voice.

...that is, they must be original, but not too original.

Students using English as an Additional Language (EAL) face particular challenges in unpacking the ambiguities surrounding acceptable recycling of language when they are still struggling to develop competency in the grammar and syntax of the target language. These research students require scaffolded learning activities in order for them to develop the competent autonomy to distinguish between appropriately using disciplinary language and engaging in unacceptable intertextuality (Eira, 2005). A scaffolded approach to learning tasks is particularly valuable in the context of language learning (Enomoto, this volume). The process we recommend in this chapter was developed from this range of previous responses towards plagiarism and developing academic voice.

Text-matching and Concordancing Software

Innovative uses of electronic technologies are central to moving university teaching practices beyond the traditional transmission mode. We can see this in the chapters by McGuigan and Rowley in this volume, which demonstrate how we can harness the strengths of these technologies to promote student learning and autonomy. Similarly, PDS has been established as a formative learning tool (Davis & Carroll, 2009; McCarthy & Rogerson, 2009) and has been used to great effect particularly in peer-assessed assignments where the students learn through scaffolded activities to advise each other and revise based on originality/text-matching reports (Ledwith & Risquez, 2008). These reports highlight the need for appropriate citation but also, through providing information on the provenance of material, open a dialogue with students on the quality of sources (Rowell, 2009). The dialogue or spoken one-on-one feedback can be used very effectively to encourage valuable reflection and learning, leading students to a clearer understanding of how to use sources.

The use of concordancing software to analyse academic corpora (bodies of writing) has proved successful as a teaching and learning strategy for academic language development. Large bodies of general academic literature such as the British National Corpus are useful for identifying and teaching academic vocabulary, collocations (words typically used together), and colligates (common grammatical/syntactical groupings), particularly for students with EAL. Student-generated corpora have also been used to identify common errors and to determine characteristics of disciplinary genres (Alsop, 2009). A more recent development has been the use of discipline-specific or topic-specific libraries of sample research articles in scaffolding the development of disciplinary language. Students are taught to develop and/or use these discipline-specific corpora along with online concordancers (text-searching tools) in order to uncover discipline-specific language structures for themselves (Cargill & Adams, 2005; Cheng, 2008; Conroy, 2010).

Our recent work has involved research students using text-matching software in combination with discipline-specific or topic-specific corpora. These students identify language that might potentially be too close to an individual source using PDS and then consider whether this language constitutes an acceptable recycling of discipline-specific language. Armed with such information, students are then in a position to make informed decisions about what constitutes plagiarism, exercising their own judgement in avoiding transgressive intertextuality. Thus, students can develop mastery over the boundaries of acceptable recycling of discipline-specific language.

Although the trials were conducted with research student participants who created their own topic-specific corpora of research articles based on their narrow areas of specialisation, it can be applied by other postgraduates, and even undergraduate students, if a disciplinary corpus is provided to the students by their lecturers/course coordinators. The lecturer/research supervisor facilitates knowledge construction (Cheng, 2008:25) by advising students on suitable texts for their topic-specific corpora and/or providing an appropriate corpus for a particular discipline, and then offers support in their exploration and independent construction of disciplinary knowledge of acceptable intertextuality and disciplinary language.

The Process

The process of using text-matching and discipline-specific corpora is carefully constructed to develop autonomous student learning and the reflective skills that such learning necessitates, thus promoting the deep learning that is advocated in other chapters in this volume (see, for example, Herbert & Leigh; Almeida & Teixeira-Dias; Elkington). Students are taken through the stages of a reflective thinking model (in line with that reported in Chan *et al.* 2002). First, the teacher/lecturer allows the student to complete a task according to their usual practice (habitual action). Next, the teacher/lecturer provides structured guidance to the student on how to categorise or unpack these habitual actions (thoughtful action). A guided reflection on the content of their work is then initiated, after which revisions to the product or changes in process are made. This is followed by a guided reflection on the process they have undergone (Chan *et al.*, 2002) and finally a critical reflection on their current state of knowledge.

This approach to developing authorial voice in research students involves two distinct stages of the process: the use of text-matching software and the use of copora and concordancing software. In the text-matching process, the students first complete their research text as per usual (habitual action), then run the text through Turnitin.com© and categorise the text matches. Turnitin is a licensed software program that uses a web crawler to search vast quantities of text online, including both published academic works and student papers. Individuals submit their writing to the process and a report is produced. It indicates the percentage of text that matches other material, highlighting strings of words and colour-code linking them to the relevant numbered source. Thus, there is clear visual evidence of the language that has potentially been plagiarised.

(1). The major end product of

n-6 pathway is arachidonic acid (AA); the major endproducts of the n-3 pathway are ecosanopentaenoic **acid (EPA) and docosapentaenoic acid** [4]

(DPA) (1). 3.1.2 n-3 LCPUFA The n-3 group that includes

docosahexaenoic acid (DHA, 22:6n-3), eicosapenatenoic **acid (EPA, 20:5n-3)** and docosapenatenoic **acid** [15]

(EPA, 20:5n-3) is called LCPUFA. n- 3 LCPUFA is rich in oily fish (ex; salmon, tuna, sardines and mackerel) and fish oil. 3.1.3 What actions do they have?

PUFA are the basic constituents of phospholipid membranes and determine cellular membrane fluidity and modulate enzyme activities, carriers and membrane receptors. They are also precursors of active metabolites known collectively as eicosanoids (prostaglandins, prostacyclins, thromboxanes and leukotrienes) which regulate cellular functions. Studies indicate that n-3 LCPUFA **have anti-inflammatory, antithrombotic, antiarrhythmic actions and immuno-modulating properties** [2]

[2].

The n- 3 LCPUFA metabolites induce eicosanoid production, alter gene expression, and modify lipid raft composition, altering T- cell signaling. [4]

Figure 1: A Sample Turnitin© Report Indicating Matched Text in Boxes and Numbers Linking that Text to the Relevant Source (bibliographic details of sources are listed separately in the report and hyperlinked).

Our students are asked to label each match according to the following categories:

too close	the text is too similar to the source and needs to be paraphrased or rewritten
not relevant	some other text has been highlighted, e.g., a formula or a bibliographic reference
discipline-specific phrase	this is the way that concept must be expressed in this context
unsure	anything else the student does not know how to categorise

Table 1: Text-matching Categories

While this is very instructive and students say that they find the concrete nature of such information enlightening, the report requires considerable interpretation. The text that is highlighted as matching that of other authors can include strings of words that are quite legitimately being recycled by students in the kind of nontransgressive intertextuality discussed earlier in this chapter.

In the second stage of the process, the students create their own discipline-/topic-specific corpus and use a concordance tool (for example, ConcApp© or AdTAT©) to explore any text match queries. ConcApp was originally developed as freeware by Chris Greaves at Hong Kong Polytechnic University, but has since become purchaseware; AdTAT©, by contrast, was developed at the University of Adelaide and can be downloaded free of charge (at at http://www.adelaide.edu.au/red/adtat/) along with detailed instructions for use.

When using either of these programs, students download the software and prepare a corpus (a body of works) to search. For research students, this corpus usually consists of the articles they have cited in their literature reviews. Individual articles need to be stripped of confounding information such as references and bibliographies and then uploaded into the concordancer as text-only files. Although this process can be time-consuming, it only has to be done once.

Students choose phrases highlighted as unoriginal in the Turnitin report that they suspect to be legitimately recycled from the field (that is, discipline-specific or standard academic expressions), which are then run through the concordancer.

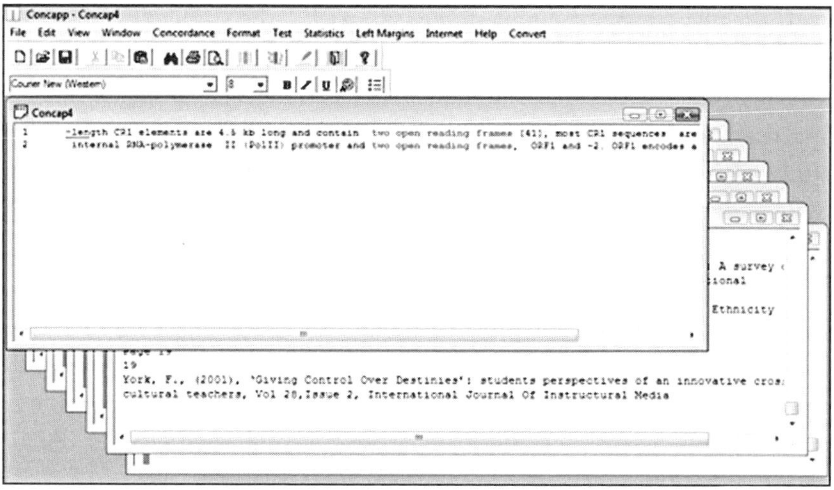

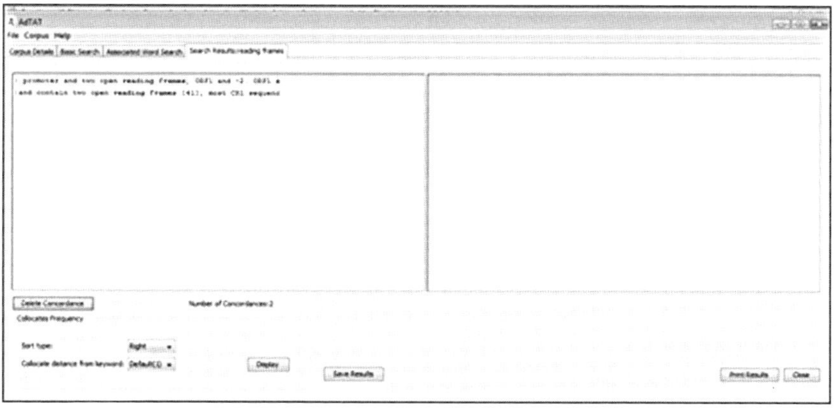

Figure 2: Sample ConcApp Report (full screen shot and enlarged text)

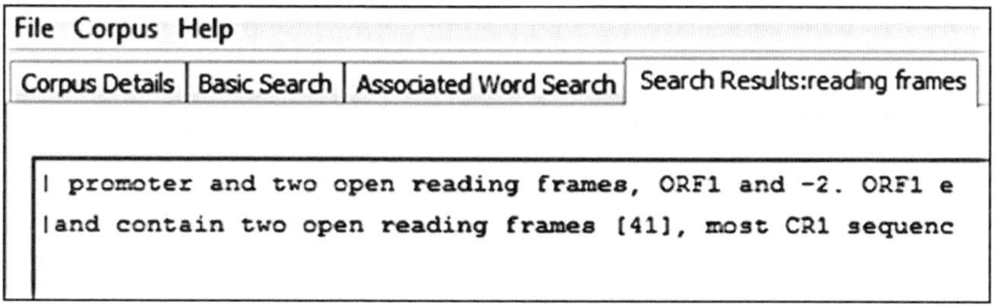

Figure 3: Sample AdTAT© Report (full screen shot and enlarged text)

If the phrase appears in a number of articles, the student can be reassured that this is indeed the language used by the discipline and therefore does not constitute plagiarism; that is, this recycling of language is entirely appropriate in the context. If the phrase appears in only one article, the student must consider whether this transgresses the rules of plagiarism (reflection on content).

After this, students revise their texts (thoughtful action), run them through the text-matching program again and finally reflect on their experiences (reflection on process) (Chan *et al.*, 2002). A further step back then allows for critical reflection on knowledge. After initial guidance through this process by the teacher/lecturer, research students can directly apply it systematically to their writing and are no longer reliant on instructors to check the originality of their texts.

Student Stories

There are three main issues facing EAL postgraduate writers that can be addressed by using the combination of text-matching and concordancing tools.

1. For those who are producing unidiomatic (that is, awkward, non-standard usage) and/or non-academic English, the concordancer is a valuable starting place, followed by text-matching to check for originality;

2. For those who are patchwriting with little understanding of referencing and citation conventions, text-matching followed by concordancing is a more instructive procedure;

3. For those who have a good grasp of both citation conventions and reasonably high-level English expression, text-matching followed by concordancing has proven to be valuable in refining their own authorial voice.

The following student stories explore each of these situations in turn and outline ways in which such students can use the relevant technology to develop their own authorial voices.

Hamda "Too original"

Like a significant number of international EAL students, Hamda began her doctoral studies with relatively poor English expression, multiple grammar issues and unidiomatic use of language. She used an online corpus and concordancer tool (in this case, the British National Corpus) to learn about collocations (especially prepositions) and to develop a sense of standard phrases in academic writing. When she ran her writing through a text-matching program, the report returned a 12% match to other texts. On further investigation, it became clear that only a few instances were in fact too close to the original academic text. In fact, many of the matches were with student writing that she had not read previously – indeed, they were texts to which she had no access, and on topics unrelated to her own area.

The matched phrases included strings such as "*It is important to note that*", "*Thus, it can be said that the use of*", "*although there are a number of studies*". There were also situations in which Hamda appeared to be using the "*sentence templates*" ("*sentence structures that could usefully be reused with different noun phrases inserted*" Cargill & O'Connor, 2006:210) that she had been taught or had developed herself from academic papers she was reading. For example, templates she had used included "*an important xxx in improving the yyy of zzz in the community*" and "*a positive correlation between xxx and yyy*". Thus, it could be argued that these matches indicate that Hamda has in fact learnt to use the language very appropriately.

A third category of matches included what we refer to as discipline-specific language. In Hamda's case, these included "*systematic random sampling technique*", "*to perform a given behaviour*" and "*carriage rate of multiple resistances*". Attempts to use one's own words in such situations would result in awkward, clumsy expression, suggesting that the author does not understand how such concepts are articulated in the disciplinary context. Instead, Hamda is clearly developing a voice in her writing that conforms to what is expected in her field that is neither plagiarised nor too original.

Weimin "Not original"

Weimin's first submission as a doctoral candidate employed very few references and no uniformity in bibliographic conventions. The writing sample included whole sentences and even paragraphs that were copied and pasted from primary sources. Clearly, this student had very little sense of his own voice in assessing and commenting on the literature in his discipline. He explained that he was in the habit of copying important chunks (sentences, paragraphs) from research articles into the chapters he is currently working on so that he can readily locate the relevant information. Unfortunately, this note-taking system is fraught with potential problems, not least that it is easy to forget precisely what has been copied verbatim unless some kind of coding system is rigorously employed. It is also markedly more difficult to synthesise the material when precise examples are within view.

In cases such as this, an even earlier first step can be introduced than we saw in Hamda's case, namely; that of training in the use of bibliographic software, such as EndNote©, to encourage consistency of presentation. This can be followed by instruction in how to organise writing by creating detailed dot-point plans. These can be built gradually, from a very broad outline of major categories/topics to more specific information to be included under those topics, down to plans for each paragraph of the chapter which are subsequently supported by citations.

Later drafts from a student in this situation included examples of phrases commonly used in general academic English (*"as the driving force behind"*, *"it is necessary to consider"*), as well as some that were more specific to his discipline (*"perceived behavioural control"*, *"market-oriented economic system"*). The student was able to check the high degree (23%) of text-matching in his article with a concordancer tool to confirm what constituted general usage or discipline-specific language, and understood that some of what remained was still unacceptable recycling of what he had copied and pasted into his document. For students in this situation, then, the combination of text-matching and concordancer tools can aid in the move towards taking ownership of the language and writing original material.

Liang Li "Refining authorial voice"

Many EAL doctoral candidates commence their studies with higher levels of English than those outlined in the previous case studies. They are at a significantly later stage of development and are working to refine their own authorial voice while simultaneously mobilising an appropriately high degree of intertextuality in the disciplinary language they employ. This is particularly the case for students researching in highly specialised areas that rely on very specific wording and jargon to describe their work.

Liang Li is a case in point. Only 7% of his own text was matched to other sources, and further inspection indicated that none of the findings constituted plagiarism. Again, several student papers appeared in the report none of which had been read by Liang Li and none of which were relevant to his topic. One example of text-matching was "*distance relay is installed*". When tested in his own topic-specific corpus of approximately 25 articles, this phrase failed to appear, and Liang Li reluctantly agreed that it would be possible to reword this phrase to avoid plagiarising. However, when put into a general Google search, many exact matches were returned, indicating that he was right to regard this as a standard phrase in his field. He had absorbed the expression along with the content in previous academic work in the area. For students in this position, the combination of text-matching and concordancing provides reassurance that they are citing the material appropriately and have developed an authorial voice that relies on nontransgressive intertextuality.

Discussion

The student stories outlined above explore common situations in which our process can aid development of authorial voice in academic writing. Each student represents a different developmental stage in the process of learning about appropriate, nontransgressive recycling of language. For Hamda, guided reflection utilising text-matching and concordancing tools enabled effective engagement with disciplinary language and norms. Such guided reflection for Weimin, in contrast, revealed the problematic nature of his note-taking system and initiated an awareness of appropriate use of sources. Liang Li, already operating at a higher level of academic language development than Hamda and Weimin, was able to critically reflect on his own writing and use the insights gained to refine his authorial voice in line with disciplinary conventions. In terms of Chan *et al.*'s (2002) reflective thinking model, we see how students can move from habitual action to thoughtful action, reflecting on their use of sources in order to develop an appropriate academic voice in their research writing. Thus, students can employ these electronic tools to become responsible for their own learning and understanding of the appropriate use of sources, no longer reliant on supervisors or lecturers to check their work for plagiarism.

Conclusion

Research students, particularly those with EAL, are required to negotiate the complex terrain around the demand to "be original, but not too original". The process outlined in this chapter combines existing technologies to aid these students in their reflection and practice as they learn the boundaries between acceptable intertextuality and plagiarism. With initial guided reflection facilitated by supervisors or lecturers, our process provides these students with an independent means of developing their own awareness of plagiarism. As students move towards autonomous research, they need tools which enable them to take responsibility for their own academic integrity, to make informed decisions about the level of originality in their writing, and hence to develop their own academic voice.

Our use of this process with EAL research students has resulted in an enhanced understanding of what constitutes plagiarism, and we have observed improved language outcomes in successive drafts of research documents. The initial implementation of this innovative combination of learning technologies indicates that it has improved students' awareness of acceptable intertextuality. Most importantly, they were able to critically *"review [their] suppositions of subject discipline and existing knowledge"* (Chan *et al.*, 2002:511) and move beyond passive acceptance of transmitted knowledge towards actively developing an autonomous voice in line with discipline expectations.

About the Authors

Michelle Picard is Director of the Researcher Education and Development Unit at the University of Adelaide, Australia. She can be contacted at this email: michelle.picard@adelaide.edu.au

Cally Guerin is a Lecturer in the Researcher Education and Development Unit at the University of Adelaide, Australia. She can be contacted at this email: cally.guerin@adelaide.edu.au

Chapter Fifteen

Communal Roleplay: Using Drama to Improve Supervision

Katarina Winka and Tomas Grysell

Introduction

The central theme of this chapter is interactive teaching methods in higher education. In particular, our examples and discussion will focus on how to implement drama as an innovative practice in order to move beyond transmission as a form of teaching in Higher Education. We will describe the drama forms "Roleplay" and "Forum Play" and a new method we have derived from these: "Communal Roleplay". The differences and similarities between them will be explained later in this chapter.

Training of postgraduate supervisors is mandatory in Sweden. This group of participants has a tendency to solve fictional supervision cases quickly by dismissing the problems or recommending instrumental solutions. We have successfully used drama in these pedagogical contexts. The purpose has been to invite the participants to actively contribute to the learning climate. By allowing different backgrounds, experiences and emotions to enrich the plays, the participants are more likely to engage actively in the learning situation.

Drama has been used in pedagogical contexts in many different forms (Boal, 1992; Byréus, 2001). According to O'Toole (2002) and Jacobsen *et al.* (2006) the main benefit of interactive teaching methods, such as drama, is increased motivation and engagement in the students. It also gives an opportunity to develop transferable competencies which are otherwise hard to obtain in more traditional higher education curricula. Biggs (1987, 2003) correlates the level of engagement of the students and the classroom climate with enhanced learning. An encouraging and secure learning environment might be even more important when non-traditional interactive teaching methods are used. According to Kolb (1984:41) the students' own experiences are also important in the learning process:

> *"Learning is the process whereby knowledge is created through the transformation of experience. Knowledge results from the combination of grasping and transforming experience".*

We have extensive experience from postgraduate supervision programs in Sweden, where training of supervisors is mandatory. The supervisors will henceforth be referred to as students, since they are participating in the pedagogical activities in a student role. Despite their higher academic ranks and extensive experience from the academic teaching and learning environment, our experience is that they respond to the pedagogical situations in much the same way as undergraduates. For instance, they adopt an instrumental approach to reading literature and performing tasks within a course. As a result, the concept of surface and deep approaches to learning introduced by Marton and Säljö (1976) is applicable also when addressing the learning processes of supervisors.

Most postgraduate supervision programs use a variety of teaching methods to address different topics and to train different skills in the students, but drama has not been implemented until recently. Our motivation to introduce these methods stems from repeated attempts to increase the students' preparedness for handling problematic supervision situations. This is one of the core learning objectives of the program at Umeå University in Sweden, and also something the students have explicitly requested.

The innovative aspect of our approach to classroom teaching is to create the opportunity to engage large groups of non-traditional students in high quality learning by integrating the different backgrounds and experiences of the students into the activities. The challenges we will address here are how to create a fruitful and safe learning climate and how to encourage as many students as possible to engage actively and deeply in the learning activities.

Learning-centred Supervision

Research training has traditionally been regarded as an apprenticeship (Walker *et al.*, 2008). The focus of the training, and supervision, was on how to ask good research questions, formulate an effective and feasible research plan, build on the work of others and communicate the results in relevant ways (Walker *et al.*, 2008; Grant & Graham, 1999). As an apprentice the research student learned these skills while observing a master – in this case an experienced researcher conducting research – and then following in a similar path. When the skills were mastered, the student was ready to defend the thesis. The only requirement on the supervisor was that he or she was an active researcher.

The learning processes of research students were put under the spotlight about two decades ago, due to an increased demand for both efficiency and quality in research education (Appel & Bergenheim, 2005). As a result of this, the supervision process and the pedagogical skills of the supervisors have been addressed in various ways (Nygaard *et al.*, 2011). In the introduction of an anthology of experienced postgraduate supervisors' advice to PhD students, Bergenheim and Ågren (2008) outlined this changed view of research supervision in a learning-centred curriculum:

> *"Today, doctoral supervision in not necessarily considered to be something directly related to competency in a particular discipline. Good supervision requires a great amount of knowledge and reflection on behalf of the individual supervisors. Supervisors also need to be given opportunities to reflect on their roles and tasks."* (translated from Bergenheim & Ågren, 2008:19)

Pearson and Brew (2002) outlined a flexible professional development programme of supervisors and corresponding programmes have been described by Appel and Bergenheim (2005) and Lee (2007). In essence, the issue is to make the supervisors aware of research supervision as a pedagogical activity and acknowledge their own role as a teacher (Taylor, 2008; Whisker, 2005). Most academic institutions agree that a central goal of postgraduate supervision is to train autonomous scholars (Golde & Walker, 2006). For the supervisors, this requires skills in working professionally with a diverse range of individuals (Johnson *et al.*, 2000). Dealing with problematic situations, or delivering critical comments on the graduate student's work, are also important tasks of the professional supervisor (Handal & Lauvås, 2006; Lia & Sealeband, 2007). These generic skills are the key to successful supervision.

So an important question is: how can these skills be enhanced and developed in a learning-centred program for supervisors? A traditional classroom teaching approach might involve reading about conflicts in supervision, discussing the literature, or perhaps listening to an expert talking about conflict management. The situation is managed by the teacher in the classroom and can result in passive students. In a more student-centred learning environment some discussions about the student's own experiences would probably be included too. Our innovative approach to moving beyond transmission is influenced by collaborative learning theory (Bruffee, 1993). It involves the use of drama to enhance student activity, to incorporate their previous experiences and varying backgrounds, and to engage all students in hands-on exercises with near-authentic supervision conflicts. These situations are administered by the teacher, but driven by the students' engagement in the exercises and shaped by their background knowledge and experiences. These conditions match the prerequisites for deep learning as described by Biggs (2003).

Forum Theatre, Forum Play and Communal Roleplay

Our work with drama methods is inspired by Augusto Boal's work with the Arena Theatre in Saõ Paulo, Brazil. During the years 1956–1971, Boal was putting on plays about the Latin American people's fight for survival and against injustice. He called this the Theatre of the Oppressed. The theatre went out to public places, often into poor areas, and acted out scenes where the audience helped the actors to reproduce their life as authentically as possible. On one occasion someone in the audience was not satisfied with the actors' performances and interrupted the play several times. Boal became annoyed with the person and asked her to step into the play – and so the method of Forum Theatre was born (Boal, 1992, 2000). Forum Theatre is a theatrical game where the illustrated conflicts are always symptoms of oppression, and it could be described as a system of different exercises, games and improvisation techniques:

> *"The Theatre of the Oppressed is a system of physical exercises, aesthetic games, image techniques and special improvisations whose goal is to safeguard, develop and reshape this human vocation, by turning the practice of theatre into an effective tool for the comprehension of social and personal problems and the search for their solutions".* (Boal, 2008:14–15).

The actors in a Forum Theatre start from an original play, but each time someone from the audience steps in – so-called "spect-actors" (an active spectator in contrast to the normally passive role of audience members) – the actors improvise a new situation based on the spect-actors' actions. The audience is invited to suggest and enact solutions. Boal means that the method itself, in addition to the theatrical dimension, has three main branches: a social, an educational and a therapeutic branch (Boal, 2008).

In Sweden the term Forum Play is more often used than Forum Theatre. The focus in a Forum Play is on the educational branch, where theatre techniques are used for analyzing, questioning, discussing and acting out sensitive topics. These could include gender equality, harassment, different types of abuse and general ethical dilemmas (Byréus, 2001). The differences between the two methods are outlined in Table 1.

The new method we have developed, Communal Roleplay, originated from a situation where a Forum Play was planned. Due to a misunderstanding with the organisers the group we faced was bigger and more heterogeneous than expected and this made us modify the layout of the activity there and then. Due to the similarities of these two methods we will first describe the organisation of a Forum Play activity before we come to the Communal Roleplay.

A Forum Play activity consists of four specific parts: warm-up (often attitude exercises), information (about the method and the topic of the play), the actual play and, finally, check-out exercises. The process is led by a person called the "Joker" whose function is to ensure the smooth running of the game and teach the audience, in our case the supervisors, the rules. These rules are explained further below. As an introduction to the entire activity, the Joker begins with some type of warm-up exercise. Because the play is often built on different kinds of attitudes, so-called attitude exercises are useful when preparing the students (Boal, 1992; Byréus, 2001).

Characteristic	Roleplay	Forum Theatre	Forum Play	Communal Roleplay
Oppressor	Sometimes present	Always present	Often present (called antagonist)	Oppression created by the situation
Oppressed	Sometimes present	Always present	Often present (called oppressed)	Often present
Freedom in role interpretation	Small	Large	Large	Large
Level of involvement	Passive spectators	More or less active spectators	More or less active spectators	Large – all are involved in the play
Significance of the Joker	No Joker needed	Large	Large	Small
Appropriate group size	10 – 30 persons	10 and up	10–30 persons	20–80 persons
Preparations	Produce detailed role descriptions	Create framework, practice with the actors	Create framework, practice with the ensemble or a group of participants	Create framework, and simple role descriptions
Time required	Very variable	15–60 minutes	15–60 minutes	45–90 minutes
Number of roles	2–more	At least 3–4	At least 3–4	3–4

Characteristic	Roleplay	Forum Theatre	Forum Play	Communal Roleplay
The audiences' knowledge of the roles and the scenario	Passive audience, sometimes with knowledge of the roles but with no chance to intervene	The audience can choose to engage themselves or not	The audience can choose to engage themselves or not	The audience is knowledgeable of the roles and the scenario, all actors have role-partners in the audience
Included parts	Play	Information Play	Warm-up Information Play Check-out	Warm-up Play Check-out
Joker in the play	No Joker needed	Can participate in the play	Can participate in the play	Should not participate in the play
Organisation of the activity	The scenario is played once according to the role descriptions, little possibility for improvisation	The scenario can be played several times, according to suggestions from the audience, large possibility for improvisation	The scenario can be played several times, according to suggestions from the audience, large possibility for improvisation	The scenario is played once according to the role interpretations of the participants, time-out gives possibility for improvisation

Table 1: Comparison of the Different Drama Methods Described in this Chapter. Translated from Grysell and Winka (2010).

It is our experience that it is important to let everybody in the room have an opportunity to say something and to be physically involved in the warm-up exercises. Then it is easier to get the students to act as spect-actors in the play. We have used different games, exercises and narrative methods (see Grysell & Winka, 2010; Boal, 2008) to create a good atmosphere in the room. Here is an example of a warm-up exercise based on the participants' attitudes: the Joker prepares a number of provocative statements related to the topic addressed later in the play. The room is organised so that the students are standing in two rows facing each other so that everyone has someone to talk to. Now the Joker calls out a statement, such as: "*it is easier to supervise male research students*", and the pairs are encouraged to discuss whether they agree or disagree with the statement. After a short while the Joker stops the conversations and asks for one or two comments from the group. Then the students in one row take a step to the right to face a new person. The exercise continues with new statements and continued discussions with new partners.

After the warm-up exercises the Joker informs the participants about the method, the theme or topic in focus, the scope of the activity and the process. Thereafter comes the play itself, or plays, depending on the time allocated.

There are a number of different techniques to let the students understand more about who the characters in the play are, and what lies behind their actions and words. For example, when someone in the audience calls out "*Stop and think*", the actors should stop the play and express their current thoughts while still in their role. The command "*Double*" means that someone from the audience can enter the play as the thought of one of the characters. If the Joker puts his or her arms like a ring over the head of an actor, this illustrates a "thought-bubble" and the audience has the opportunity to express what they think that special character is thinking about. All sessions end with a check-out exercise to put the students in a relaxed mode after the often intense engagement in the Forum Play. One such technique is called "hearing". The audience can pose questions to the actors while they still remain in their roles. In this way the enacted situation can become even more complex, or realistic, as the thoughts and objectives of each character become apparent.

The Joker

The leader of a forum activity is not really equivalent to a teacher or an instructor; the leader should rather act as a "difficultator" (in the terms of Boal) than as a facilitator (Boal, 2008). The leader in a Forum Theatre and Forum Play is termed Joker (but do not confuse this with Batman's enemy or associate it with the idea of playing jokes). A Joker is the most complex figure in an ordinary deck of cards. He is black and red, and represents all suits at the same time. A Joker is a colourful figure and this is also the role of the Joker in a forum activity: to float between the performers and the audience just as he floats between the suits in a deck of cards. A Joker has the function to grasp and reinforce the complexity of a situation, and to undermine simplified conclusions or judgments from the performers and the audience (Boal, 2008). He or she is, depending on the different contents and contexts, sometimes a trainer, a coach, director, referee, workshop leader, performer, "edutainer" and a person who encourages the ideas of an audience to be expressed in theatrical form. He or she has the task to lure the audience, a group of students, into acting, questioning and analyzing their preconceptions and conditions within the framework of the forum activity (Boal, 1992).

Table 1 shows that in some forum activities the Joker role is very prominent. However, in a Communal Roleplay the Joker is more like a process leader and should not participate in or influence the play. The focus is instead on questioning and analyzing the situation to help the students understand and reflect on the topic in focus.

Communal Roleplay – Layout and Pedagogical Principles

Communal Roleplay mainly follows the organisation of a Forum Play, but with more elements of traditional roleplay. For example, the play is prepared with a framework and often with a simple role description. The main difference between Forum Play and Communal Roleplay is that the latter method becomes a collective activity since all students in the room are involved, both in creating the roles and acting out the case (Table 1).

After an initial warm-up exercise the students are divided into the same number of groups as there are roles in the play. Our recommendation is to use three or four roles to create a sufficiently complex situation in the play. The groups have less than 30 minutes initially to read the materials for their respective role: a description of the scenario, the role itself and the role's relationship to the problems in the scenario (Figure 1). In addition, there is a suggestion regarding the desirable outcome of the meeting with the other roles. This material has been prepared in advance by the Joker. If there is too little information in the material the students are encouraged to make their own assumptions. This means that the final solution of the roleplay is rarely evident and can take any direction depending on the students' background, experiences, emotions and attitudes. All of the involved roles have an honest intent with their actions so there are no obvious scapegoats that provide a simple solution for the problem. Each group also needs to agree on a representative who will begin acting in the play.

When the different roles meet, the intentions of the other characters become apparent. Therefore the initial strategies formed by the groups may not hold for long. Anyone is allowed to stop the play by calling for a five minute time-out. During this short break the groups reconvene to sharpen their arguments or change their strategies before the play proceeds. The groups may substitute their actor if they wish to. It is also possible to use the Forum Play techniques "Stop and think" and "Double". The play is led by the Joker and continues until the groups are satisfied with the outcome.

Role 1: Supervisor

One of your doctoral students is very dependent on you and requires much more of your attention than the other students do. He/she hands in half-done manuscripts for you to look at, as soon as possible. You have indicated that you don't have time for this, but nothing has changed. Your other doctoral students are much less demanding and you don't have to spend as much time supervising them.

In your opinion, you are really trying to be a good supervisor, but there must be a limit on how much time you should devote to the students. You travel a lot in your work, and when you are at the department this student occupies most of your time. Sometimes he/she calls you at home at weekends, not to mention all the emails you receive from him/her. The student is never pleased and you know he/she complains to the others. You are getting tired of this. The student has asked for a meeting and you are convinced it will be full of complaints.

You want the student to work more independently, and to feel more responsible for the project.

Role 2: Doctoral student

You are not getting the help from you supervisor that you need. He/she travels a lot and you think he/she is rarely available. Even your emails are replied only sporadically. Sometimes you have had to call him/her at home because it was impossible to meet up at work.

The supervisor has many doctoral students but you feel you have lowest priority. From what you can see, the supervisor interacts much more frequently with the others. When you leave a manuscript to the supervisor it takes too long to get it back with comments, sometimes it takes weeks! But, when you do get comments they are very good and helpful. Your supervisor is a well-known researcher, and you have great respect for him/her. Now you have built up the courage to ask for a meeting.

You want the supervisor to devote more time to you, and to be available more often.

Figure 1: A Scenario with Two Role Descriptions in a Communal Roleplay

In a Communal Roleplay the students are encouraged to adapt the scenario to their own background and experiences. A framework or a case for Communal Roleplay should be quite simple so that the group of students can interpret and create a scene from their own viewpoint and understanding. There are several opportunities for reflection about the theme in focus, both through the discussions before the play and in the discussions that take place during time-outs. The actors do not need to feel abandoned because each student is a representative for a group where they have discussed their way through the situation, how to interact, and the potential strategies to reach their objectives. Rather, the actors become a communication link between the group and the enacted scenario.

The activities can be described as both teacher-driven and student-driven. As an organiser of a Communal Roleplay, the Joker has the opportunity to prepare a scenario, a framework, involving a theme or situation to put in focus. Sometimes careful investigation is necessary to be able to create cases that are as authentic as possible. The students will then turn the roleplay into their own by discussing the scenario and the conditions of the role from their own perspectives. They can use their own experiences and knowledge to produce new content or reproduce a previous situation. The framework for the roleplay functions as a map for the situation without too much steering of the students' actions. This setup creates excellent conditions for a concluding meta-discussion regarding the theme, the course of events, and the outcomes, because by then there is a basis of more or less common knowledge and experience within the group.

The key pedagogical principle behind Communal Roleplay is social constructivism, which focuses on an individual's learning that takes place through interactions in a group in a collective learning environment (Vygotsky, 1978; Dobozy, this volume). However, although organising students into groups may increase their potential for discussions, it does not mean they will automatically discuss or learn collaboratively. What also is needed is a shared knowledge base, a sense of relevance and a safe learning environment (Ramsden, 2003). These criteria are all met by the Communal Roleplay method.

The outcome of a Communal Roleplay depends on what a group of people believes at a particular moment. The outcome could be completely different with another group of people, even if they were using the same simple role descriptions. These variations come from the students' backgrounds, experiences, emotions, attitudes *et cetera*, and are also characteristic of the other forum activities (Boal, 2008). The wide range of applications is one of the strengths of using forum activities. Communal Roleplay is also influenced by Paulo Freire's dialogic philosophy of education (Freire, 2002). Instead of the performance turning into an individual activity, which is often the case in a roleplay or sometimes in a Forum Play, a Communal Roleplay is always a collective activity.

Many traditional pedagogical methods give us an opportunity to discuss and reflect on complex subjects and areas, such as gender issues, power relationships and cultural differences. Most of them also allow us to hide ourselves behind political or social correctness. Often we know what we are allowed to say in a specific situation, for example concerning gender equality, and how we are expected to answer. However, to promote deep learning and to develop both knowledge and skills we need to be connected to our inner thoughts and feelings, and understand the complexity of the problems. Because of the interactions in the activities, Communal Roleplay is a method where everyone participates with their rational thinking as well as their feelings and emotions. You can actually say that the students are using their whole body and soul for learning and understanding. In this innovative and interactive pedagogical method, based on collaborative and active learning, the students are allowed to express and explore opinions that might be perceived as politically incorrect (Boal, 2008).

Empirical Evidence from Students

The most common reactions among the students after a Forum Play or a Communal Roleplay are that the scenarios feel authentic and that the activity was a very useful exercise. We would like to illustrate this statement with two examples. Both courses in these examples had similar learning objectives, namely; to gain insight in the different roles of students and supervisors, to gain knowledge about supervision as a process and its different phases as well as awareness of the role of ethnicity and gender, experience of communication as a tool for supervision, and practical skills in how to handle conflicts and problems that can arise in a supervision situation.

In the autumn of 2010 Tomas Grysell organised a course for 23 students (16 female and 7 male supervisors). They were from different research areas and had varying experiences as supervisors. One of the themes in focus during the second day of the course was cultural diversity and handling of conflicts. A Communal Roleplay was used with a scenario around a research student who got little guidance and attention from his supervisors ... and the time of the *viva* was approaching.

Everyone in the room was deeply involved and enthusiastic about discussing the case and acting in the play. There were a lot of time-outs and the scenario developed in several directions. During the time- outs the students started to reflect on why the supervisors in the scenario never asked the research student about his social life and his situation at the department. All the questions raised early on were about the progress and the quality of the research student's work. It later became quite clear that the student had a complex situation with his family life, a new baby was coming soon, and he was not feeling comfortable at the department because his background was different from most of the others in the department.

In the course evaluation, 87 % of the students (20 of 23) agreed that this approach had given them important and new thoughts regarding their own behaviour in similar situations. These were some of the comments from the course evaluation:

> *"Communal roleplay is a good way to start discussions about topics that are normally difficult to speak about, more of that in a future course!" (Man).*

> *"One of the most exiting pedagogical methods in the course was the Communal Roleplay. It gave us a great opportunity to act and reflect over sensitive matters." (Woman).*

> *"We should work more with case and forum activities because it lets us meet around subjects and topics without being so politically correct – it gave us a mentally pedagogical 'mindset'."* (Woman).

In the spring of 2009, Katarina Winka organised an international course for 29 students from 10 countries (12 female and 17 male supervisors). When planning the course, extra care was taken when preparing the scenarios for a Communal Roleplay. The intention was to make the situations general, yet complex, so they would be experienced as relevant within an internationally heterogeneous group.

One afternoon was devoted to Communal Roleplay under the theme "Conflicts and problems – identifying problems and finding solutions". The scenario centred on a research student who had failed to follow the individual study plan, and included the student, supervisor, co-supervisor and head of department who each had their own ways of handling the situation. The groups needed extra time when preparing their strategies since their backgrounds were quite diverse. But when the roleplay started, the actors and their respective groups quickly became involved in the activity and found new ways to address the situation. Afterwards, the students in groups were asked to write down "what are you taking with you from this afternoon?" The replies varied from insights and ideas that were new to them as well as comments on the pedagogical method. The following four excerpts from the course evaluation typify these points.

> *"Roleplay! Excellent way to visualise and make us reflect on real situations."*

"This was a most interesting exposure to a practical situation – it is good to explore possible situations that can arise to cause conflicts."

"The session creates a sense of awareness that research training and supervision is not a conflict-free process."

"The role play was an excellent and dynamic activity, taking roles is always a good method for learning and facilitate reflection."

Although the method has strong support from the majority of our students, the Communal Roleplay approach does not suit everyone. The contrast to some strict academic traditions can be too great and yield reactions such as:

"I found some of the teaching formats difficult to relate to; for example roleplay".

Individual differences, such as learning styles, may also influence the level of engagement in the activities (Almeida & Teixeira-Dias, this volume).

Remarks on the Method's Applicability

There are several pedagogical gains with Communal Roleplay both on an individual level as well as on the group level. It is a collective activity that builds on the students' engagement, knowledge and skills and their will to share these. As Biggs (2003) points out, a high level of involvement has a positive effect on our learning processes.

The flexible and adaptable methodology of Communal Roleplay is highly suitable for complex problems and heterogeneous groups, with students from different subject backgrounds or academic positions. The students develop together and adapt the play according to their own experiences of hierarchies and relationships to create a common knowledge base (O'Toole, 2002; Jacobsen *et al.*, 2006; Ramsden, 2003). The method has been shown to work in different pedagogical contexts and with students from very different backgrounds, even in very heterogeneous international groups.

Some attention has been given to the problems surrounding development of generic skills, or transferable competencies, in higher education (Drummond *et al.*, 1998; Enomoto, this volume). Traditional higher education curricula may not promote skills for dealing with obstacles and crises, identifying and managing ethical issues, delegating responsibility, motivating others, and some of the other skills we have described in our learning objectives. When the students are engaged in forum activities the scope of the possible learning outcomes becomes wider (Byréus, 2001). Achievement of reflective skills or very practical skills may require hands-on exercises and in-depth discussions (Biggs, 2003). Our hope is that this approach will lead our students to be more innovative and to adopt a more scholarly approach to their supervisory practice.

Forum Play can enhance the understanding of experiences from work practice placements for students in teacher education (Byréus, 2001). They can use the method to understand and analyse problems they have experienced during work practice in public schools when they are back in their own educational setting. If Communal Roleplay were to be used instead the students could themselves create frameworks for the plays, based on their experiences in primary school. These could then be used to illustrate different situations and everyone could contribute to the understanding and solution of the problems. This would create a collaborative situation where the students share important knowledge and skills for the future workplace and at the same time guide each other to ways of understanding, reflecting and solving difficult problems (Marton *et al.*, 2005).

Conclusion

We believe that most education programs could use these methods to help the students to understand better the academic environment, the future career paths available to them, and to increase their professionalism. The exercises could be prepared by allowing the students to read relevant literature or visit new environments in advance.

Our student groups have mainly consisted of postgraduate supervisors, but the method can also be used with other groups. Actually, supervisors have a reputation for being especially reluctant to participate in pedagogical training (Appel & Bergenheim, 2005; Handal & Lauvås,

2006). So, if it works with supervisors it is likely to work in other student groups as well.

About the Authors

Katarina Winka is a senior lecturer at the Centre for Teaching and Learning, Umeå University, Sweden. She can be contacted at this email: katarina.winka@upc.umu.se

Tomas Grysell is a guest lecturer at the Division for Development of Teaching and Learning, Uppsala University, Sweden. He can be contacted at this email: tomas.grysell@uadm.uu.se

Collected Bibliography

Abhayawansa, S. & L. Fonseca (2010). Conceptions of learning and approaches to learning – a phenomenographic study of a group of overseas accounting students from Sri Lanka. *Accounting Education*, Vol. 19, No. 5, pp. 527–550.

Abraham, R.R., P. Vinod, M.G. Kamath, K. Asha & K. Ramnarayan (2008). Learning approaches of undergraduate medical students to physiology in a non-PBL- and partially PBL-oriented curriculum. *Advances in Physiology Education*, Vol. 32, pp. 35–37.

Abrandt Dahlgren, M., A. Reid, L. Dahlgren & P. Petocz (2008). Learning for the professions: lessons from linking international research projects. *Higher Education*, 56(2), pp 129–148.

Abt, C. (1968). Games for Learning. In Boocock, S. & E. Schild (Eds.). *Simulation Games in Learning*. Beverly Hills, U.S.A.: Sage Publications, pp. 65–84.

Ackoff, R. (1974). *Redesigning the future: A systems approach to societal problems*. New York: John Wiley & Sons.

ACO (2005). *Careers by Country*. www.eui.eu/ProgrammesAnd Fellowships/AcademicCareersObservatory/AcademicCareersbyCountry/Finland.aspx [Accessed 12 December 2010].

Acs, Z.J. & L. Szerb (2007). Entrepreneurship, Economic Growth and Public Policy. *Small Business Economics*, 28, pp 109–122.

Adams, D. (1973). *Simulation Games: An Approach to Learning.* Worthington, U.S.A.: Charles A. Jones Publishing.

Adamy, P. & N. Milman (2009). *Evaluating Electronic Portfolios in Teacher Education.* Charlotte, NC: Information Age Publishing.

Aghion, P., M. Dewatripont, C. Hoxby, A. Mas-Colell & A. Sapir (2008). *Higher aspirations: An agenda for reforming European universities.* Brussels, Belgium: Bruegel. http://www.econ.upf.edu/~mcolell/research/Bruegel%20blue.pdf [Accessed 1 May 2011].

Akcil, U. & I. Arap (2009). The opinions of education faculty students on learning processes involving e-portfolios. *Procedia Social and Behavioral Sciences.* No 1, pp. 395–400.

Åkerlind, G. (2005). Variation and commonality in phenomenographic research methods. *Higher Education Research & Development,* Vol. 24, No. 4, pp. 321–334.

Akister, J., A. Bannon & H. Mullender-Lock (2000). Poster Presentations in Social Work Education Assessment: a Case Study, *Innovations in Education and Training International,* Vol.37, No:3. Available at http://www.tandf.co.uk/journals [Accessed on 12 June 2010].

Almeida, P. A. (2010). Scholarship of teaching and learning: an overview. *Journal of the World Universities Forum,* Vol. 3, pp. 143–154.

Alsop, S. (2009). Issues in the development of the British Academic Written English (BAWE) corpus. *Corpora,* Vol. 4, No. 1, pp. 71–83.

Anderson, C. & D. Hounsell (2007). Knowledge practices: 'doing the subject' in undergraduate courses. *The Curriculum Journal,* Vol. 18, pp. 463–478.

Anderson, L.W., D.R. Krathwohl & B.S. Bloom (2002). *A taxonomy for learning, teaching, and assessing: a revision of Bloom's taxonomy of Educational Objectives.* New York: Longman.

Antonovsky, A. (1987). *Unravelling the mystery of health: how people manage stress and stay well.* San Francisco, CA: Jossey-Bass.

Appel, M. & Å. Bergenheim (2005). *Reflekterande forskarhandledning. [Approaches to postgraduate supervision]* Lund: Studentlitteratur.

Aragno, A. (2009). Meaning's vessel: A metaphoric understanding of metaphor. *Psychoanalytic Inquiry,* Vol. 29, No. 1, pp. 30–47.

Argyris, C. & D. Schön (1974). *Theory in Practice.* San Francisco: Jossey-Bass.

Arkoudis, S., L. Hawthorne, C. Baik, G. Howthorne, K. O'Loughlin & E. Bexter (2009). The impact of English language proficiency and workplace readiness on the employment outcomes of tertiary international students. Melbourne, VIC: Centre for the Study of Higher Education, the University of Melbourne. http://www.aei.gov.au/AEI/PublicationsAndResearch/Publications/ELP_Full_Report_pdf.pdf [Accessed 27 April 2011].

Asselin, M. E. (2003) Insider research: issues to consider when doing qualitative research in your own setting. *Journal for nurses in staff development*, Vol. 19, No.2, pp. 99–103.

Australian ePortfolio Project (AeP.2) (2010). Researching ePortfolios in education, employment and community. http://www.eportfoliopractice.qut.edu.au [Accessed 21 February, 2011].

Baeten, M., F. Dochy & K. Struyven (2008). Students' approaches to learning and assessment preferences in a portfolio-based learning environment. *Instructional Science*, Vol. 36, pp. 359–374.

Bailey, J. (2000). Students as clients in a professional/client relationship. *Journal of Management Education*, Vol. 24, No. 3, pp. 353–365.

Ball, S. (1995). Enriching student learning through innovative real-life exercises, *Education + Training*, Vol. 37: 4, pp.18–25.

Bandura, A. (1971). *Social Learning Theory*. New York: General Learning Press.

Bandura, A. (1997). *Self-efficacy: the exercise of control*. New York: W.H. Freeman.

Barbian, J. (2001). Get Simulated. *Training*, Vol. 38, No. 2 (February), pp. 66–70.

Barnett, R. (2000). *Realising the University in an age of supercomplexity*. Buckingham: The Society for Research into Higher Education and Open University Press.

Barnett, R. (2004). Learning for an unknown future. *Higher Education Research and Development*, Vol. 23, No. 3, pp. 247–260.

Barnett, R. (2007). *A Will to Learn: Being a Student in an Age of Uncertainty*. Berkshire: Open University Press and Society for Research into Higher Education.

Barton, R. (1970). *A Primer on Simulation Gaming*. Englewood Cliffs, U.S.A.: Prentice-Hall.

Beale, R. & C. Creed (2009). Affective interaction: how emotional agents affect users. *International Journal of Human-Computer Studies*, Vol. 67, No. 9, pp. 755–776.

Becher, T. & P. R. Trowler (2001). *Academic Tribes and Territories*. (2nd edition) Buckingham: The Society for Research into Higher Education & Open University Press.

Bennett, S., K. Maton & L. Kervin (2008). The 'digital natives' debate: a critical review of the evidence. *British Journal of Educational Technology*, Vol 39, No 5, pp. 775–786

Bergenheim, Å. & K. Ågren (Eds.) (2008). *Forskarhandledares robusta råd. [Robust advice on postgraduate supervision]* Lund: Studentlitteratur.

Biggs, J. & C. Tang (2007). *Teaching for Quality Learning at University* (3rd edition). Maidenhead: McGraw Hill.

Biggs, J. (1978). Individual and group differences in study processes. *British Journal of Educational Psychology,* Vol. 48, pp. 266–279.

Biggs, J. (1987). *Student approaches to learning and studying.* Hawthorne: Australian Council for Educational Research.

Biggs, J. (1994). Approaches to learning: nature and measurement of. In Husen, T. & T.N. Postlethwaite (Eds.) *The International Encyclopedia of Education,* pp. 319–322. Oxford: Pergamon.

Biggs, J. (1999), *Teaching for quality learning at university: What the student does.* SRHE, Oxford University Press.

Biggs, J. (2003). *Teaching for Quality Learning at University.* Maidenhead: SRHE & Open University Press

Birt, D. & J. Nichol (1975). *Games and Simulations in History.* London, England: Longman Group.

Blackburn, R.T., G.R. Pellino, A. Boberg & C. O'Connell (1980). Are Instructional Programs Off-Target? *Current Issues In Higher Education* Vol 1: pp 32–48.

Blake, N., P. Smeyers, R. Smith & P. Standish (2003). *The Blackwell guide to the philosophy of education.* Malden, MA: Blackwell publishing.

Bloom, B., M. Englehart, E. Hill & D. Krathwohl (1956). *Taxonomy of Educational Objectives: The Classification of Educational Goals by a Committee of College and University Examiners.* New York, U.S.A.: Longmans.

Boal, A. (1992). *Games for Actors and Non-Actors.* London: Routledge.

Boal, A. (2000). *Theatre of the Oppressed.* London: Pluto Press.

Boal, A. (2008). *The Rainbow of Desire. The Boal Method of Theatre and Therapy.* London and New York: Routledge.

Boden, R. & D. Epstein (2006). Managing the research imagination? Globalisation and research in higher education. *Globalisation, Societies and Education,* Vol. 4, No. 2, pp. 223–236.

Bolt, J. (1990). How Executives Learn: The Move from Glitz to Guts. *Training and Development Journal,* Vol. 44, No. 5, (May), pp. 83–88.

Boocock, S. & E. Schild (1968). Introduction. In Boocock, S. & E. Schild (Eds.). *Simulation Games in Learning.* Beverly Hills, U.S.A.: Sage Publications, pp. 13–26.

Booth, P., P. Luckett & R. Mladenovic (1999). The quality of learning in accounting education: the impact of approaches to learning on academic performance. *Accounting Education,* Vol. 8, No. 4, pp. 277–300.

Bostock, S (1998). Constructivism in Mass Higher Education: a case study. *British Journal of Educational Technology* 29 (3), pp 225–240.

Boud, D. (1995). *Enhancing learning through self-assessment.* London: Routledge.

Bowden, J. (2009). The process of customer engagement: A conceptual framework. *The Journal of Marketing Theory and Practice,* Vol. 17, No. 1, pp. 63–74.

Bracher, L., J. Cantrell & K. Wilkie (1998). The process of poster presentation: a valuable learning experience. *Medical Teacher,* Vol.20, No:6 , pp 552–557. Available at Informalhealth.com [Accessed 30 April].

Braun, V. & V. Clarke (2006). Using thematic analysis in psychology. *Qualitative Research in Psychology,* No. 3, pp. 77–101.

Bridges, W. (2003). *Managing Transitions – Making the Most of Change* (2nd edition). Cambridge, MA: Perseus Publishing.

Brockbank, A. & I. McGill (2003). *Facilitating reflective learning in higher education.* Buckingham: Open University Press.

Broscow, D. & B. Kleiner (1991). Skill Training Needed by Tomorrow's Executives. *Industrial and Commercial Training,* Vol. 23, No. 3, pp. 26–32.

Brown, R.D. & L. Krager (1985). Ethical issues in graduate education: Faculty and student responsibilities. *The Journal of Higher Education,* Vol. 56, No. 4, pp. 403–418.

Brown, S., C. Rust, & G. Gibbs (1994). *Strategies for Diversifying Assessment.* Oxford Centre for Staff Development.

Bruffee, K. A. (1993). *Collaborative learning: Higher education, Interdependence, and the authority of Knowledge.* Baltimore: The Johns Hopkins University Press.

Bruner, J. (1960). *The Process of Education,* Cambridge, Mass.: Harvard University Press.

Brush, T. & J. Saye (2001). The use of embedded scaffolds in a technology-enhanced student-centred learning activity. *Journal of Educational Multimedia and Hypermedia,* Vol. 10, No. 4, pp. 333–356.

Brush, T. & J. Saye (2002). A summary of research exploring hard and soft scaffolding for teachers and students using a multimedia supported learning environment. *The Journal of Interactive Online Learning,* Vol. 1, No. 2, pp. 1–12.

Burke, L.A. & B. Rau (2010). The Research-Teaching Gap in Management. *Academy of Management Learning & Education,* 9(1). pp 132–143.

Byréus, K. (2001). *Du har huvudrollen i ditt liv. [You play the leading role in your life].* Stockholm: Liber.

Cadman, K. & M. Grey (2000). The 'action teaching' model of curriculum design: EAP students managing their own learning in an academic conference course. *EA Journal.* Vol. 18, No. 2, pp. 21–36.

Callois, R. (1961). *Man, Play and Games*. New York, U.S.A.: Free Press.

Cargill, M. & P. O'Connor (2006). Developing Chinese scientists' skills for publishing in English: Evaluating collaborating-colleague workshops based on genre analysis. *Journal of English for Academic Purposes*, Vol. 5, No. 3, pp. 207–221.

Cargill, M. & R. Adams (2005). Learning discipline-specific research English for a world stage: A self-access concordancing tool?. *Higher Education in a Changing World: Proceedings of the HERDSA International Conference*, Sydney, pp. 86–92.

Carlson, J. & M. Misshauk (1972). *Introduction to Gaming: Management Decision Simulations*. New York, U.S.A.: John Wiley and Sons.

Case, J. & D. Gunstone (2003). Going deeper than deep and surface approaches: a study of students' perceptions of time. *Teaching in Higher Education*, Vol. 8, No. 1, pp. 55–69.

Case, J. & D. Marshall (2009). Approaches to learning. In Tight, M., K. H. Mok, J. Huisman & C. C. Morphew (Eds.) *The Routledge International Handbook of Higher Education*, pp. 9–22, Routledge.

Cazden, C., B. Cope, N. Fairclough & J. Gee (1996). A pedagogy of multiliteracies: Designing social futures. *Harvard Educational Review*, Vol. 66, No. 1, 60–92.

Chan, C. C., M. S. Tsui,, M. Y. C. Chan & J. H. Hong (2002). Applying the Structure of the Observed Learning Outcomes (SOLO) Taxonomy on Student's Learning Outcomes: An empirical study. *Assessment & Evaluation in Higher Education*, Vol. 27, No. 6, pp. 511–527.

Chandrasoma, R., C. Thompson & A. Pennycook (2004). Beyond plagiarism: Transgressive and nontransgressive intertextuality. *Journal of Language, Identity and Education*, Vol. 3, No. 3, pp. 171–193.

Cheng, W. (2008). Concgramming: A corpus-driven approach to learning the phraseology of discipline-specific texts. *CORELL: Computer Resources for Language Learning*, Vol. 1.

Chevalier, A. (2007). Financing higher education. *European Educational Research Journal*, Vol. 6, No. 2, pp. 190–196.

Chickering, A. W. & Z. F. Gamson (1987). *Seven principles for good practice in undergraduate education*. AAHE Bulletin. 39 (7) pp. 3–7.

CITE: Critical Integrative Teacher Education (2011). https://www.jyu.fi/edu/laitokset/okl/integraatio/en [Accessed June 2011].

Clayson, D. (2009). Student evaluations of teaching: Are they related to what students learn? A meta-analysis and review of the literature. *Journal of Marketing Education*, Vol. 31, No. 1, pp. 16–30.

Coates, H. (2005). The value of student engagement for higher education quality assurance. *Quality in Higher Education,* 11:1, pp. 25–36.

Cohen, L. & L. Manion (1996). *Research Methods in Education.* London: Routledge.

Conroy, M. (2010). Internet tools for language learning: University students taking control of their writing. *Australasian Journal of Educational Technology,* Vol. 26, No. 6, pp. 861–882.

Corkill, H. (2010). A most ingenious paradox?: building a 'transition pedagogy' from foundation to bachelor degrees. In Atlay M. & A. Coughlin (Eds.), *Creating Communities,* pp. 216–231. Luton: University of Bedfordshire.

Costello, M. (1991). *The Greatest Games of All Times.* New York, U.S.A.: John Wiley and Sons.

Crowley-Long, K., J. L. Poweel & C. Christensen (1997). Teaching students about research: Classroom poster sessions. *The Clearing House,* Vol.70, No.4, pp 202–205. Available at Proquest 5000, [Accessed 10 February 2011].

Csikszentmihalyi, M. (1990). *Flow: The Psychology of Optimal Experience.* New York, NY: Harper & Row.

Csikszentmihalyi, M. (1997) Flow and Education. *The NAMTA Journal,* Vol. 22, No.2, pp. 2–35.

Csikszentmihalyi, M. (2002) Thoughts about education. In Dickinson. D (Ed.) (2002). *Creating the Future: Perspectives on Educational Change.* Johns Hopkins University School of Education, New Horizons for Learning. http://education.jhu.edu/newhorizons/future/creating_the_future/ [Accessed 18 July 2011].

Culin, S. (1975). *Games of the North American Indians.* New York, U.S.A.: Dover Publications.

Curtin University (2010). iPortfolio – it's all about your website. https://iportfolio.curtin.edu.au/index.cfm [Accessed 21 February, 2011].

Dahlgren, L. O., M. A. Dahlgren, H. Hult, H. Hård af Segerstad & K. Johansson (2005). *Students as Journeymen Between Communites of Higher Education and Work, EU Research on Social Sciences and Humanities.* Brussels: European Commission.

Dale, A. & C. Klasson (1964). *Business Gaming: A Survey of American Collegiate Schools of Business.* Austin, U.S.A.: Bureau of Business Research, University of Texas at Austin.

Darling-Hammond, L., Ancess, J. & Falk, B. (1995). *Authentic Assessment in Action: Studies of Schools and Students at Work.* NY: Teachers College Press.

Davidson, H. (1997). *Even More Offensive Marketing: An Exhilarating Guide to Winning in Business*. London, England: Penguin Books.

Davidson, R. A. (2002). Relationship of study approach and exam performance. *Journal of Accounting Education*, Vol. 20, No. 1, pp. 29–44.

Davis, M. & J. Carroll (2009). Formative feedback within plagiarism education: Is there a role for text-matching software? *International Journal for Educational Integrity*, Vol. 5, No. 2, pp. 58–70.

Day, C. (1999). *Developing teachers: The challenges of life long learning*. London: Falmer.

Denzin, N. & Y. Lincoln (Eds) (2000). *Handbook of Qualitative Research*. Thousand Oaks: Sage.

Dewey, J. (1952). *Experience and education*. New York: The Macmillan Company.

Diseth, A. (2003). Personality and approaches to learning as predictors of academic achievement. *European Journal of Personality*, Vol. 17, No. 2, pp. 143–155.

Dobbins, K. (2009). Feeding innovation with Learning Lunches: contexualising academic innovation in higher education. *Journal of Further and Higher Education*, 33:4, pp 411–422.

Dobozy, E. (2007). *The learning of democratic values: How four 'out-of-the-ordinary schools' do it*. Frenchs Forest, NSW, Australia: Pearson Education.

Dobson, R. & S. Hölttä (2001). The internationalization of university education: Australia and Finland compared. *Tertiary Education and Management*, Vol. 7, No. 3, pp. 243–254.

Dobson, R. (2007). Full circle: The return to user-pays in Australian higher education. *The 1st international annual Réseau d'Etude sur l'Enseignement Supérieur (RESUP) conference*. Paris, France, 1–3 February. http://www.resup.u-bordeaux2.fr/manifestations/conferenceinternationaleparis2007/Actes/DOBSON_RESUP2007.pdf [Accessed 9 February 2011].

Dow, K., B. Adams, J. Dawson & D. Philips (2009). *Report advising on the development of the Victorian tertiary education plan*. Melbourne, VIC: Skills Victoria. http://www.skills.vic.gov.au/__data/assets/pdf_file/0003/162894/Report-advising-on-the-development-of-the-Victorian-tertiary-education-plan.pdf [Accessed 27 April 2011].

Drucker, P. F. (1985). *Innovation and Entrepreneurship. Practice and Principles*. New York: Harper and Row.

Drummond, I., I. Nixon & J. Wiltshire (1998). Personal transferable skills in higher education. *Quality Assurance in Education*, Vol. 6, No. 1, pp. 19–27.

Dukes, R. & C. Seidner (Eds.) (1978). *Learning with Simulations and Games*. Beverly Hills, U.S.A.: Sage Publications.

Dunbar-Hall, P., J. Rowley, M. Webb & M. Bell (2010). ePortfolios for music educators: parameters, problems and possibilities. In proceedings of the *29th Conference of the International Society for Music Education*, Beijing, pp. 61–64.

Dunn, L., C. Morgan, S. Parry & M. O'Reilly (2004). *The Student Assessment Handbook*. New York: Routledge.

Dunstan, M. & P. Bassinger (1997). An Innovative Model: Undergraduate poster sessions by health profession majors as a method for communicating chemistry in context. *Journal of Chemical Education*, Vol.74, No.9. Available at Proquest 5000, [Accessed 10 February 2011].

Editor (1972). Widespread Use of Simulation Games. *Computing Newsletter*, Vol. 6, No. 1, p. 1.

Eira, C. (2005). Obligatory intertextuality and proscribed plagiarism. *2nd Asia-Pacific Educational Integrity Conference.*

Elkington, S. (2010). Articulating a Systematic Phenomenology of Flow: An experience-process perspective. *Leisure/Loisir*, Vol. 34, No. 3, pp. 327–260.

Ellington, H., E. Addinall & F. Percival (1981). *Games and Simulations in Science Education*. London, England: Kogan Page.

El-Shamy, S. (2001). *Training Games: Everything You Need to Know About Using Games to Reinforce Learning*. Sterling, U.S.A.: Stylus Publishing.

Enomoto, K. (2010). Promoting self-regulated learning: a feedback-based study skills action plan for students from diverse cultural, linguistic and disciplinary backgrounds. In Morrel E. & M. Barr (Eds.) *Crises and Opportunities: Proceedings of the 18th Biennial Conference of the ASAA, 2010, Adelaide*. Canberra: ASAA, Inc.

Entwistle, N. J. & E. R. Peterson (2004). Conceptions of learning and knowledge in higher education: relationships with study behaviour and influences of learning environments. *International Journal of Educational Research*, Vol. 41, No. 6, pp. 407–428.

Entwistle, N. J. (2008). Taking stock: teaching and learning research in higher education. Review prepared for an international symposium on *Teaching and Learning Research in Higher Education*, April, 25–26, 2008, Guelph, Ontario, Canada: www.kcl.ac.uk/content/1/c6/02/63/41/Entwistle-Ontariopaper.doc [Accessed 3 June 2011].

Entwistle, N. J. (2009). *Teaching for understanding at university. Deep approaches and distinctive ways of thinking*. London: Palgrave Macmillan.

Entwistle, N. J., V. McCune & P. Walker (2001). Conceptions, styles and approaches within higher education: analytic abstractions and everyday experience. In Sternberg R. J. & L. F. Zhang (Eds.) *Perspectives on Cognitive, Learning and Thinking styles*, pp. 103–136. Mahwah, NJ: Lawrence Erlbaum Associates.

Farber, E. & S. Penhale (1995). Using Poster sessions in Introductory Science Courses: An Example at Earlham. *Research Strategies*, Winter, Available at Proquest 5000 [Accessed 23 June 2010].

Faria, A. (1987). A Survey of the Use of Business Games and Simulations in Academia and Business. *Simulation and Games*, Vol. 18, No. 2, pp. 207–224.

Fibæk-Laursen, P. (1998). Forskningsbaseret undervisning. In Fibæk-Laursen, P. & T. S. Gabrielsen (Eds.) (1998) *At undervise i humaniora*, Frederiksberg: Samfundslitteratur. pp 93–109.

Firth, M. (2006). Using Poster Presentation with ESL students. *The Internet TESL Journal*, Vol.12, No.11, November. Available at http://iteslj.org/Lessons?Firth-PosterPresentation.html [Accessed 23 June 2010].

Fister, S. (1999). CBT Fun and Games. *Training*, Vol. 36, No. 5, pp. 68–78.

Flecha, R. (2000). *Sharing words: theory and practice of dialogic learning.* Lanham, MA: Rowman & Littlefield.

Flowerdew, J. & Y. Li (2007). Plagiarism and second language writing in an electronic age. *Annual Review of Applied Linguistics*, Vol. 27, pp. 161–183.

Franz, R. (1998). Whatever you do, don't treat your students like customers! *Journal of Management Education*, Vol. 22, No. 1, pp. 63–69.

Freire, P. (1970/2002). *Pedagogy of the Oppressed*. Harmondsworth, UK: Penguin.

Freire, P. (1994). *Pedagogy of Hope: Reliving Pedagogy of the Oppressed*. New York: Continuum.

Fullan, M. (1997). *What's worth fighting for in the principalship*. New York & London: Teachers College Press.

Gabriel, T. (2010). Plagiarism lines blur for students in digital age. *The New York Times*. 1st August.

Gammon, S. & L. Lawrence (2004). Developing and evaluating the application of leisure-related psychological theory (the concept of flow) to student and lecturer assessment strategies in higher education (a summary of final support), *Learning and Teaching Support Network (LTSN)*.

Gardner, H. (1999). *The Disciplined Mind: What All Students Should Understand*. New York, U.S.A.: Simon & Schuster.

Garrett, B. & C. Jackson (2006). A mobile clinical e-portfolio for nursing and medical students, using wireless personal digital assistants (PDAs). *Nurse Education in Practice*. Vol 6, pp. 339–346.

Geoghegan, W. (1994). Whatever happened to instructional technology? *Paper presented at the 22nd Annual Conference of the International Business Schools Computing Association:* http://eprints.ecs.soton.ac.uk/10144/ [Accessed on May 1st 2011].

Gibbons, M. (1997). *What kind of University? Research and teaching in the 21st century*. Victoria University of Technology: 1997 Beanland Lecture.

Gibbons, M., C. Limoges, H. Nowotny, S. Schwartzman, P. Scott & M. Trow (1994). *The New Production of Knowledge: the dynamics of science and research in contemporary societies*, London: Sage.

Gibbs, G. (1999). *Using assessment strategically to change the way students learn*, In Brown S. & A. Glasner (Eds.) *Assessment Matters in Higher Education: Choosing and Using Diverse Approaches*. Maidenhead: SRHE/Open University Press.

Gijbels, D., M. Segers & E. Struyf (2008). Constructivist learning environments and the (im)possibility to change students' perceptions of assessment demands and approaches to learning. *Instructional Science*, Vol. 36, pp. 431–443.

Gilmore, J., D. Strickland, B. Timmerman, M. Maher & D. Feldon (2010). Weeds in the flower garden: An exploration of plagiarism in graduate students' research proposals and its connection to enculturation, ESL, and contextual factors. *International Journal for Educational Integrity*, Vol. 6, No. 1, pp. 13–28.

Giroux, H. (1988). *Teachers as Intellectuals: Toward a Critical Pedagogy of Learning*. New York, NY: Bergin & Garvey.

Giroux, H. (1994). Toward a pedagogy of critical thinking. In Walters K. (Ed.) *Re-Thinking Reason: New Perspectives in Critical Thinking*. Albany, NY: State University of New York Press, pp. 200–211.

Giroux, H. (2007). *The university in chains: Confronting the military-industrial-academic complex*. Boulder, CO: Paradigm.

Giroux, H. (2010). Bare pedagogy and the scourge of neoliberalism: Rethinking higher education as a democratic public sphere. *The Educational Forum*, Vol. 74, No. 3, pp. 184–196.

Golde, C. M. & G. E. Walker (2006). *Envisioning the future of doctoral education: Preparing stewards of the discipline*. The Carnegie Foundation for the advancement of teaching. San Fransisco: Jossey-Bass.

Goodman, J. & J. Kuzmic (1997). Bringing a Progressive Pedagogy to Conventional Schools: Theoretical and Practical Implications from Harmony. *Theory into Practice*, Vol. 36, No. 2, pp. 79–86.

Goodman, S. B. (2006). Autonomy and guidance in doctoral advisement relationships: A dialectical study. *Humanistic Psychologist*, Vol. 34, No. 3, pp. 201–222.

Goodyear, P. (1999). Pedagogical frameworks and action research in open and distance learning, *European Journal of Open and Distance Learning*. http://www.eurodl.org/materials/contrib/1999/goodyear/ [Accessed 18 July 2011]

Gore, J. M., T. G. Griffiths & J. G. Ladwig (2004). Towards better teaching: productive pedagogy as a framework for teacher education. *Teaching and Teacher Education*. 20, 375–387

Grant, B. & A. Graham (1999). Naming the game: reconstructing graduate supervision. *Teaching in Higher Education*, Vol. 4, No. 1, pp. 77–89.

Greenblat, C. (1988). *Designing Games and Simulations: An Illustrated Handbook*. London, England: Sage Publications.

Grupp, H. & S. Maital (2001). *Managing New Product Development and Innovation. A Microeconomic Toolbox*. Cheltenham: Edward Elgar Publishing.

Grysell, T. & K. Winka (Eds) (2010). *Gestaltandets utmaningar – forumaktiviteter och lärande. [The challenges of performance – forum activities and learning]*. Lund: Studentlitteratur.

Gurr, G. M. (2001). Negotiating the "rackety bridge": A dynamic model for aligning supervisory style with research student development. *Higher Education Research & Development*, Vol. 20, No. 1, pp. 81–92.

Handal, G. & P. Lauvås (2006). *Forskarhandledaren*. Lund: Studentlitteratur.

Hannan, A. & H. Silver (2000). *Innovating in Higher Education. Teaching, Learning and Institutional Cultures*. Buckingham: Open University Press.

Hapgood, F. (2001). Not Just Playing Around. *CIO*, Vol. 14, No. 17, pp. 174–176.

Harvey, J. B. (1999). *How Come Every Time I Get Stabbed in the Back my Fingerprints Are on the Knife?* San Fransisco: Jossey-Bass.

Harvey, L. & S. Drew, M. Smith (2006). *The first-year experience: a review of literature for the Higher Education Academy*. http://www.heacademy.ac.uk/assets/York/documents/ourwork/archive/first_year_experience_full_report.pdf [Accessed 9 February 2011]

Hasbro Games (1998). *RISK®*. Pawtucket, U.S.A.: Hasbro Games.

Haskel, R. (1997). Academic freedom, tenure, and student evaluation of faculty: Galloping pools in the 21st century. *Education Policy Analysis Achieves*, Vol. 5, No. 6, pp. 36–39.

Hautamäki, A. (2006). *Kestävä innovointi. Innovaatiopolitiikka uusien haasteiden edessä.* [Sustainable development. Innovation policy faces new challenges]. Sitra reports 76.

Hawke, J. (1983). The way ahead. John Curtin Memorial Lecture. http://john.curtin.edu.au/jcmemlect/hawke1983.html [Accessed 9 February 2011].

Hayes, M. (2008). Threshold and transformation. *European Journal of Management*, Vol. 8, No. 3, pp. 24–46.

HEFCE (2001). Strategies for learning and teaching in higher education: a good practice guide: http://www.hefce.ac.uk/pubs/hefce/2001/01_37/01_37.pdf [Accessed on May 1st 2011].

Heikkinen, H. L. T., H. Jokinen & P. Tynjälä (2010). *VERME. Vertaisryhmämentorointi työssä oppimisen tukena* [Supporting learning at work through Peer Group Mentoring]. Helsinki: Tammi.

Henning, J. E., J. M. Stone & J. L. Kelly (2009). *Using action research to improve instruction. An interactive guide for teachers.* New York: Routledge.

Herrington, J. & R. Oliver (2000). An instructional design framework for authentic learning environments. *Educational Technology Research and Development*, Vol. 48, No. 3, pp. 23–48.

Hess, G. R. & E. N. Brooks (1998). The class poster conference as a teaching tool. *Journal of Natural Resources and Life Sciences*, Vol 27, pp 155–158, Available at agronomy.org. [Accessed 30 April 2011].

Hickman, L. & T. Alexander (1981). *The essential Dewey, Vol. 1: Pragmatism, Education, Democracy.* Bloomington, IN: Indiana University Press.

Hoban, V. (2001). It's Learning, Jim, But Not as We Know It. *Management Today*, November, pp. 96–98.

Honey, P. & A. Mumford (1982). *The Manual of Learning Styles.* Maidenhead, UK: Peter Honey Publications.

Horn, R. & A. Cleaves (Eds.) (1977). *The Guide to Simulations/Games for Education and Training.* 4th ed. Cranford, U.S.A.: Didactic Systems.

Howard, R.M. (1995). Plagiarisms, authorships, and the academic death penalty. *College English*, Vol. 57, No. 7, pp. 788–806.

Howe, E.R. (2006). Exemplary teacher induction: An international review. *Educational Philosophy and Theory*, Vol. 38, No. 3, pp. 287–297.

Huba, M.E. & J.E. Freed (2000). *Learner-Centered Assessment on College Campuses: Shifting the Focus from Teaching to Learning.* Needham Heights, MA: Allyn & Bacon.

Hunt, S. (2000). *A General Theory of Competition: Resources, Competences, Productivity, Economic Growth.* London, England: Sage Publications.

Hunt, S. (2002). *Foundations of Marketing Theory: Toward a General Theory of Marketing.* Armonk, U.S.A.: M.E. Sharpe.

Ingersoll, R. (2003). *Is there really a teacher shortage? A report co-sponsored by the center for the study of teaching and policy and the center for policy research in education.* Seattle: University of Washington, Center for the Study of Teaching and Policy.

Irzik, G. (2001). Back to Basics: A Philosophical Critique of Constructivism, *Studies in Philosophy and Education* Vol 20, pp 157–175.

Jacobsen, T., A. Baerheim, M. R. Lepp & E. Scheil (2006). Analysis of role-play in medical communication training using a theatrical device: the fourth wall. *BMC Medical Education,* Vol. 6, No. 51.

Jacobson, M. J., C. Maouri, P. Mishra & C. Kolar (1996). Learning with hypertext learning environments: theory, design, and research. *Journal of Educational Multimedia and Hypermedia,* Vol 5, No.3/4, pp. 239–281.

Johnson, L., A. Lee & B. Green (2000). The PhD and the Autonomous Self: gender, rationality and postgraduate pedagogy. *Studies in Higher Education,* Vol. 25, pp. 135–147.

Johnston, B. (2010). *The first year at university: teaching students in transition.* New York: Society for Research into Higher Education and Open University Press.

Jones, K. (1985). *Designing Your Own Simulations.* London, England: Methuen and Company.

Jones, K. (1987). *Simulations: A Handbook for Teachers and Trainers.* 2nd ed. London, England: Kogan Page.

Kahn, D. (2003). Montessori and optimal experience research: Toward building a comprehensive education reform. *The NAMTA Journal,* Vol. 23, No. 1, pp. 1–10.

Kaye, M. (1973). *The Story of Monopoly, Silly Putty, Bingo, Twister, Frisbee, Scrabble, Et Cetera.* New York, U.S.A.: Stein and Day.

Kemp, K. M. & J. A. Clark (1992). Teaching Geology Using Poster Assignments. *Journal of Geological Education,* Vol.40, No:5, pp 398–403.

Keys, B. & J. Wolfe (1988). Management Education and Development: Current Issues and Emerging Trends. *Journal of Management,* Vol. 14, No. 2, pp. 205–230.

Keys, B. & J. Wolfe. (1990). The Role of Management Games and Simulations in Education and Research. *Journal of Management,* Vol. 16, No. 2, pp. 307–337.

Kift, S. (2009). *Articulating a Transition Pedagogy.* Sydney: ALTC.

Kirkpatrick, D. L. (1975). Techniques for Evaluating Training Programs. In Kirkpatrick D. L. (Ed.) *Evaluating Training Programs.* Alexandria, VA: American Society for Training and Development.

Klein, J. (1985). The Abstraction of Reality for Games and Simulations. *The Journal of the Operational Research Society*, Vol. 36, No. 8, pp. 671–679.

Knobloch, E. (2006). Alexander von Humboldt: The explorer and the scientist. In Kokowski, M. (Ed.) (2006) The Global and the Local: The History of Science and the Cultural Integration of Europe. *Proceedings of the 2nd ICESHS*. Cracow, Poland, September 6–9. http://www.2iceshs.cyfronet.pl/2ICESHS_Proceedings/Chapter_2/Plen_Lec_Knobloch.pdf [Accessed 18 July 2011].

Knowles, M. (1973). *The Adult Learner*. Houston, U.S.A.: Gulf Publishing Company.

Knowles, M., E.F. Holton & R.A. Swanson (2005). *The Adult Learner*. (Sixth Edition). New York: Butterworth-Heinemann,

Knowles, M.S. (1975). *Self-Directed Learning. A guide for learners and teachers*. Englewood Cliffs: Prentice Hall/Cambridge.

Kolb, D.A. (1984). *Experiential learning: experience as the source of learning and development*. Englewood Cliffs, NJ: Prentice Hall.

Koshy, S. (2008). Group work for freshmen students: A positive learning experience? In proceedings of the *Conference of the International Journal of Arts and Sciences*, Germany, November 2008.

Koshy, S. (2009). Innovative Assessments: The Workshop Method. *Conference of the International Journal of Arts and Sciences* 1(17), pp 122–129.

Krashen, S. (2003). *Explorations in Language Acquisition and Use*. Portsmouth: Heinemann.

Krathwohl, D. R., B. S. Bloom & B. B. Masia (1956). *Taxonomy of educational objectives: the classification of educational goals: handbook 2: affective domain*. London: Longmans, Green & Co.

Kwiek, M. (2009). The changing attractiveness of European higher education in the next decade: Current developments, challenges and major policy issues. *European Educational Research Journal*, Vol. 8, No. 2, pp. 218–235.

Lam, A. & B.-A. Lundvall (2007). The Learning Organisation and National Systems of Competence Building and Innovation. In: Lorenz, N. & B.-A. Lundvall (Eds.) *How Europe's Economies Learn: Coordinating Competing Models*. Oxford University Press, pp. 110–139.

Lam, A. (2004). Organizational innovation. In Fagerberg J., D. Mowery & R. Nelson (Eds.) *Handbook of Innovation*. Oxford University Press.

Lambert, C., A. Parker & M. Neary (2007). Teaching entrepreneurialism and critical pedagogy: Reinventing the higher education curriculum. *Teaching in Higher Education*, Vol. 12, No. 4, pp. 525–536.

Lammers, W. J. & J. J. Murphy (2002). A Profile of Teaching Techniques Used in the University Classroom: A Descriptive Profile of a US Public University *Active Learning in Higher Education,* 3: 54.

Land, R. (2000). Orientations to Educational Development. *Education Developments,* 1:2, pp 19–23.

Lane, D. (1995). On the Resurgence of Management Simulations and Games. *The Journal of the Operational Research Society,* Vol. 46, No. 5, pp. 604–626.

Larréché, J. (1987). On Simulations in Business Education and Research. *Journal of Business Research,* Vol. 15, No. 6, pp. 559–572.

Laurillard, D. M. (2002). *Rethinking University Teaching: A Conversational Framework for the Effective Use of Learning Technologies* (2nd edition). London: Routledge.

Lave, J. & E. Wenger (1999). Legitimate Peripheral Participation in Communities of Practice. In McCormick, R. & C. Paechter (Eds.), *Learning and knowledge.* London: SAGE Publications Ltd., pp 21–35.

Leadbeater, C. (2005). *The shape of things to come: personalised learning through collaboration.* Nottingham: DfES.

Ledwith, A. & A. Risquez (2008). Using anti-plagiarism software to promote academic honesty in the context of peer reviewed assignments. *Studies in Higher Education,* Vol. 33, No. 4, pp. 371–384.

Lee, A. (2007). Developing effective supervisors: Concepts of research supervision. *South African Journal of Higher Education,* Vol. 21, No. 4, pp. 680–693.

Levy, P., S. Little, P. McKinney, A. Nibbs & J. Wood (2010). *The Sheffield companion to inquiry-based learning.* Brook Hill, Sheffield, UK. http://www.shef.ac.uk/content/1/c6/10/88/63/Sheffield_IBL_Companion.pdf [Accessed 15 December 2010].

Lia, S. & C. Sealeband (2007). Managing criticism in Ph.D. supervision: a qualitative case study. *Studies in Higher Education,* Vol. 32, No. 4, pp. 511–526.

Lindblom-Ylänne, S., A. Nevgi & T. Kaivola (2003). Tentistä tenttiin -oppimisen arviointikäytäntöjen kehittäminen. In Lindblom-Ylänne, S. & A. Nevgi (Eds.) (2003). *Yliopisto- ja korkeakouluopettajan käsikirja.* Vantaa: WSOY. pp. 268–294.

Little, B. & R. Williams (2010). Students' roles in maintaining quality and in enhancing learning: Is there a tension? *Quality in Higher Education,* Vol. 16, No. 2, pp. 115–127.

Lutz, J. (2009). Flow and sense of coherence. *Global Health Promotion*, Vol. 16, pp. 64–67.

Mandelson, P. (2009). Speech at the CBI higher education summit in London. http://highereducation.cbi.org.uk/media/latest_news/00248/ [Accessed 27 August 2010].

Mäntylä, H. (2007). *On "Good" Academic Work: Practicing Respect at Close Range*. Helsinki School of Economics: http://hsepubl.lib.hse.fi/ EN/ diss/?cmd=show&dissid=337 [Accessed 14 January 2011].

Marquardt, M.J., S. Leonard, A. Freedman & C. Hill (2009). *Action learning for developing leaders and organizations*. Washington, DC: American Psychological Press.

Marton, F. & R. Säljö (1976). On qualitative differences in learning: I. Outcome and process. *British Journal of Educational Psychology*, Vol. 46, pp. 4–11.

Marton, F. & R. Säljö (1997). Approaches to learning. In Marton, F., D. Hounsell & N. Entwistle (Eds.), *The experience of learning*, pp. 39–58. Edinburgh: Scottish Academic Press.

Marton, F., D. Hounsell & N. Entwistle (Eds) (2005). *The Experience of Learning: Implications for Teaching and Studying in Higher Education* (3rd internet edition.). Edinburgh, UK: University of Edinburgh, Centre for teaching, Learning and Assessment.

Marvel, J., D. M. Lyter, P. Peltola, G. A. Stirizek & B. A. Morton (2007). *Teacher attrition and mobility: Results from the 2004–2005 teacher follow-up survey*. Washington: Government Printing Office.

Maslach, C. & S. E. Jackson (1981). The Measurement of Experienced Burnout. *Journal of Occupational Behaviour*, Vol. 2.pp 99–113. Available at Proquest 5000, [Accessed 10 February 2011].

Mayo, P. (2009). Competitiveness, diversification and the international higher education cash flow: The EU's higher education discourse amidst the challenges of globalisation. *International Studies in Sociology of Education*, Vol. 19, No. 2, pp. 87–103.

Mbajiorgu, N. & N. Reid. (2006). *Factors Influencing Curriculum Development in Chemistry*. Hull: Higher Education Academy Physical Sciences Centre.

McCarthy, G., & A. Rogerson (2009). Links are not enough: Using originality reports to improve academic standards, compliance and learning outcomes among postgraduate students. *International Journal for Educational Integrity*, Vol. 5, No. 2, pp. 47–57.

McCready, T. (2007). Portfolios and the assessment of competence in nursing: A literature review. *International Journal of Nursing Studies*. Vol 44, pp. 143–151

McCulloch, A. (2009). The student as co-producer: Learning from public administration about the student-university relationship. *Studies in Higher Education*, Vol. 34, No. 2, pp. 171–183.

McFarlane, F., J. McKenney & J. Seiler (1970). *The Management Game: Simulated Decision Making*. New York, U.S.A.: The Macmillan Company.

McGowan, U. (2008a). International Students: A conceptual framework for dealing with unintentional plagiarism. In: Roberts T.S. (Ed.) *Student Plagiarism in an Online World: Problems and Solutions*. Hershey, New York: Information Science Reference. pp. 92–107.

McGowan, U. (2008b). *Avoiding Plagiarism: Achieving Academic Writing*. http://www.adelaide.edu.au/clpd/plagiarism/ [Accessed 12 January 2011].

McGuire, C., L. Solomon & P. Bashook (1976). *Construction and Use of Written Simulations*. San Antonio, U.S.A.: The Psychological Corporation.

McKenney, J. (1967). *Simulation Gaming for Management Development*. Boston, U.S.A.: Harvard University Press.

McKenzie, J., S. Alexander, C. Harper & S. Anderson (2005). *Dissemination, Adoption and Adaptation of Project Innovations in Higher Education*. www.altc.edu.au/resource-dissemination-adoption-uts-2005 [Accessed 12 December 2010].

McKinsey & Company. (2007). *How the world's best performing school systems come out on top*. http://www.mckinsey.com/clientservice/socialsector/resources/pdf/Worlds_School_Systems_Final.pdf [Accessed 19 December 2009].

McMillan, J. H. (Ed.) (2007). *Formative Classroom Assessment-Theory into Practice*. New York: Teachers College Press.

Meltzer, D. E. & K. Manivannan (2002). Transforming the lecture-hall environment: The fully interactive physics lecture. *American Journal Physics*, Vol. 70, pp. 639–654.

Merriam, S. B., R. S. Caffarella & L. M. Baumgartner (2007). *Learning in Adulthood: A comprehensive guide*, (3rd edition). San Francisco: Jossey-Bass

Meyer, J. H. F. & R. Land (2003). Threshold concepts and troublesome knowledge: Linkages to ways of thinking and practising within the disciplines. In Rust C. (Ed.) *Improving student learning: Improving student learning theory and practice – Ten years on*. Oxford: Oxford Centre for Staff and Learning Development.

Mezirow, J. (1997). Transformative Learning: Theory to Practice. In: Cranton, P. (Ed.) (1997). Transformative Learning in Action: Insights from Practice. *New Directions for Adult and Continuing Education*. No. 74, pp. 5–12. San Francisco: Jossey-Bass.

Mezirow, J. (2000). *Learning as Transformation*. San Francisco, CA: Jossey-Bass.

Miller, M. (2005). Teaching and Learning in Affective Domain. In: M. Orey (Ed.), *Emerging perspectives on learning, teaching, and technology*. http://projects.coe.uga.edu/epltt/index.php?title=Teaching_and_Learning_in_Affective_Domain [Accessed 10 February 2011].

Milne, F. (2001). *The Australian universities: A study in public policy failure*. Working Paper 1080. Kingston, Canada: Queens University. http://www.econ.queensu.ca/working_papers/papers/qed_wp_1080.pdf [Accessed 9 February 2011]

Minasian-Batmanian, L. C., J. Lingard & M. Prosser (2006). Variation in student reflections on their conceptions of and approaches to learning biochemistry in a first-year health sciences' service subject. *International Journal of Science Education*, Vol. 28, No. 15, pp. 1887–1904.

Moody, J. (2007). Plagiarism or intertextuality?: Approaches to teaching EFL academic writing. *The Asian EFL Journal*, Vol. 9, No. 2, pp. 195– 210.

Moon, J. (2004). *A Handbook of Reflective and Experiential Learning: Theory and Practice*. Oxon: Routledge Farmer.

Moore, G. (1991). *Crossing the Chasm*. HarperBusiness, New York.

Moradi, B. & D. T. Townsend (2006). Raising Students' Awareness of Women in Psychology. *Teaching of Psychology*, Vol.33, No.2, pp 113–117, Available at Proquest 5000, [Accessed 24 June 2010].

Mori, T. & T. Yoshida (1990). *Data Analysis Technical Book for Psychology*. Kyoto: Kitaoji-Syobo.

Mulnix, A. & S. J. Penhale (1997). Modeling the Activities of Scientists: A Literature Review and Poster Presentation Assignment. *The American Biology Teacher*, Volume 59, No.8. Available at http://earlham.edu/~libr/documents/publications/Modeling.pdf [Accessed 12 June 2010].

Musashi, M. (1974). *A Book of Five Rings: The Classic Guide to Strategy*. Woodstock, U.S.A.: The Overlook Press.

Nash, R. (1990). Bourdieu on education and social and cultural reproduction. British *Journal of Sociology of Education*, Vol. 11, No. 4, pp. 431–447.

National Curriculum Board. (2009). *The Shape of the Australian Curriculum*. http://www.ncb.org.au/communications/publications.html [Accessed 9 May 2010].

Naughton, C., J. Roder & J. Smeed (2010). The strategic learner goes digital: Web 2.0 and the implications of assessment when transferring from distance education to online learning. In Steel, C. H., M. J. Keppell, P. Gerbic & S. Housego (Eds.) *Curriculum, technology & transformation for an unknown future*. In proceedings of ascilite 2010 Sydney, pp 673–683. http://ascilite.org.au/conferences/sydney10/procs/Naughton-full.pdf [Accessed 14 February 2011].

Neary, M. (2009). Student as producer: Risk, responsibility and rich learning environments. Proceedings of the *Centre for Learning and Teaching Conference* 2008. http://staffcentral.bton.ac.uk/clt/events/conf/2009/Post-conf.%2708%20spreads%20.pdf#page=5 [Accessed 23 June 2010].

Nikkola, T., P. Räihä, P. Moilanen, M. Rautiainen & S. Saukkonen (2008). Towards a Deeper Understanding of Learning in Teacher Education. In Nygaard C. & C. Holtham (Eds.) *Understanding Learning-Centered Higher Education*. Frederiksberg: Copenhagen Business School Press, pp. 251–263.

Nygaard, C. & C. Holtham (2008). The Need for Learning-Centred Higher Education. In Nygaard, C. & C. Holtham (Eds.), *Understanding Learning-Centred Higher Education*: Copenhagen Business School Press, pp. 11–29.

Nygaard, C. & C. Holtham (2008). *Understanding Learning-centred Higher Education*. Copenhagen Business School Press.

Nygaard, C., N. Courtney, & L. Frick, (2011). *Postgraduate Education: Form and Function*. Oxfordshire, Libri Publishing.

Nygaard, C., T. Højlt, & M. Hermansen (2008). Learning-based curriculum development. *Higher Education*, Vol. 55, No. 1, pp. 33–50.

O'Keeffee, D. (2011). Higher education on the up. *Education Review*, 28 April 2011. http://www.educationreview.com.au/pages/section/article.php?s=Breaking+News&idArticle=20746 [Accessed 29 April 2011].

OECD (2005). *Teachers matter: Attracting, developing and retaining effective teachers*. Paris: OECD.

Oliver, B., P. Nikoletatos, B. von Konsky, H. Wilkinson, J. Ng, R. Crowley, R. Moore & R. Townsend (2009). Curtin's iPortfolio: An online space for creating, sharing and showcasing evidence of learning. In *Same places, different spaces. Proceedings ascilite Auckland 2009*. http://www.ascilite.org.au/conferences/auckland09/procs/oliver-poster.pdf [Accessed 21 February, 2011].

Olssen, M. & Peters, M. (2005). Neoliberalism, higher education and the knowledge economy: From the free market to knowledge capitalism. *Journal of Education Policy*, Vol. 20, No. 3, pp. 313–345.

Orsmond,P., S. Merry & K. Reiling (2002). The Use of Exemplars and Formative Feedback when Using Student Derived Marking Criteria in Peer and Self-assessment. *Assessment and Evaluation in Higher Education*, Vol.27, No.4, pp 309–323. Available at Proquest 5000 [Accessed 10 February 2011].

O'Toole, J. (2002). *Drama: The Productive Pedagogy*. Melbourne Studies in Education, Vol. 43, No 2, pp. 39–52.

Palomba, C. A. & T. W. Banta (1999). *Assessment Essentials: Planning, Implementing and Improving Assessment in Higher Education*. San Francisco: Jossey-Bass.

Papastephanou, M. (2006). Education, risk and ethics. *Ethics and Education*, Vol. 1, No. 1, pp. 47–63.

Papinczac, T., L. Young, M. Groves & M. Haynes (2008). Effects of a metacognitive intervention on students' approaches to learning and self-efficacy in a first year medical course. *Advances in Health Sciences Education*, Vol. 13, pp. 213–232.

Passer, M. W. & R. E. Smith (2011). *Psychology:The Science of Mind and Behaviour*. New York: McGraw-Hill.

Pearson, M. & A. Brew (2002). Research Training and Supervision Development. *Studies in Higher Education*, Vol 27, pp. 135–150.

Pecorari, D. (2003). Good and original: Plagiarism and patchwriting in academic second language writing. *Journal of Second Language Writing*, Vol. 12, No. 4, pp. 317–345.

Pedrosa de Jesus, H., P. Almeida & M. Watts (2005). Orchestrating teaching and learning in interdisciplinary chemistry. *Canadian Journal of Science, Mathematics and Technology Education*, Vol. 5, No. 1, pp. 81–94.

Pedrosa de Jesus, H., P. Almeida, J. J. C. Teixeira-Dias & M. Watts (2006). Students' questions: building a bridge between learning styles and approaches to learning. *Education + Training*, Vol. 48, No. 2/3, pp. 97–111.

Pennycook, A. (1996). Borrowing others' words: Text, ownership, memory, and plagiarism. *TESOL Quarterly*, Vol. 30, No. 2, pp. 201–230.

Phillips, R. A. (2005). Challenging the Primacy of Lectures: the Dissonance between Theory and Practice in University Teaching. *Journal of University Teaching and Learning Practice*, 2(1), 1–12. http://jutlp.uow.edu.au/2005_v02_i01/phillips003.html [Accessed 24 May 2011].

Picard, M., R. Warner & L. Velautham (2011). Enabling postgraduate students to become autonomous ethnographers of their disciplines. In Nygaard C., C. Holtham & N. Courtney (Eds.) *Postgraduate Education - Form and Function*. Faringdon, Oxfordshire: Libri Publishing Ltd.

Pourmand Nordic, K. (2005). A critical look at student resistance to non-traditional law school professors, *Western New England Law Review,* Vol. 27, No. 2., pp. 173–192.

Prosser, M. & K. Trigwell (1999). *Understanding Learning and Teaching.* Buckingham, UK: Open University Press.

Prosser, M., K. Trigwell, E. Hazel & F. Waterhouse (2000). Students' experiences of studying physics concepts: the effects of disintegrated perceptions and approaches. *European Journal of Psychology of Education,* Vol. 15, No. 1, pp. 61–74.

Queensland University of Technology (QUT) (2009). QUT student ePortfolio: http://www.studenteportfolio.qut.edu.au [Accessed 21 February, 2011].

Ramsden, P. (2003). *Learning to teach in higher education* (2nd edition). Abingdon: RoutledgeFalmer.

Räsänen, K. (2009). Understanding academic work as practical activity – and preparing (business-school) academics for praxis? *International Journal for Academic Development,* Vol. 14, pp. 185–195.

Rautiainen, M., T. Nikkola, T, P. Räihä, S. Saukkonen & P. Moilanen (2010). "From Disorder to New Order: The Complexity of Creating a New Educational Culture". In Nygaard C., C. Holtham & N. Courtney (Eds.) *Teaching Creativity – Creativity in Teaching.* Faringdon, Oxfordshire: Libri Publishing, pp. 189–202.

Reibstein, D. & M. Chussil (1999). Putting the Lesson Before the Test: Using Simulation to Analyze and Develop Competitive Strategies. *Competitive Intelligence Review,* Vol. 10, No. 1, pp. 34–48.

Revans, R. (1980). *Action learning: New techniques for management.* London: Blond & Briggs, Ltd.

Revans, R. (1983). *The ABC of Action Learning.* Bromley: Chartwell-Bratt.

Reynolds, J. (2006). Learning-centred learning: A mindset shift for educators. *Inquiry,* Vol. 11, No 1, pp. 55–64.

Ries, A. & J. Trout (1986). *Marketing Warfare.* New York, U.S.A.: McGraw-Hill.

Ringleb, A., & Rock, D. (2009). NeuroLeadership in 2009. *NeuroLeadership Journal,* Vol. 2, No. 1. pp. 1–7. http://www.neuroleadership.org/files/INTRO_US.pdf [Accessed 23 June 2010].

Robinson, C., J. Sebba, D. Mackrill & S. Higgins (2008). *Personalising learning: The learner perspective and their influence on demand.* Coventry: BECTA. http://research.becta.org.uk/index.php?section=rh&catcode=_re_rp_02&rid=14551 [Accessed 27 August 2010].

Rogers, C. (1969). *Freedom to Learn: A View of What Education Might Become*. Columbus, Ohio: Charles Merill.

Rogers, E. M. (1962). *Diffusion of Innovations*. Free Press, New York. [with reprinted/revised editions in 1983, 1995 & 2003].

Rowell, G. (2009). TurnitinUK: Plagiarism detection software? *The Journal of Hospitality, Leisure, Sport & Tourism Education*, Vol. 8, No. 2, pp. 157–162.

Rowland, S. (2006). *The Enquiring University: Compliance and Contestation in Higher Education*. Open University Press, Maidenhead.

Rowley, J. & P. Dunbar-Hall (2009). Integrating e-portfolios: putting the pedagogy in its place. *Same Places, Different Spaces. Proceedings ascilite (Australian Society for Computers in Learning in Tertiary Education) Conference*, Auckland, pp. 898 – 901. http://www.ascilite.org.au/conferences/auckland09/procs/rowley.pdf [Accessed 21 February, 2011].

Rowley, J. & P. Dunbar-Hall (2010). Integrating ePortfolios for music teachers: a creative and pedagogic undertaking. *Proceedings of the Society for Information Technology & Teacher Education International Conference*, San Diego, pp. 213–215.

Ruohotie-Lyhty, M. & P. Kaikkonen (2009). The difficulty of change: the impact of personal school experience and teacher education on the work of beginning language teachers. *Scandinavian Journal of Educational Research*, Vol. 53, No. 3, pp. 295–309.

Rupp, A., M. Gushta, R. Mislevy & D. Shaffer (2010). Evidence-centred design of epistemic games: Measurement principles for complex learning environments. *Journal of Technology, Learning and Assessment*, Vol. 8, No. 4, pp. 4–42. www.tla.org/ [Accessed 30 April 2011].

Sadler, D. R. (1998). Formative assessment: revisiting the territory. *Assessment in Education: Principles, Policy and Practice*. Vol 5, pp. 77–84.

Sadler, D. R. (2005). Interpretations of criteria-based assessment and grading in higher education. *Assessment and Evaluation in Higher Education*, 30, pp. 175–194.

Saunders, M. (2000). Beginning an Evaluation with RUFDATA. *Evaluation* 6:1, pp 7–21.

Scheopner, A. J. (2010). Irreconcilable differences: Teacher attrition in public and catholic schools. *Educational Research Review*, Vol. 5, No. 3, pp. 261–277.

Schön, D. A. (1987). *Educating the reflective practitioner*. San Francisco, CA: Josey-Bass.

Schön, D. A. (1995). The New Scholarship Requires a New Epistemology. *Change*. (November/December): pp 27–34.

Schrage, M. (2000). *Serious Play: How the World's Best Companies Simulate to Innovate*. Cambridge, U.S.A.: Harvard Business School Press.

Schumpeter, J. (1934). *The Theory of Economic Development*. Harvard University Press.

Scott, W.R. (1998). *Organizations: Rational, Natural, and Open Systems* (4th edition.). Upper Saddle River, New Jersey: Prentice Hall International, Inc.

Scottish Executive (2006). *Professional Standards for Lecturers in Scotland's Colleges*. http://www.scotland.gov.uk/Resource/Doc/129678/0030901.pdf [Accessed 14 February 2011].

Seligman, M.E.P. (1975). *Helplessness: depression, development and death*. New York: W H Freeman.

Semler, L. (2007). The culture shock of campus life: Universities speak a different language from schools. *The Australian, November* 21. http://www.theaustralian.news.com.au/story/0,25197,22792734–27702,00.html [Accessed 23 June 2010].

Senge, P. (1990). *The Fifth Discipline: The art and practice of the learning organization*. New York: Doubleday.

Share, P. (2006) Managing intertextuality – meaning, plagiarism and power. *Proceedings of the 2nd International Plagiarism Conference*, UK 2006, http://m23.nlearning.co.uk/plagiarismconference.org/media/2006papers/PerryShare.pdf [Accessed 12 January 2011].

Siltala, R., J. Alajääski, S. Keskinen & A. Tenhunen (2009). Opetusalan asiantuntijoiden käsityksiä opettajan pedagogisesta innovatiivisuudesta. [Educational experts' conceptions of a teacher's pedagogical innovativeness]. *Aikuiskasvatus* [*Adult Education*], Vol. 29, No. 2, pp. 93–103.

Silver, H. (1999). Managing to innovate in higher education. *British Journal of Educational Studies*, Vol. 47, No. 2, pp. 145–156.

Smart, D. & G. Ang (1993). The Origins and Evolution of Commonwealth Full Fee Paying Overseas Student Policy 1975–1992. In Peachment A, & J. Williams (Eds.). *Case Studies in Public Policy*. Public Sector Research Unit. Perth, WA: Curtin University Press.

Snowman, J., E. Dobozy, J. Scevak, F. Bryer, B. Bartlett & R. Biehler (2009). *Psychology Applied to Teaching*. Milton, QLD: John Wiley & Sons Australia.

Spronken-Smith, R., R. Walker, J. Batchelor, B. O'Steen & T. Angelo (2011). Enablers and constraints to the use of inquiry-based learning in undergraduate education. *Teaching in Higher Education*, Vol. 16, No. 1, pp. 15–28.

Stolley, K. & A. Brizee (2010). Avoiding plagiarism: Overview and contradictions. Purdue Online Writing Lab. http://owl.english.purdue.edu/owl/resource/589/01/ [Accessed 12 January 2011].

StratX (2002). *MarkStrat*. Boston, U.S.A.: StratX.

Struyven, K., F. Dochy, S. Janssens & S. Gielen (2006). On the dynamics of students' approaches to learning: the effects of the teaching/learning environment. *Learning and Instruction*, Vol. 16, pp. 279–294.

Stunkel, K. R. (1998). The Lecture: a Powerful Tool for Intellectual Liberation, *The Chronicle of Higher Education*, 26th June, http://abyss.uoregon.edu/~js/ast121/tool_lecture.html [Accessed 18 July 2011].

Suits, B. (1967). What is a Game? *Philosophy of Science*, Vol. 34, pp. 148–156.

Sun-Tzu, P. (1983). *The Art of War*. New York, NY.: Delacorte Press.

Suomala, J., V. Taatila, R. Siltala & S. Keskinen (2005). Liiketalousinnovaatioiden keksiminen on myös kognitiivinen prosessi. [Inventing business innovations is also a cognitive process]. *Aikuiskasvatus* [*Adult Education*], Vol. 9, No. 3, pp. 180–190.

Syed, J., J. Mingers & P. A. Murray (2010). Beyond rigour and relevance: A critical realist approach to business education. *Management Learning*, 41(1): pp 71–85.

Tait, H. & N. Entwistle (1996). Identifying students at risk through ineffective study strategies. *Higher Education*, Vol. 31, No. 1, pp. 97–116.

Taylor, S. (2008). Thinking of research supervision as a form of teaching. Lancaster University, Centre for the Enhancement of Learning and Teaching. *http://www.lancaster.ac.uk/celt/celtweb/current_journal* [Accessed 7 June 2011].

Tella, S. & K. Tirri (1999). *Educational Innovations in Finnish and European Contexts: an Analysis of the Aims and Outcomes of "The European Observatory" of the European Commission (1994–1998)*. University of Helsinki Department of Teacher Education, Research Report 200.

Tennant, M., C. McMullen & D. Kaczynski (2010). *Teaching, learning and research in higher education: A critical approach*. New York and London: Routledge.

Thurik, R. & S. Wennekers (2004). Entrepreneurship, Small Business and Economic Growth. *Journal of Small Business and Enterprise Development*, 11: pp 140–149.

Tidd, J., J. Bessant & K. Pavitt (2005). *Managing innovation: integrating technological, market and organizational change*. (3rd edition). Chichester: John Wiley & Sons.

Tinto, V. (1999). Taking Retention Seriously: Rethinking the First Year of College. *NACADA Journal*, Vol. 19, No. 2, pp. 5–9.

Tracy, B. (2002). *Victory! Applying the Proven Principles of Military Strategy to Achieve Greater Success in Your Business and Personal Life*. New York, U.S.A.: Amacom.

Trigwell, K. & P. Ashwin (2006). An exploratory study of situated conceptions of learning and learning environments. *Higher Education*, Vol. 51, No. 2, pp. 243–258.

Trilling, B. & C. Fadel (2009). *21st century skills: Learning for life in our times*. San Francisco, CA: Jossey-Bass.

Trowler, V. & P. Trowler (2010) *Student Engagement evidence summary*, Higher Education Academy [online]: http://www.heacademy.ac.uk/assets/York/documents/ourwork/studentengagement/StudentEngagementEvidenceSummary.pdf [Accessed 1 May 2010].

Tynjälä, P., V. Slotte, J. Nieminen, K. Lonka & E. Olkinuora (2006). From University to Working Life: Graduates' Workplace Skills in Practice. In: Tynjälä, P., J. Välimaa & G. Boulton-Lewis (Eds.), *Higher Education and Working Life - Collaborations, Confrontations and Challenges*. Oxford: Elsevier, pp 73–88.

Ursin, J. (2011). *Muuttuva yhteikunta – sopeutuva korkeakoulutus? Järjestelmäteoreettinen näkökulma. [Changing society – adaptive higher education? A systems theory viewpoint]*. In Lasonen J. & J. Ursin (Eds.) *Koulutus yhteiskunnan muutoksissa: jatkuvuuksia ja katkoksia. [Education and training amidst social changes: continuities and interruptions]*. Suomen kasvatustieteellinen seura. Kasvatusalan tutkimuksia 53, [Finnish Educational Research Association. Educational studies 53], pp. 22–42.

Valadas, S., F. Gonçalves & L. Faísca (2009). Approaches to studying in higher education Portuguese students: a Portuguese version of the approaches and study skills inventory for students. *Higher Education*, Vol. 59, No. 3, pp. 259–275.

Van Rossum, R. J. & S. M. Schenk (1984). The relationship between learning conception, study strategy and learning outcome. British Journal of Educational Psychology, Vol. 54, No. 1, pp. 73–83.

Verenikina, I. (2004). What does the metaphor of scaffolding mean to educators today? *Outlines*, No. 2, pp. 5–15.

Vidgrén, M. (2009). *Koulutusinnovaatiotoiminan tukemisen ja johtamisen mallintaminen: tapaustutkimus monialaisen ammattikorkeakoulun terveys- ja liiketaloudesaloilta. [Modelling educational innovation management: a case study about multidisciplinary University of Applied Sciences in the field of nursing and business studies]*. Kuopion yliopiston julkaisuja E. Yhteiskuntatieteet 178. [Kuopio University publications E. Social sciences 178].

Vygotsky, L.S. (1978). *Mind in Society: The development of higher psychological processes.* Cambridge, MA: Harvard University Press.

Walker, G. E., C. M. Golde, L. Jones, A. C. Bueschel & P. Hutchings (2008). *The Formation of Scholars. Rethinking doctoral education for the twenty-first century.* The Carnegie Foundation for the advancement of teaching. San Fransisco: Jossey-Bass.

Walker, S. (2005). Poster poster on the wall: whose is the fairest assessment of all? *Journal of Family Therapy,* Vol.27, No.4, pp 285–288. Available at Proquest 5000, [Accessed 24 June 2010].

Warner, R. (2010). Giving feedback on assignment writing to international students – the integration of voice and writing tools. In: Chan W.M., K.N. Chin, M. Nagami & T. Suthiwan (Eds.) *Media in Foreign Language Teaching and Learning,* pp.355–381, Singapore: National University of Singapore.

Watson, S. (2003). Closing the feedback loop: Ensuring effective action from student feedback, *Tertiary Education and Management,* Vol. 9, No. 2, pp. 145–157.

Watts, H. (1985). When teachers are researchers, teaching improves. *Journal of Staff Development,* Vol. 6, No. 2, pp. 118–127.

Weiss, R. (2000). Brain-Based Learning. *Training and Development Journal,* Vol. 54, No. 7, pp. 21–24.

Wetzel, K. & N. Strudler (2005). The diffusion of electronic portfolios in teacher education: Next steps and recommendations from accomplished users. *Journal of Research on Technology in Education.* Vol 38, pp. 231–243

Whitehouse, P. (2011). Networked teacher professional development: The case of Globaloria. *Journal of Interactive Learning Research,* Vol. 22, No. 1, pp. 139–165.

Whitson, C. & Consoli, J. (2009). Flow theory and student engagement. *Journal of cross-disciplinary perspectives in education,* Vol. 2, No. 1, pp. 40–49.

Wilson, B. (Ed.) (1996). *Constructivist Learning Environments,* Englewood Cliffs, N.J.: Educational Technology Publications.

Wisker, G. (2005). *The Good Supervisor.* Basingstoke: Palgrave Macmillan.

Wolfe, J. (1975). Effective Performance Behaviors in a Simulated Policy and Decision-Making Environment. *Management Science,* Vol. 21, No. 8, pp. 872–882.

World Bank (2008). *Economics of Education.* http://web.worldbank.org/WEBSITE/EXTERNAL/TOPICS/EXTEDUCATION/0,,contentMDK:20264769~menuPK:63701~pagePK:148956~piPK:216618~theSitePK:282386,00.html [Accessed 03 November 2010].

Yorke, M. & B. Longden (2008). *The first year experience of higher education in the UK*. http://www.heacademy.ac.uk/assets/York/documents/resources/publications/FYEFinalReport.pdf [Accessed 12 February 2011].

Yorke, M. (2003). Formative Assessment in Higher Education: Moves towards theory and the enhancement of pedagogic practice. *Higher Education Research & Development* Vol. 45, pp. 477–501.

Yunker, P. & Yunker, J. (2003). Are student evaluations of teaching valid? Evidence from an analytical business course. *Journal of Education for Business,* Vol. 78, No. 6, pp. 313–317.